Preconception, Pregnancy and Postnatal Yoga

A guide for Yoga Teachers

Author
Yogacharini Deepika Giri

ISBN 978-0-9927841-9-5

First Published November 2024

Designed. Printed & Published by Design Marque

Printed in Great Britain by www.designmarque.co.uk

Dedication

I dedicate this work to my lineage of Gurus to whom I am indebted for showing me the path of ultimate light and timeless wisdom that is Yoga. To Yogamaharishi Dr Swami Gitananda Giri Guru Maharaj, Ammaji Meenakshi Devi Bhavanani and Dr Ananda Balyogi Bhavanani.

I also dedicate this book to my three sons, Siddha, Mahadev and Krishna, to whom I am grateful for every day of my life!

Blessings from the Guru Parampara

Yoga is a wholistic and integral science of life dealing with physical, mental, emotional and spiritual health of the individual and society. It is a way of life that provides a rare opportunity to leave the madness of world behind and attain inner peace.

It is indeed the original mind body medicine and is one of the greatest treasures of the living Indian cultural heritage. Yogic lifestyle, Yogic diet, Yogic attitudes and various Yogic practices help strengthen ourselves and develop positive health. This Yogic "health insurance" is achieved by normalizing the perception of stress, optimizing the reaction to it and by releasing it effectively through various practices.

We need to remember that Yoga is something that we "live" until our last breath, and even that last breath should be completed with awareness.

This book by my dearest Yogacharini Deepika is an excellent addition to modern Yoga literature and deals with one of the most important aspects of life, which is birth. She has rightly included both the pre conception as well as the post natal periods in a woman's life that are vital for a healthy experience of motherhood.

"Healthy mothers will more often than not, bring forth healthy progeny" is something that common sense tells us. Thus we all need to work together in Yoga with a focused intent (Sankalpa) towards manifesting the birthright of humanity, health and happiness.

She has brought into this compilation an immense amount of knowledge and it exudes wisdom that has come forth from her own lived experience as a Yogic mother. It is well illustrated and easy to read for everyone and hence I hope that it will have high acceptance and readership all over the world. It has a mixture of tradition and science and the personal sharing goes straight to the heart of the expectant reader.

She has brought out the essence of Yogic motherhood through each and every page of this excellent treatise. Param Pujya Ammaji, our Divine Mother blesses Deepika abundantly for this great Yoga Seva that will empower each and every woman who aspires to be a Yogic mother.

May she always be blessed by the Divine Consciousness and manifest her inherent potential as a loving blessing for humanity.

With blessings in Yoga.

Yogacharya Dr Ananda Balayogi Bhavanani, MD, DSc, C-IAYT
Ashram Acharya and Chairman ICYER at Ananda Ashram, Pondicherry, India
www.icyer.com

With Gratitude

This work would never have been possible if it were not for my three sons who have enabled me to grow and evolve spiritually in a way I would never have imagined possible! My first thanks has to go to them who are the root of my life as a mother! Their father Yogacharaya Jnandev has done much to guide me as a new mother who had little experience with babies or children. Jnandev also guided several yoga adaptations and is always helping me on the path of Yoga and for that I am ever grateful.

A huge thanks to Yogacharini Cathy Davis who has been key to putting together these Yoga (asana) sequences. Cathy's deep knowledge of the Gitananda practices and experiences of midwifery have proved invaluable and I have felt honoured to have had such support from Cathy.

Also to Dr Ananda Balyogi Bhavanani who provided me with literature and materials for me to work with, from his own work and research with pregnant women and of course his vast knowledge of Yoga.

Last and not least, Ammaji Meenakshi Devi Bhavanani has always been a great example for me of a saintly life of a mother who is leading an extraordinary life and brought up a brilliant son pioneering authentic Yoga in the world today! I am grateful for having had the good karma to have been trained under Ammaji's guidance and have had Ammaji's support and love throughout. Ammaji, for me has truly been a catalyst in my life that changed and moved my being onto a more conscious evolved yogic lifestyle for which I am eternally grateful and pray that I will never lose or let go of the rope of this Paramparai (lineage) keeping me firmly in the light.

Thank you to my pregnant models, Alex, Jodie & Kerry, you all look fabulous!
Illustrations by Jessica Saunders, also by Peter Kay. Thanks to Sarah Ray at Design Marque for design work!

Contents

Introduction

This book is designed to equip yoga teachers with some specific yoga work that will be of benefit to women preparing themselves for pregnancy, (the pre-conception phase is often overlooked) going through pregnancy and post-natal changes. Our aim is to keep mum fit, healthy and as relaxed as possible throughout pregnancy and to be able to prepare her body to be able to cope well with labour, delivery and recovery afterwards.

Throughout the book we will work through some Jattis (warming up/ loosening up movements), Kriyas (movements to use with the breath), Asanas (holding postures), Pranayamas (energy breath work), chanting (sound work and vibration healing) and some relaxation techniques.

In addition to this we will also address topics such as lifestyle and diet and give a basic understanding of the process the body goes through during pregnancy.

My work is mostly influenced by our own teachers who are founders of The International Centre for Yoga Education and Research (ICYER) based in India. In particular Dr Ananda Balayogi Bhavanani who is a senior medical doctor and has established a Yoga Therapy department in one of the most well reputed University hospitals in India. Dr Ananda has put together specific yoga work, which he has researched, in his medical profession. Dr. Ananda is now part of the first medical University in the world offering post graduate Yoga therapy training (ISCM (Institute of salutogenesis and complementary medicine)) of Sri Balaji Vidyapeeth.

Also Yogachariya Jnandev and myself have created and grown 3 healthy baby boys and my own experiences of pregnancy and yoga, I will be sharing with you in this text and in our Yoga lessons. Primarily we come from an ancient and authentic yoga tradition and our practices reflect this.

The sequences used here have been created from classical hatha yoga jointly with Yogacharini Cathy Davis who is a senior Yoga teacher at ICYER and a direct student of Dr Swami Gitananda Giriji; Cathy has practiced as a midwife for over 25 years, until she recently retired. To all my great teachers I am sincerely grateful for their guidance without which this work would not have been possible.

This work has also been informed by those I have been delivering the course with, physiotherapists, midwives, Doulas, breast-feeding counsellors and nutritionists, my grateful heart goes out to them. Also not forgetting the yoga work done with Yogachariya Jnandev.

The course we teach here at the Ashram includes several presentations from specialist, however this book will focus primarily on the yoga practices, with a section by Jyoti Vora, a physiotherapist who assists me with my training courses. I would recommend that anyone wishing to teach pregnancy yoga needs to find a good course that covers all aspects to get a fuller picture.

YOGA: A BOON FOR MATERNAL AND CHILD HEALTH

Yogacharya Dr ANANDA BALAYOGI BHAVANANI
Chairman: International Centre for Yoga Education and Research
(ICYER) at Ananda Ashram, Pondicherry. www.icyer.com

INTRODUCTION:

Having been a medical practitioner for more than a decade now, and having been exposed to the benefits of Yoga as a way of life for the past 30 years, it amazes me that Yoga hasn't yet become an integral part in the preparation of this 'life changing experience' of pregnancy and childbirth. It is deeply concerning to witness the lack of support an expectant mother receives towards preparing herself for childbirth leading to a feeling of stressful dread and debilitating exasperation.

It is often said that the knowledge of how to give birth without outside interventions lies deep within each woman and that successful childbirth depends on an acceptance of the process. Yoga as a way of life is an excellent tool to help the expectant mother dwell deep within herself and develop this spiritual awareness of her strengths with the realization of her blessings.

We must always remember that pregnancy and childbirth are a period of great change for the mother as well as for the entire family. It provides the opportunity to take another look at our life, bring about the necessary changes, and finally become a better human being as the result of this entire process that engineers a great sense of joy and confidence in the individual.

We must never forget that Yoga is not merely a preparation for pregnancy and child birth, but is a continuous preparation for the experience of one's whole life. Yoga is a boon that enables us to realise our blessings and manifest our potential. Pujya Swamiji, Gitananda Giri Guru Maharaj used to often say, "Yoga is not all about changing the world but is all about changing oneself".

EMOTIONAL AND PHYSICAL PREPARATION:

Many of the stories from Indian tradition can educate us about the maternal-child bonding that begins with conception and warn us against underestimating the power of this psychic bond. The great Rishi Ashtavakara, Prahalada and Abimanyu are just a few examples of so many incidents where the child in the womb was able to fully comprehend for itself the external environment and be born with amazing abilities.

Modern medicine has finally come to realize the importance of the maternal mental and emotional status in smoothening the entire process of pregnancy and childbirth.

This has taken a long time in the coming and Grantly Dick-Read was one of the first medical doctors to suggest in the 1950's that emotional and physical preparation for birth encouraged more natural births. This concept that has been part of Indian traditional thought since time immemorial, revolutionized the management of pregnancy in the west as it enabled the medical profession to understand that fear causes pain, which in turn causes more fear, which then causes more pain!

To facilitate better pregnancy and childbirth experiences, Grantly Dick-Read codified preparation classes that involved practicing deep relaxation, which could then be practiced during labour to reduce tension and pain. These techniques have been used for antenatal preparation for labour ever since but in recent times it is sad that these sessions have mostly become a place to share information rather than to prepare expectant mothers physically, mentally and emotionally for their 'life changing' experience of motherhood.

YOGA FOR A HEALTHY PREGNANCY:
Yoga has enormous potential to help expectant mothers prepare themselves physically, mentally, emotionally for this grand experience that can be a very spiritual one for so many. Yoga as a way of life focuses on right living and right thinking while utilizing various tools for the overall psycho-physiological health of the mother and child.

The Jathis, Kriyas and Asanas help promote the healthy functioning of all body systems while Pranayama creates psycho-somatic harmony with a Pranic energisation of every cell of the body. Various Mudras and Bandhas such as Aswini Mudra and Moola Bandha can help tone up the pelvic musculature while others like the Yoni Mudra induce a sense of inner wellbeing. The various concentrative and contemplative practices help achieve an inner peace with the development of a deep sense of self-understanding. Yogic relaxation practices facilitate a balanced and relaxed anabolic inner environment that promotes the healthy growth and development of the baby with the facilitation of healing at all levels of being.

A Yogic diet with a stress on natural life-giving foods and adequate hydration helps the mother nurture the child growing within herself and fortify herself for the challenging events to come. A balanced lacto-vegetarian diet rich in calcium, iron and other essential vitamins and minerals is advocated with training in the preparation of soups, salads and sprouts. Foods of the Sattwic nature elevate the mother's consciousness thus helping to create an uplifting psycho-mental-spiritual inner environment developing the inherent potential of the child in a wonderful manner.

SCIENTIFIC EVIDENCE OF THE BENEFITS OF YOGA IN PREGNANCY:
Preliminary evidence from various scientific studies supports Yoga's potential efficacy, particularly if started early in the pregnancy. A study by Beddoe et al., (2009) showed that women practicing Yoga in their second trimester reported significant reductions in physical pain from baseline to post intervention compared with women in the third trimester whose pain increased. Women in their third trimester showed greater reductions in perceived stress and trait anxiety.

Another study by Sun et al., (2009) reported that women who took part in the prenatal Yoga programme reported significantly fewer pregnancy discomforts at 38-40 weeks of gestation. The subjects who participated in the Yoga programme exhibited higher outcome and self-efficacy expectancies during the active stage of labour and the second stage of labour. They also suggested that the provision of booklets and videos on Yoga during pregnancy may contribute to a reduction in pregnancy discomforts and improved childbirth self-efficacy.

Satyapriya et al., (2009) concluded that Yoga reduces perceived stress and improves adaptive autonomic responses to stress in healthy pregnant women while Chuntharapat et al., (2008) concluded that Yoga produced higher levels of maternal comfort during labour and 2 hours post-labour, with a decrease in subject evaluated labour pain. They also reported a shorter duration of the first stage of labour, as well as the total time of labour in the subjects practicing Yoga.

A study by Narendran et al., (2005) reported a lower trend in the occurrence of complications of pregnancy such as pregnancy-induced hypertension (PIH), intrauterine growth retardation (IUGR) and pre-term delivery in subjects who practiced Yoga. He also concluded that an integrated approach to Yoga during pregnancy is safe. It improves birth weight, decreases pre-term labour, and decreases IUGR either in isolation or associated with PIH, with no increased complications (2005).

A review by Field (2008) reported that alternative therapies have been found effective for reducing pregnancy-related back and leg pain and nausea and for reducing depression and cortisol levels and the associated prematurity rate. It also said that the labour research generally shows that alternative therapies reduce pain and thereby the need for medication.

SUGGESTED YOGA PRACTICES DURING PREGNANCY:
The entire duration of the pregnancy is traditionally divided into three trimesters and hence the Yoga practices may be advised under this classification, too.

In the 1st trimester, standing postures such as Ardhakati Chakra Asana and Trikona Asana can be introduced to create a sense of stability. 'On the floor' postures such as Nikunja or Bala Asana along with the Chatushpada Asana, Chatushpada Kriya and the Vyagraha Pranayama can be taught to reduce the potentiality of back pain. Postures such as Eka Pada and Dwi Pada Uttanpada Asana, Hala Asana and Sarvanga Asana may be taught if the person has some previous experience of Yoga as they create a healthy neuroendocrine feedback along with the toning-up of the abdomino-pelvic musculature. Variations of the Utkat Asana as well as the Baddhakona Asana and Kriya are to be introduced right away to help open up the pelvis to facilitate the healthy delivery later. Aswini Mudra and Moola Bandha create a healthy flow of Pranic energy in the urogenital region. Relaxation practices such as Shava Asana with the Savitri Pranayama are to be taught. Pranava Pranayama creates a harmonious inner environment that is conducive to the creation of a healthy child right from day-one.

Continuing into the 2nd trimester, practices such as the Supta Baddhakona Asana, Mehru Asana, Nava Asana may be introduced while the Nikunja Asana, Baddhakona Asana and Kriya are continued with Aswini Mudra and Moola Bandha. Jathara Parivrittana Asana may be introduced if possible to open up the pelvis in a healthy manner. Relaxation practices such as Kaya Kriya, Tala Kriya and Yoga Nidra may be introduced. Practices on the face may not be possible and if there is too much tension in Shava Asana, then the relaxation may be done in Nishpanda Asana on the side. Kukkriya Pranayama is added to strengthen the diaphragm and create a sense of optimistic energy.

In the 3rd trimester, the main practices are the Chatus Pada Asana and Chatus Pada Kriya along with the Vyagraha Pranayama. Moola Bandha and Aswini Mudra in Baddhakona Asana are continued while Bhramari Pranayama is added to reduce stressbased anxiety levels. Yoga Nidra, Anuloma Viloma Kriya and other practices can be used to produce a calm and steady mind with an optimistic outlook.

During the delivery, deep breathing may be done and the abdomino-pelvic muscular strength obtained from previous months of practice is used to facilitate a healthy delivery through the flexible pelvis. A positive attitude with the feeling of a deep sense of love towards the new born will enhance the spiritual nature of the whole process.

Post natal practices may be started in a few weeks time following the delivery and are aimed at enhancing a swift and healthy physiological return to the pre-pregnant state. Baddhakona Asana and Kriya along with the Chatus Pada Asana and Kriya are key elements of this programme. Vyagraha Pranayama, Pranava Pranayama and Savitri Pranayama in Shava Asana help to repair tissue damage as well as facilitate healing at all levels. Aswini Mudra and Moola Bandha help focus the energies in the pelvis while the Uddiyana Bandha, Eka Pada Uttanpada Asana, Dwi Pada Uttanpada Asana and Nava Asana help the mother to regain abdomino-pelvic muscular tone at the earliest.

Pavanamukta Kriya and the Vakra Asana help to correct any spinal displacements while the Surya Pranayama helps burn up excess weight that accumulated in the pregnant period. The importance of the right diet and positive attitude towards parenting is to be encouraged at all stages to produce a state of excellent psycho-physiological health and harmony.

The role of the father in the whole process must never be underestimated and his involvement in both the practical Yoga sessions as well as in the adoption of a Yogic diet with positive attitudes is vital for the success of the programme. Yoga can help the family to bond together and such a bond is a boon to the entire social unit that is based on healthy inter-personal relationships.

A word of caution: All Yoga practices must be learnt from a competent and qualified Yoga teacher / therapist and performed with a common-sense based approach. Postures such as Dhanur Asana and other "on the face postures" that exert great pressure on the uterus and impair flow of blood to the fetus must be avoided. Inverted postures may result in 'falls' that can cause many complications while the rapid breathing practices such as Kapalabhati must be done with caution. The mother must be helped to develop an inner sense of knowing what is happening within her own body during the practices and if she senses anything wrong must stop the practice immediately and consult the Yoga therapist immediately. In the final trimester it is better to be aware of how even simple things like jumping into postures or sudden change in position may cause premature rupture of membranes. The list of practices that are safe / unsafe will of course depend on the mother's previous Yoga experience, on how long she has been practicing Yoga, and on the type of practices she has been doing previously. On the whole, it is better to be safe at all times rather than sorry later.

CHILDBIRTH– A NATURAL STATE OF BLISS:
My beloved mother and Guru Ammaji, Yogacharini Meenakshi Devi Bhavanani has so beautifully said, "I must confess that bearing, delivering and raising my son has been the single most significant spiritual experience of my life, my first real initiation into the blissful state of Yoga – a oneness and communion with the Universe on a nearly mystical level".

In her book on Yoga for expectant mothers and others, she has beautifully described the Samadhi-like experience of my birth 38 years ago as follows:

"I really felt as though I had slipped into a Samadhi by mistake. Completely drained, relaxed, limp, receptive, I felt a bliss, which I had never felt before in my whole life. As though a purpose had been accomplished, as though I had achieved what I had set out to do, difficult though the task had been, as though I had somehow repaid a

debt, which I had contracted by my own birth. I felt tremendous love for everyone, for my husband, for the doctors, for the nurses, for the Universe, for the good green earth, and the beautiful warm sun…but most all, I felt an immense, overpowering love and devotion to the small little creature that the doctors immediately put into my arms. It was mine, and from that day, I would be responsible for the growth into light of another little human soul. My baby smiled at me, he really did, even though he could not see, and I smiled and smiled back at him, for surely, he was the most beautiful, perfect, intelligent and fantastic child ever born to the Universe! And even as I thought that thought, I realized how many others must have experienced the same feelings, looking for the first time at the first child born to them, and I felt wonderful communion with all mothers who had ever lived and all those who would ever pass through this marvellous experience. Certainly, we shared a secret; certainly, we had something more precious than the most rare of gems; certainly, we were blessed by life itself to be brought so close to that mystical core which creates, out of nothing but a few cells of matter and a few sparks of energy, such a marvellous creature as the new-born child". "I took my pen to paper and wrote these words. "I was given life… I gave life… a debt repaid with interest… I have returned what I was given a hundred- fold. Was there such perfect beauty in my own body… once, long, long ago…Did my mother also see…God move one step beyond herself…in me? And thus, on the crest of these overpowering, ecstatic emotions, did the Yoga of Motherhood rush into my life… a whole new phase of my Yoga Sadhana had begun… with Ananda!"

CONCLUDING THOUGHTS:

Indian culture understands this and respects the mother as the 'First God', even before 'Father' and 'Guru'. It may be said that motherhood is the ultimate Yoga Sadhana. The attainment of motherhood is the height of ego-less-ness, which is the goal of all spirituality.

To be such a 'Mother', one who is consciously aware of the great spiritual nature of pregnancy and childbirth, it is necessary that our young girls start the practice of Yoga at the earliest and continue it into their adulthood. When this is done, healthy and conscious conception is facilitated. This along with the inculcation of healthy and positive attitudes towards child bearing and child rearing will lay down a firm foundation for the production of healthy and spiritually potent children who can transform the future of our planet into a 'Garden of Eden'.

REFERENCES:

1. Beddoe AE, Paul Yang CP, Kennedy HP, Weiss SJ, Lee KA. The effects of mindfulness-based Yoga during pregnancy on maternal psychological and physical distress. J Obstet Gynecol Neonatal Nurs. 2009 May-Jun;38 (3):310-9.

2. Bhavanani Ananda Balayogi. Yoga Therapy Notes. Dhivyananda Creations, Iyyanar Nagar, Pondicherry. 2007

3. Bhavanani Ananda Balayogi. A Primer of Yoga Theory. Dhivyananda Creations, Iyyanar Nagar, Pondicherry. 2008.

4. Bhavanani Meenakshi Devi. The Yoga of Motherhood. www.discover-Yogaonline. com/pregnancy-and-Yoga.html

5. Chuntharapat S, Petpichetchian W, Hatthakit U. Yoga during pregnancy: effects on maternal comfort, labour pain and birth outcomes. Complement Ther Clin Pract. 2008 May;14(2):105-15.

6. Field T. Pregnancy and labour alternative therapy research. Altern Ther Health Med. 2008 Sep-Oct;14(5):28-34.

7. Narendran S, Nagarathna R, Gunasheela S, Nagendra HR. Efficacy of Yoga in pregnant women with abnormal Doppler study of umbilical and uterine arteries.
J Indian Med Assoc. 2005 Jan;103(1):12-4, 16-7.

8. Narendran S, Nagarathna R, Narendran V, Gunasheela S, Nagendra HR. Efficacy of Yoga on pregnancy outcome. J Altern Complement Med. 2005 Apr;11(2):237 44.

9. Polly Ferguson. Yoga for Pregnancy. Thesis submitted to ICYER, Ananda Ashram, Pondicherry for Yoga step-by-step correspondence course final certification examination.
10. Satyapriya M, Nagendra HR, Nagarathna R, Padmalatha V. Effect of integrated Yoga on stress and heart rate variability in pregnant women. Int J Gynaecol Obstet. 2009 Mar; 104(3):218-22. Epub 2008 Dec 25.
11. Sun YC, Hung YC, Chang Y, Kuo SC. Effects of a prenatal Yoga programme on the discomforts of pregnancy and maternal childbirth self-efficacy in Taiwan. Midwifery. 2009 Feb 24.

10. Satyapriya M, Nagendra HR, Nagarathna R, Padmalatha V. Effect of integrated Yoga on stress and heart rate variability in pregnant women. Int J Gynaecol Obstet. 2009 Mar; 104(3):218-22. Epub 2008 Dec 25.

11. Sun YC, Hung YC, Chang Y, Kuo SC. Effects of a prenatal Yoga programme on the discomforts of pregnancy and maternal childbirth self-efficacy in Taiwan. Midwifery. 2009 Feb 24.

Planning Pregnancy – Preconception Practices

If you're planning to get pregnant the first and most basic advice we can give anyone is related to lifestyle, by cleaning up our lifestyle, we thereby clean up our body, which will become the baby's home! If you want to encourage life, a fertile and good environment is needed. So if someone has unhealthy habits, such as smoking or drinking alcohol, these should be stopped altogether to promote a healthy pregnancy. Once these issues are curtailed, we should encourage a good diet of fresh fruits and vegetables and if someone is not vegetarian it would be beneficial to introduce more beans, pulses etc. into the diet and cut down on meat as our body does not digest meat well, particularly red meat. As Yogic living people we encourage a vegetarian diet. That said I do believe allowances should be made for different body constitutions and our living, climate, medical conditions and other factors. Growing a baby takes incredible amounts of energy and it is very important mum is happy and feeling like she is getting enough of the right foods. I personally have come to think that if it's easier to manage your life in this challenging time of growing another body inside of you, eating the occasional bit of fish or chicken to help keep you going if your struggling, is not the end of the world.

Our diet is not the only thing – there is much more we need to clean up if we want to bring an evolved soul into our life! Our mind for example, is sometimes full of even worse things that our intestines! In yoga we can learn to calm down our mind, to try to create more positive thoughts all of which will create a better environment for the baby to live and grow in, after all the mind and body are intrinsically connected and linked. We have a complete set of practices which we would recommend for anyone planning to have a baby which is renowned to bring the body into balance, physically, mentally, hormonally and emotionally. These sets of practices are called the loma-viloma set and primarily balance the masculine (solar) and feminine (luna) aspects within us on all levels. Remember the most powerful practice is that which is done with your full consciousness and awareness, people do not need to get into acrobatic positions – but they do need to develop their self awareness. The Loma-viloma series is very potent for re-balancing your entire body system, and energetic system but it must be done consciously. This Loma viloma sequence will follow later in the book that we use in preparation for motherhood.

Proper Breathing

There is little doubt in my mind that the vast majority of people on the planet are not breathing well, fully or properly. Our breathing is something that is very easily taken for granted if you have a healthy pair of lungs and have never experienced any kind of breathing disorder, it is difficult to comprehend how debilitating poor breathing due to a number of various respiratory disorders can be.

I grew up with acute asthma and spent a lot of time in hospital as a child and was even on life support for several days at the age of 8. Thankfully I survived and after finding Yoga in my teens, specifically Pranayama my quality of life improved ten-fold. I often say that had it not been for Yoga I do not believe I could have managed 3 healthy pregnancies, births and child raising as these take such huge amounts of energy (Prana) which is accessed mostly through the breath. Think about it, we stop eating we will die in a month or two, if we stop drinking maybe a week or two… if the breath stops we have minutes. Breathing and the lungs feed oxygen into the rest of our body, via the heart pumping around oxygenated blood back round to the heart once the oxygen has been 'harvested' from the body. If this process is done effectively we will feel healthy and strong, however if it is not, dis-ease and ailments can occur, as well as a general lack of energy.

Breathing is of course an automatic function of the body, after all if we had to think about every single breath we wouldn't get much else done, but through the practice of Pranayama we begin to bring the breath under some conscious control. What we typically see in people from birth to death is that we are born making long deep 'belly' abdominal breaths as babies, then as we grow up the stresses and strains of life without any kind of management or self-interventions slowly but surely shortens and weakens our breath. Many older people have very short breath until our last breath is literally 'croaked' out right up in the high chest or throat. How to breath properly is not something taught in general health care or GP surgeries, even under specialist respiratory care much of the work done is around risk managing acute attacks or effectively taking medication or medication management. Some work is done through hydrotherapy which I was lucky enough to have myself as a child to try to train me to breath deeper, however compared to the classical yoga practices on the lungs this is really very little. In childhood it is more difficult to work consciously on the lungs for obvious reasons, however in adulthood when we have the ability to concentrate we can cleanse and strengthen the lungs through the yogic practices.

Respiration - Essence of life

"The breath is the vehicle of our mind. The main purpose of meditation is the perception of the soul or the psyche. The breath is the process of perceiving the prana and finally reaches to the psyche or the soul". (Upanishads)

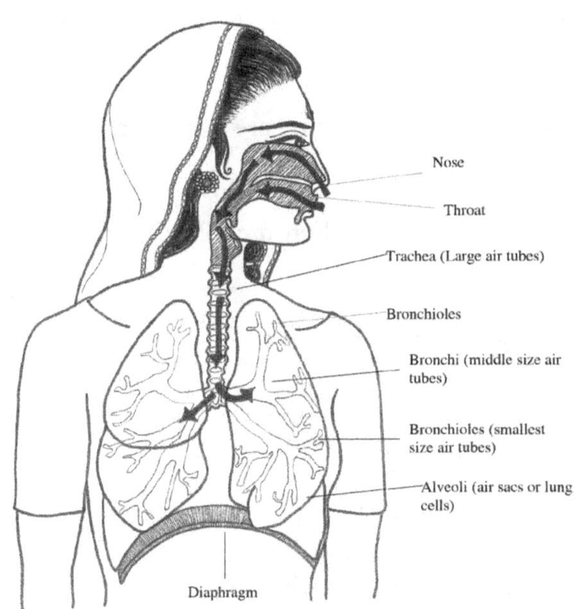

It is known that oxygen plus glucose, meets the basic energy needs of the human body. The former aids in the process of elimination of waste products of the oxidation process, while glucose supplied with oxygen nourishes the body cells in the flow of respiration.

The respiratory system is the gateway of purifying the body, mind and intellect. The key to this is the Deep-breath perception. Respiration is essential for human life. The person is said to be alive up to when there is breath in the body.

Normal breathing per minute is 16-18 breaths. Fresh air containing life giving oxygen is breathed in and the air containing the carbon dioxide from the body cells is breathed out. The movements of the rib cage and diaphragm maintain the rhythmic inflation of the soft-combed bellows of the lungs.

One breathing cycle consists of three parts:
- Inhalation (Puraka)
- Exhalation (Rachaka)
- Retention (Kumbhaka or Shunyaka)

Respiration may be classified into the following four types-

1. High or clavicular breathing, where the relevant muscles of the neck participate actively and mainly the upper part of the lungs are used in breathing.

2. Inter-coastal or mid-breathing, where only the central parts of the lungs are activated.

3. Low or diaphragmatic breathing, where the lower part of the lungs is activated chiefly, while the upper and central parts remain less active.

4. Total or deep-rhythmic breathing

Respiration can also be classified in various phases:

- External Respiration – Where air in inhaled and exhaled between the external and internal environment.

- Internal Respiration - Here oxygen and carbon-dioxide are exchanged between lung cells and blood.

- Intra-cellular respiration - Here oxygen and carbon-dioxide are exchanged between blood and cells or tissues.

The Respiratory system consists of the following structures-

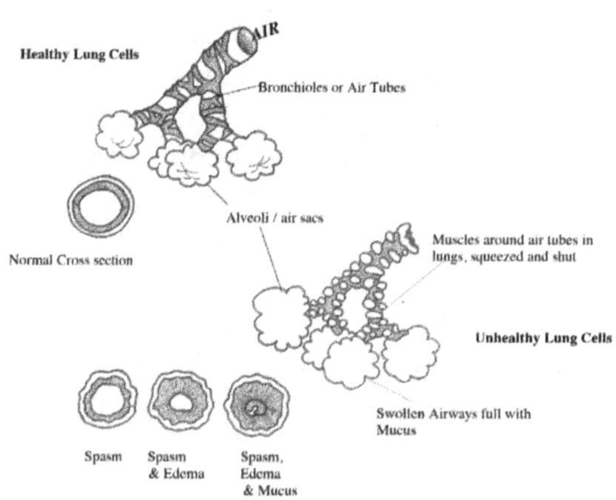

1. Nasal cavity,
2. Pharynx,
3. Larynx,
4. Trachea,
5. Bronchi,
6. Bronchioles,
7. Alveoli,
8. Lungs.

The bronchial system connecting the windpipe and the alveoli is based in the thoracic cage. It resembles an inverted tree with its root in the gullet, while branches spread out downwards towards the diaphragm and the sidewalls of the chest cavity.

The windpipe in the throat is a tube about four inches long and less than an inch wide. The windpipe branches out into two primary bronchi, one leading into each lung. Both branch out in tiny numerous passages called bronchioles. At the end of each bronchiole are the alveoli; the tiny air sacs clustered like branches of grapes, some 300 million lining each lung.

The two lungs - right lung and left lung, differ in size, shape and capacity. The left lung is smaller and divides into the two lobes. The right lung divides into the three lobes.

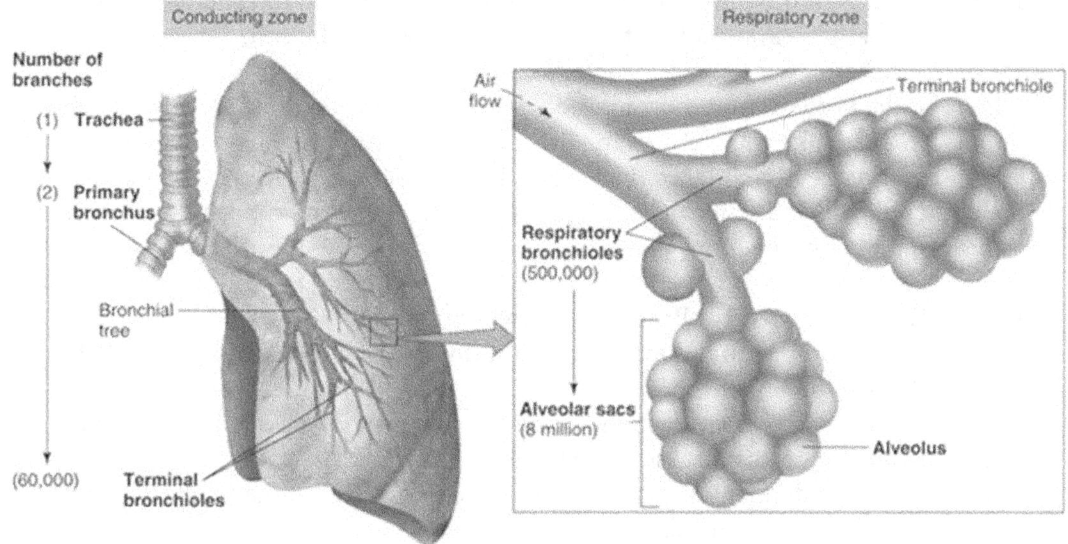

The lungs are covered with a membrane called the pleura that helps in the expansion of the lungs like the bladder of a football.

The dome of the right diaphragm is higher than the left dome. beneath it lays the largest solid abdominal structure, less compressible and depressible than the stomach and spleen lying below the left diaphragm. In order to equalise the filling of both lungs from base and side, special effort and attention must be directed to diaphragmatic and chest wall movements on the right side.

Around the outer wall of the alveoli lie minute blood vessels. An exchange of gases takes place between the alveoli and the red blood cells and plasma of the blood via the fluid in the alveoli or interstitial space.

The air in the alveoli contains more oxygen and less carbon dioxide than blood passing through the capillaries in the lungs. During the exchange of oxygen and carbon dioxide, the molecules of oxygen diffuse into the blood and carbon dioxide diffuse into the lungs from the blood.

Pregnancy and Breathing

As your womb grows and baby bump expands your belly gets bigger during pregnancy, you will lose space for the lower lungs to breath fully, hence breathing can get difficult as pregnancy grows. As a long-term asthma patient, I was automatically placed under consultant care with my first child to observe how I coped with pregnancy, everything was fine of course due to yogic breathing! You might feel difficulty in breathing even during small tasks in the third trimester. So, it is quite common to experience some shortness of breath in expectant mothers, especially towards the end.

Some of the causes:

- Increase in progesterone hormone causes you to breath more deeply, which makes you feel like you are working harder to get enough air.
- The Enlarging uterus takes up more space, putting pressure against the diaphragm, which doesn't allow lungs to expand to their full capacity, especially the lower lobes of the lungs.

What do Health and Medical Professionals recommend?

- Maintain a good posture, don't slouch as it doesn't give lungs enough room to expand when you breathe.
- Using more pillows when sleeping especially around the upper body, to reduce the pressure the uterus places on the lungs.
- Keep things moderate, don't over work, or over exercise. Take your time and respond to your body's needs.

Yoga and preparation for Pregnancy (Preconception)

The first and most important part is to prepare our body fully for pregnancy. Yoga can do that magic for you, if you can learn and choose some Hatha Yoga practices to prepare all parts of your body which are going to help you to go through a healthy pregnancy.

Working on your abdominal and pelvic muscles will help to gain health, strength and flexibility which can help accommodate and support all the changes you will go through.

Also making sure that you have a healthy and strong back to support your postures is very important.

Key recommendations are:

- Surya Namaskars
- Loma-Viloma series
- Pelvic or hip openers
- Spinal Postures

You will also need to build strong and healthy lungs to improve your breathing capacity. Awareness of breathing can help tremendously as the minute we become aware of our breath, naturally we breath more deeply, easily and rhythmically. Hathenas, and Vibhaga Pranayama are unique sets of hatha yoga kriyas and can help by preparing and developing this healthy and complete breathing from the Gitananda tradition. Sukha Purvaka Pranayama can be practised right through pregnancy.

Pranava Sadhana
(extract from the Gitananda Yoga tradition publications)

Pranava, or Aum is the most powerful and sacred mantra in Hindism. In the Vedas, Upanishadas, Puranas, and other sacred literature it is stated that aum is the root of all the sounds and mantras. The pranava is representation of isvara or God. Chanting aum with concentrating on its meaning with deep heart and faith is the easy way to attain Samadhi or enlightenment according to the Yogasutras of Patanjali. Pranava is the mantra of all the mantras. Aum is the name of God in vibration, in sound. To intone the Pranava aum, "the mantra of mantras", "the sound of sounds", is to intone and evoke, the most potent of all powers in a mantra, a vibratory rune. Pranava is comprised of three symbols- a, u and m. The following illustration is to relate pranasva with various symbols of yoga and Hinduism

Syllables of pranava Mantras God Chakra Sound-
>*A Akaar Brahma Anahata Aaa*
>*U Ukaar Vishnu Vishuddha Uuu*
>*M Makaar Mahesh Sahsrara Mmm*

AUM in the Worldwide Scripture
This is a commonly used mantra by Hindus, Jains, Buddhists, Sikhas, etc. While aum is also found in sacred mantras of other religious. Muslims use the aum as OM-IM (amin) to evoke Allah and as a close to their prayer. The Christians use AUM-EN (amen) similarly. In all religions a sign from God is called an OM-en (omen), while to leave God out of your life is OM-it (omit). As a supreme God he is OM-nipotent (omnipotent). He is OM-niscient (omniscient), all light resplendent, effulgent, all knowing. He is OM competent (omnicompetent), all-law; OM-niflic (omniflic), all creating; OM-nifarious (omnifarious), in all things; OM-nigenous (omnigenous), all kinds and species. He is Omnipresent (omnipresent), far as well as near, ubiquitous, being constantly met with; Omnivorous (omnivorous), he feeds on anything, even on himself.

AUM in Yoga Sutra of Patajali
(Yoga Sutra I-27)
Isvara (Supreme Self / God) is expressed and represented (vachakah) by the vibratory energy contained in the pranava (the sacred syllable, aum).
Isvara cannot be defined or limited because Isvara by definition is indefinable infinite mind, however he can be symbolically represented by the expression of pranava - by the vibratory essence that the sacred sound, aum. Thus isvara is often accessed through the pranava which is aum. Tasya means 'that'. Vacakah means 'expression' from the root vac to speak. Pranavah means "the sacred syllable AUM" derived from 'pra' (before) and 'nava' (sound). From my limited experience of Infinite Mind (isvara),

I think that the intoning of AUM is a conveyer, a pathway, a sadhana which leads us into the greater vibration, pulsation, and interdimensional energetic hologram which has no beginning or end -- where both sound and words have little meaning. Patanjali actually said that the pranava is the expression of isvara -- the omniscient teacher of all the teachers. Practically speaking however all vital and living religions agree, that is to focus on the creator in creation. That is spiritual practice. So the practical meaning would be the same i.e., practice intoning aum and/or listening for aum as the self-existing expression of isvara (the divine purusha). Patanjali is thus offering this sutra as one practice that may be effective in clearing out the vrittis and obscuration leading us eventually to Infinite Mind.

(Yoga-Sutra. I 28)
Through generating (bhavanam) constant repetition (taj-japa) of the pranava (aum) the meaning (artha) behind the sound is realized and becomes manifest (bhavanam). The vibratory energy contained in the vibration of the sound, Aum (the pranava), connects with isvara. Japa means the repetition of mantra. Thus japa (mantra repetition of aum) is given as a practice.

(Yoga-Sutra. I 29)
Thence through the practice of the pranava, aum, as a dedication toward realizing isvara (through isvara pranidhana) consciousness (cetana) is redirected inwards (pratyak) toward the realization (adhigamo) of the intrinsic light of consciousness (pratyak-cetana-adhigamo) and (ca) also (api) obstacles and hindrances (antarayah) are thus removed (abhava).

Prana Mudras of Vibhaga Pranayama or Sectional Breathing

Hasta mudras control our physical, mental, emotional and psychic flows. One of the easiest examples to check the physical control is vibhaga pranayama mudras. Our lungs are divided in three lobular parts: the inferior or the lower abdominal lobe, a middle intra-costal lobe, between the ribs and the clavicular or superior lobe. Because of the position of the heart left lung has only two lobes.

Each of these lobes are controlled by different sections of the brain, called aprakasha bindu. It is the Respiratory Centre in the medulla oblongata. This respiratory centre is divided in three general areas, each one governing one lobe of the lungs. The lower area called chin-bindu controls the abdominal breathing. The mid area called chinamaya bindu governs the middle chest breathing. The upper most section known as adhi bindu regulates the upper clavicular breathing. The entire aprakash bindu is divided in two parts, one regulates inspiration and other regulates expiration.

Autonomic impulses arising from the lower area of this segment, sending nerve impulses through the phrenic nerve. This impulse excites the diaphragmatic breathing known as the adham pranayama. The mudra used to control this breathing is china mudra.

Conscious impulses arousing in the cerebral cortex on the top of the brain arouse impulses in the mid-section of aprakasha bindu, sending signals to the middle chest breathing known as the madhyama pranayama. Chinamaya mudra is used to control this breathing.

The superior breathing is stimulated by the impulses arising from the cerebral cortex part of the brain. This is governed by the upper part of the aprakasha bindu, and the mudra used to control this section of breathing is adhi mudra.

Brahma mudra is used for the total or the complete breath. Brahma mudra governs all segments of the aprakash bindu. When you do this, first your low lobes then middle and finally upper lobes will be inflated. Primarily Brahma was associated with the breath, and this is really interesting, as well as being depicted as having four heads (4 breath parts).

By our ancient yogis, Rishij more than hundreds of mudras were practiced to control the body, mind, emotions and spirit to arouse the kundalini power to attain the oneness or the union with the 'self' or the 'supreme self'.

Pranava Sadhana-Process

All the four could be chanted in the 1x2, 1x3, 1x4, … ratio, i.e., if you inhale in 4 counts than produce the sound for 12 counts in 1x3 pranava pranayam. In complete pranava you can divide it in three equal parts, i.e., 4x4x4.

CHIN MUDRA

Akar Pranayam

Sit straight in vajrasana with the hands in the **chin mudra**. Now inhale slowly while expanding the diaphragm muscles downward, adhyam pranayama. While exhaling produce the sound aa.. with concentrating from the navel to heart.

Touch the tips of the thumb and the index finger together making a circle. Keep the remaining three fingers straight. Now place the hands at the root of each leg over the thighs, so that the circle of the thumb and index finger will come close to the pelvic area and the remaining fingers rest over the inner area of the thigh. This mudra is known as china mudra. This is to stimulate the lower lobes of the lungs.

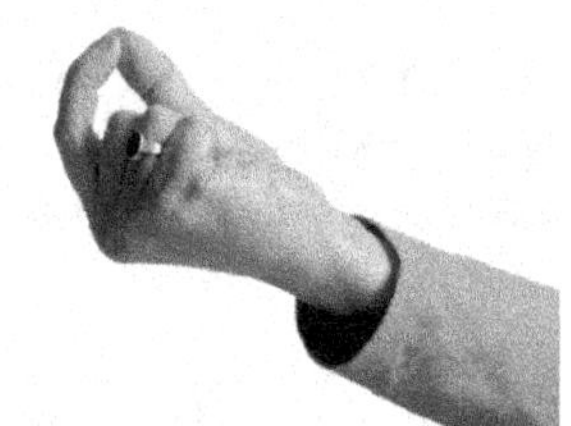

CHINAMAYA MUDRA

Ukar Pranayam

Sit straight in vajrasana with the hands in the **chinamaya mudra.** Now inhale slowly while expanding the middle chest muscles outward, madhyam pranayama. While exhaling produce the sound uu.. with concentrating from the heart to visuddha chakra.

Touch the tips of the thumb and the index finger together making a circle. Press the centre of the palm with the remaining three fingers. Now place the hands at the root of each leg over the thighs, so that the circle of the thumb and index finger will come close to the pelvic area and the fist faces downward to the thigh. This mudra is known as chinamaya mudra. This is to stimulate the middle lobes of the lungs.

ADHI MUDRA

Makar Pranayam

Sit straight in vajrasana with the hands in the **adhi mudra.** Now inhale slowly while expanding the upper chest muscles, adham pranayama. While exhaling produce the sound mm.. with concentrating from the vishuddha to sahasrara chakra.

Place the tip of the thumb at the root of the small finger and press the thumb by closing the remaining four fingers. Now place the fists at the root of each leg over the thighs, so that the thumb will come close to the pelvic area and the remaining part of the fist rests over the thigh. This mudra is known as adhi mudra. This is to stimulate the upper lobes of the lungs.

Mahat Yoga Pranayam

Sit straight in vajrasana with the hands in the **brahma mudra.** Now inhale slowly breathing into all three parts of the lungs. Exhaling with the sounds aa.. uu.. mm.. Visualise from the naval to the sahasrara chakra.

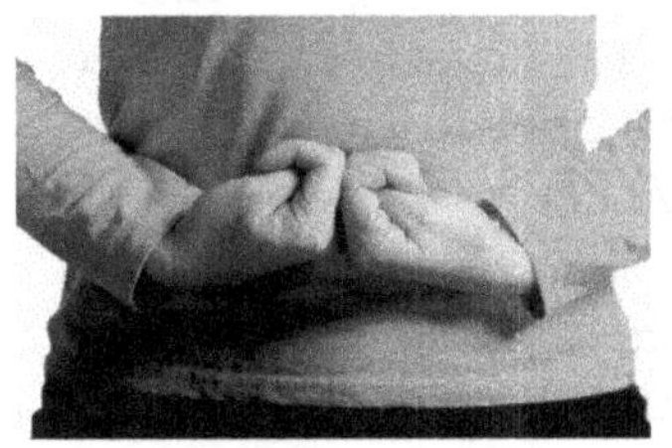

BRAHMA MUDRA

Place the tip of the thumb at the root of the small finger and press the thumb by closing the remaining four fingers. Now place both the fists touching together below the navel, with the fingers turned upwards and the little fingers next to the abdominal area. This is known as brahma mudra. This is to stimulate the lower, middle and upper lobes of the lungs. This mudra is also known as mahat-yoga mudra.

Pranava Aum with Mudras

Begin by sitting in Vajra asana (ideally if its comfortable, otherwise crossed legged is fine but put a cushion under your buttocks to lift your torso up straight, it tends to prevent us from collapsing the spine and slightly compressing the lungs)

Before we start using the Hasta mudras it is useful to gain or increase our awareness of the lungs using vybhaga pranayama or sectional breathing simply with the touch of our hand or sparsha mudra.

Bring the palms of the hands around the lower lobes of the lungs, feel the front sides and back of the lower lobes and take some long slow inhalations and exhalations. Feel the movement of the rib cage expanding and contracting. Repeat this with the mid lobes and the upper lobes of the lungs.

 Then we can start to use the Hasta Mudras – the gestures of the hands. These mudras are based in the yogic knowledge that we have 72,000 nadis or subtle energy currents travelling and running through our physical body and surrounding our body connecting us to the Universe. These energy flows also connect and gather at certain vortex points commonly known as Chakras. There are many chakras points in the body but 7 are well known located at different points up the line of the spine to the top of the head. The Hasta mudras will gesture to the energy currents to make connections which stimulate the different sections of the lungs to expand and contract. We work from the lower lobes up to the upper lobes and complete with linking all three parts to the full yogic breath or Mahat Yoga Pranayama.

We relax the shoulders, lengthen the spine and bring the hands into CHIN MUDRA where the thumb and forefinger are touching, and the other three fingers are extended, straight and resting on top of the thigh. This will primarily draw the air into our lower lobes.

Use a 6 count in breath and a 6 count out SUKKHA RHYTHM for 3 rounds or 6 rounds.

Then add the vibrational sound on the out breath for the lower lung:

AAAAAHHHHHHH for 3 rounds

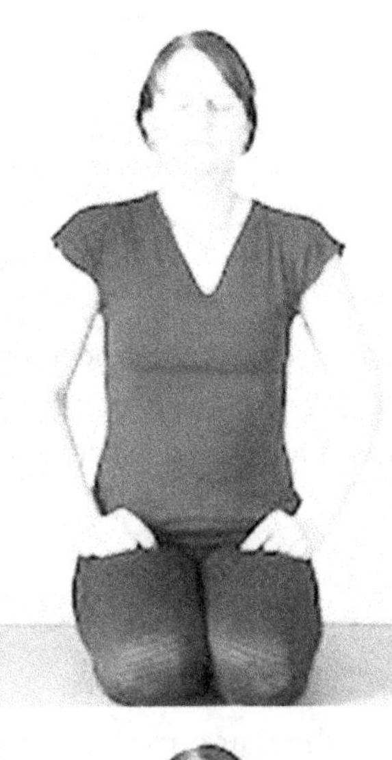

For the Mid lung area we use CHIN MAYA MUDRA, bringing the thumb and forefinger together as before, this time the three fingers are curled in towards the palm and again resting on top of the thighs.

Breath consciously into the mid chest area using the 6x6 SUKKHA RHYTHM, for another 3 - 6 rounds. Then add the vibrational sound on the out breath for the intercostal area:

OOOOOOOOOOOO for 3 rounds

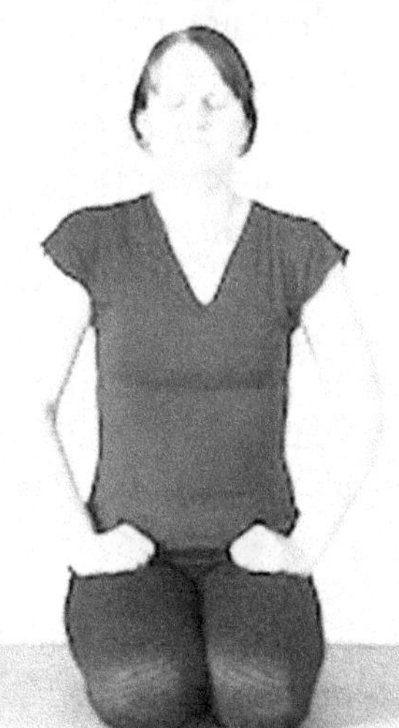

The Upper most part of the lungs, using ADHI MUDRA the clavicular area is one of the most difficult part to isolate as generally, most of us have some stale, trapped air here.

Bring our thumb inside the fist and again bring the hands on top of the thigh.

Breath consciously into the upper lung area using the 6X6 sukkha rhythm for 3 - 6 rounds.

Then add the vibrational sound on the out breath for the upper lung area:

MMMMMMMMM for 3 rounds

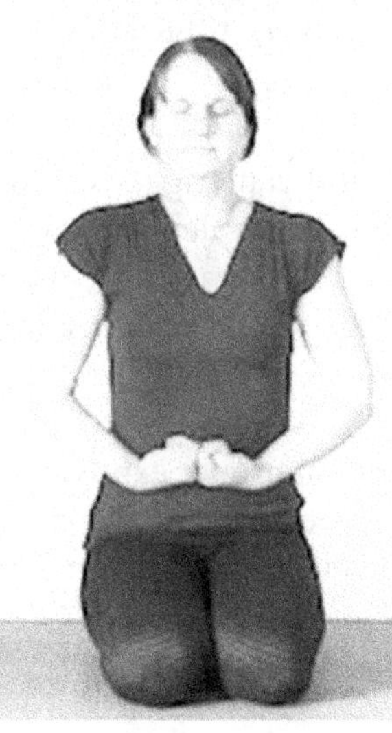

Finally completing with BRAHMA MUDRA connecting all three parts of the lungs and breath flow in sequence. Bring the hands into Brahma mudra with the backs of the fists together, thumbs inside the fist with hands resting around the naval region.

Breath in and out evenly using the 6X6 SUKKHA RHYTHM, feel the air flowing from the lower lobes first, to mid and then to the upper lobes of the lungs, as you exhale in the same order.

Then add the sound AAAAA-UUUUU-MMMMM making the sound equal in each part. This is called the Pranava AUM.

Aruna Surya Namaskar
salutation to the red sun

Sun Light- Essence of the Life

We all know that we need calcium for strong bones and teeth, to prevent osteoporosis, to keep the heart muscles and nerves functioning well and even to prevent blood clotting. What most of us do not know is that for calcium to do its work, vitamin-D must pitch in too.

The crucial calcium-vitamin-D connection is a medically well-established fact, though few people know of it.

It is especially important for post-menopausal women as they are particularly vulnerable to osteoporosis and osteomalacia (softening of the bones). This information is also crucial for infants and growing children, because deficiency of calcium or vitamin-D may cause deformed bones and rickets. Vitamin-D is also instrumental in controlling the movement of calcium in between bone and blood and vice-versa.

Vitamin-D is also known as the sunshine vitamin. Our body manufactures vitamin-D only on exposure to the sunlight. This is a hormone like fat-soluble vitamin. It regulates the formation of the bones and absorption of the calcium and phosphorus from the intestines. Lactating and expecting women need about 400-500 IUs of vitamin-D per day.

In the northern countries like the UK where there is less exposure to sun and the whole body is kept covered with clothes - these are more prone to calcium and vitamin-D deficiencies. In hot countries like India, although the dress code is to cover the body, the cloth worn is usually thin cotton and the sunlight can still be absorbed to a large degree through this.

However, an excess of the vitamin-D can be determinant and can trigger off loss of appetite, weight loss, nausea, headache, depressions, and calcium deposits in the kidneys. This may lead to excess secretion of the calcium from the bones which may be deposited in the soft tissues of body organs like heart, kidneys and may result in formation of stones, vomiting and muscle weakness.

During the wintertime vitamin-D deposits in the liver depend on proper exposure to the sun light during the summer. People with vitamin-D deficiency are more prone to cancers of the colon, prostate, breast and even ovaries. This vitamin also regulates the cell growth.

The best time to have a 'sunbath' absorbing this natural energy is the early morning at the time of the sun rising. Go out and stand facing the sun. Open your hands a little wide with the palms facing towards the front. Surrender yourself to the sun. Do some deep breathing and try to inhale the energy with the breath. Concentrate on your hands and then over the whole body and feel the warm sensations of the golden pranic energy that you are receiving from the solar energy.

Sources of Prana: the Vital Energy

Hindu's do not generally say the word 'death' instead they say your prana departs from the body. Whilst there is prana; there is life in the body. Sometimes when you meet someone, you feel charged, light and very happy. While at other times you feel dull, lethargic and even sad after meeting someone. The reason in yogic thought is the levels of pranic energy; one person is a very rich source of the prana and emanates prana whilst the other one is lacking in prana and just like a vacuum, they absorb your prana. Perhaps you can feel or experience this many times in your day-to-day life. Once you are starting to grow on the yogic path and be aware of those who give energy and those who absorb we can make the necessary changes in our own lives to avoid these people.

The people that we have in our life is also something to be contemplated. We should try to spend a bit of time asking ourselves why certain people are in our lives? We have a lot of choice over the people we spend our time with who like it or not will influence our quality of life tremendously. In Yoga we use the word 'satsanga' which means a gathering or group of 'truth-seekers' or we can also think of this as like-minded people. The Yogic scriptures encourage us to surround ourselves with spiritual, evolved souls if we hope to grow and evolve ourselves. In fact, they say that if we do not there is no chance of progression on the spiritual path. Of course, the spiritual path is not for everybody in this life, because it involves making many sacrifices from a life of 'Bhoga' which means a worldly life or comforts, desires and living selfishly rather than selflessly.

Maybe the Yogic spiritual life is not for you, nevertheless we need to improve our environment for a new baby! This event turns many people's lives around, who suddenly find they will need to become responsible for another human being who will arrive helpless, vulnerable and totally dependent upon its mother or guardian. Then we can look at our lives and see what and who is an uplifting influence in our lives and what and who drains us out? We want to create a good life for a new child, so this event often gives people's lives a natural 'cleanse' of many aspects of our lives. If we clean up our lives we are also cleaning up our pranic energy.

Most of the prana we receive from the air we inhale. Although it is not the air itself we are referring to, but the energy created from 'breathing well' which harmonises and replenishes our inner energies. But we also receive it in some extent from the food and drink. Some part is also absorbed directly in the skin from the atmosphere. The Sun is also a very good source of prana.

Prana is not the oxygen or the other gases we inhale and not the nutrients we take in from the food. The truth is that behind using all these nutrients and the gases for breathing, this divine energy prana plays the role as the catalyst. Prana is absorbed through the exposed nerve endings of the body and especially in the nostrils, mouth and back of the throat. For example, we should eat slowly and chew enough to allow the releasing and absorbing of the prana. Water should be sipped slowly to allow the absorption of prana in throat and mouth.

Therefore, the richest source of the prana is the air we breathe in. That's why all the practices of pranayama emphasise to do slow deep breathing, to allow the free absorption of the prana in the nostrils and the inner parts of the body.

According to yogic philosophy one can easily survive without eating food, these practitioners are known as the breatharians. If you have ever read the book 'auto biography of a yogi', the author Paramahansa Yogananda (1893–1952) talks about having met a woman in her 60's who had not eaten food since being a child. In India you can still hear stories of people today who live this way, they are mostly living in solitude and often in the Himalayan region of India.

The fresh air, the water sources, green plantations, hills, rivers, ocean, forests, morning fresh air, is very rich in prana, whereas the filtered air using air conditioners, electric devices, etc. have a lesser amount of prana. Polluted air sources have no prana or will be dramatically decreased, which is a problem in densely populated areas.

Thus to get enough prana, try to go for an early morning walk; outings in nature or places positioned close to natural water sources, springs and trees are the best way to fulfil our need for prana.

Second to the air, the richest source of the prana is water. Even water functions as the vehicle of prana. Clean, fresh, non-refrigerated, and taken from its natural source, is good source of prana. One important observance is to never gulp water; try to sip it like tea or coffee. Allow it to stay in your mouth for a while so that the prana can be absorbed. Keep yourself hydrated. Drink plenty of clean water. A large number of the people in the world die, because of the dehydration and it is a common fact that generally humans are dehydrated, which is worsened with a stressful over busy life where we do not have enough time to regularly drink water. Dehydration blocks the flow of the prana in our body. So always keep your mouth and the throat moist with water, if it feels dried out this is a sign that you are already dehydrated.

Food is the third source of the prana. Prana is available in food. Fresh vegetables, fruits, green leaves, cereals, dry fruits have excess prana. Your food should be fresh, seasonal and related to the area you are living in.

All non-vegetarian food, preserved food, fast foods and refrigerated foods have little or no prana.

To release the prana from the food it should be chewed properly before swallowing. Eating with awareness also increases prana absorption from the food. Emotions used during cooking the food will also affect the prana or vital energy in the food. So be positive and happy when you are cooking food for you or your family! It's also quite important to sit down and relax whilst we are eating rather than eating on the go or walking around whilst eating, this simply aids our digestion process.

One can also get prana directly from space (environment) and the sunlight. This needs high sensitivity and awareness. You can start absorbing the prana through your skin by using your deep feelings of getting the prana through the skin. This could be used as the tool of relaxation and dharana (concentration).

what are the factors adversely affecting your access to prana?
- Your negative thoughts and emotions
- Bad habits
- Unhealthy lifestyle
- Imbalance of rest and action
- Unhealthy/negative surroundings or companions
- Ignorance
- Imbalanced dietary habits
- Smoking, alcohol, drug-addiction, etc.

This brings us to a great way to start building up prana, which is through the classical Yoga practice, Surya Namaskar or Sun salutations!

Some benefits of Surya Namaskar:
- Regular performance of Surya namaskar has effects on all the parts of the body. It is especially effective for stiffness of the joints, which can be reduced or removed. The backbone also becomes more flexible.

- It enhances digestive capacity and can be curative in diseases pertaining to the neck and the stomach. Neck, back and joints pains are improved or cured.

❖ By this Kriya the chest is widened and the waist slimmed. This Asana reduces the fat of the abdominal region. Improves problems with constipation and the kidneys are strengthened.

❖ Spiritual awareness and a state of peace and concentration of mind are achieved by performing Surya namaskar with recitation of mantras. It helps in awakening the 'serpent power', or Kundalini.

❖ Exhale during the bending positions and inhale during upward and stretching movements. This is complete process of pranayama. Suryanamaskar improves asthma, bronchitis, sinusitis, cold, cough and other respiratory problems.

❖ The digestive system is activated and regulated. The secretions of liver, spleen, kidney, and stomach are specially regulated.

❖ When you practice Surya Namaskar outside to the morning sun, the movements are designed to allow the pranic sun energy to enter your body through different chakra points or centres.

Surya Mantras
(these should be chanted before practicing Surya Namaskar)

1. Om Mitraya namah (salutation to one who is friend to all),

2. Om Ravaye namah (salutation to one who is praised by all),

3. Om Suryaya namah (salutation to one who is guide to all),

4. Om Bhanave namah (salutation to one who is bestower of beauty),

5. Om Khagaya namah (salutation to one who is stimulator of senses),

6. Om Pushne namah (salutation to one who is nourisher of life),

7. Om Hiranyagarbhaya namah (salutation to one who is promoter of virility),

8. Om Marichaye namah (salutation to one who is destroyer of diseases),

9. Om Adityaya namah (salutation to one who is inspirer of love),

10. Om Savitre namah (salutation to one who is Begetter of life),

11. Om Arkaya namah (salutation to one who is inspirator of Awe) and

12. Om Bhaskaraya namah (salutation to one who is effulgent one).

By chanting these mantras, we can bring our mind into the deeper meanings of the Surya Namaskar practice.

Aruna Surya Namaskar - Salutation to the Red Sun
(as taught by the Rishi Culture Ashtanga - Gitananda Tradition)

Aruna is one of the names of the sun, which means red colour. This Surya Namaskar has different ten positions. Stand straight in the Samasthiti Asana keeping palms facing the sun and hands little wide open.

This series is good to gain flexibility and align the body structure. Those who are willing to reduce the weight and get rid of problems associated to obesity must do at least twelve rounds of it daily.

Step-1.   Slowly raise up both your hands in the Anjali Mudra while inhaling. Stretch whole body and look the sky.

Step-II.   Open your palms to face the sun and slowly bend in front, place the palms on ground near the feet. Touch the head to the knees while exhaling the breath. Keep your legs straight. This is Hasta-Pada-Asana.

Step-III.   Stretch your neck in front and look in front. Your spine, neck and head should come in the straight position while breathing in.

Step-IV.   Jump back and balance whole of your body weight on the two hands and two feet. Other parts of body should not touch the ground. Perform this while exhaling.

Step-V.   Slowly raise up your head, stretch the chest upside while breathing in. Try to look to the sky and keep the toes tucked. This is the Kokila-Asana.

Step-VI.   Now come to Meru-Asana while inhaling. Balance whole body on both hands and feet, while raising the buttocks as high as possible. Your legs and spine should be straight. Now perform few rounds of the Nasarga-Mukha- Bhastrika. In this inhale from the nose and blast exhale from the mouth, with hissing sound, and exerting the diaphragm forcefully.

Step-VII.   Jump to place both the feet in middle of the both the palms. Look forward while stretching the neck and spine forward to come back to the position III while inhaling.

Step-VIII.   Slowly bent down your head and touch the head with the knees while exhaling the breath. Your legs should be straight. This is Hasta-Pada-Asana.

Step-IX.   Slowly move up to the position one, Anjali Mudra while inhaling and stretch the whole body.

Step-X.   Slowly raise down your hands and come back to the Sama-sthiti-asana, while exhaling the breath. Your palms should be facing the sun to absorb the prana and energy from the sun light.

Aruna Surya Namaskar with back bend

Aruna is one of the names of the sun, which means red colour. This surya namaskar has different twelve positions. Stand straight in the Samasthiti Asana with keeping palms facing the sun and hands little wide open.

Step-1.   Slowly raise up both your hands in the Anjali Mudra while inhaling. Stretch whole body and look the sky.

Step-II.   Open your palms to face the sun and slowly bend in back as much as possible. You can keep holding the breath in and eyes open in beginning.

Step-III. To X. Repeat as the Aruna-Surya-Namaskar (position II to IX).

Step-XI.   Open your palms to face the sun and slowly bend in back as much as possible. You may keep holding the breath in.

Step-XII. Slowly raise down your hands with opening them in the wide circle and come back to the Samasthiti-Asana, while exhaling the breath. Your palms should be facing the sun to absorb the prana and energy from the sun light.

"I have always been bemused by the fact that
many pregnant women spend longer preparing
the nursery for the baby than their bodies"
Dr. Gowri Motha.

Pancha Kosha (Five Bodies, Sheaths or Layers)

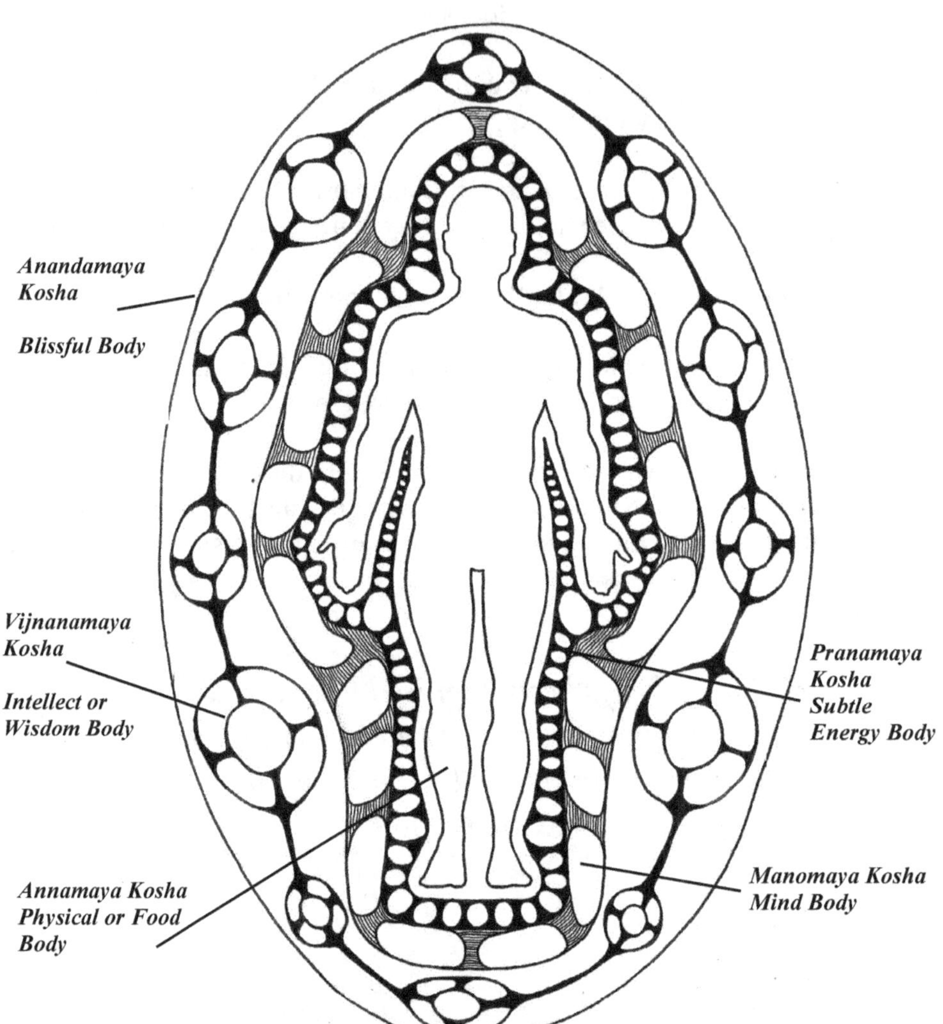

Pancha Kosha or Five Energy Bodies

Pancha Koshas- Yoga and Tantra Science explains the five body concept. Pancha means five and Kosha means sheath or layer. Yoga believes in the five body concept. It is very important to understand this concept to understand the concept of Chakras and Kundalini and the true essence of Hatha Yoga Kriyas from Tantric perspectives.

Annamaya Kosha -Physical or Food Body – This is the first layer, made up of food and five elements. Anna means atom or food. This body is a tool or instrument for all the other bodies. This is nourished through fulfilling our biological needs of hunger, thirst and sex. This body has a vital role in the life and death process as well as our evolution. We cannot experience anything in this world without this body. In Upanishads it is stated that even Gods have to come in human forms and have this body to experience and fulfil the duties they need to do. There are so many examples of incarnations of divinities like Krishna, Buddha, Jesus, Mahavira, etc.

Hatha Yoga provides a wide range of asana, mudra, pranayama and cleansing practices to keep the body healthy, strong and full of vitality.

Pranamaya Kosha- Subtle Energy Body – This is the second layer, composed of the subtlest cosmic vital forces. Prana means vital, psychic and cosmic energy. Prana literally means "the energy which exists before the beginning of the universe". This body has 72,000 nadis or subtle energy channels. This Prana, or life force, governs all our physical and psychological functions.

In yoga prana is described as the eternal life force, which governs all the physical, psychic and spiritual functions of the whole universe. It also carries all the knowledge, wisdom, processes, and formulas of manifestation, sustaining the evolution of all living and non-living activities. It is like the DNA in our body, which carries all the genetic code of our life process.

Manomaya Kosha- Mind Body –This is third energy body or layer. Manas means mind. This is the mind or mental body and is composed of all our thoughts, feelings, emotions, memories and life experiences from all the life times we have been through. This body is interlinked between our physical and pranic bodies and has a direct influence on both of them as well as being influenced by them also.

Vijnanamaya Kosha -Intellect or Wisdom Body –This is the fourth body. Vijnana means wisdom or knowledge of life and the universal process. This is the conscious body which governs our insights, intuition, reasoning, and conscience. Only through meditation and spiritual practices one can access this body which is known as transcendental awareness or realisation.

Anandamaya Kosha - Blissful Body- Ananda means joy or bliss. This is purest of energy bodies in the form of pure love, joyfulness, and bliss. This body is the realm of super-consciousness or higher-self. In this body one achieves self-realisation or Samadhi. All the layers are interconnected with each other, imagine a 'blue-tooth' connectivity.

Loma Viloma Vidya

Hatha yoga and all the Tantric practices are based on the concept of the loma-viloma. The Sanskrita word 'hatha' is derived from joining of 'ha' and 'tha'. 'Ha' is the solar energy represented by the warm golden sun. 'Tha' is the lunar energy represented by the cool silvery moon. The aim of all the hatha yoga and tantric practices is union and balance of the 'ha' and 'tha'; solar and lunar energies.

The Pranamaya or Subtle energy body is beyond scientific explanation for now. Also, you will need to go beyond your physical body through yoga and meditation to experience this energy body.

Chakras are a very well-known concept in the Yoga world and it fascinates most of us. There are many theories, ideas and myths around the idea of chakras and kundalini energy. In Yoga, we know that there are five bodies (Pancha-koshas). Here try to merely understand that the first layer is our physical body (Sthula Sarira), we all know this very well as we can see it, we can touch it, and we can feel it. The second group of bodies is known as Sukhsama Sarira or the subtle body. This layer is composed of vital life forces (prana), our thoughts, ideas, emotions and experiences (manas or mind), our karma or deeds and soul or spirit (Purusha or atman). Here the Pranic body is most important to understand. All our chakras have their location in our Pranic Body, and they work as connecting or linking points between the pranic and physical body.

We could think of the chakras like that of an electro-magnetic dynamo, which can produce electricity if it is spun in the magnetic field. Our Chakras spin at various speeds to transform the subtlest prana into multiple forms of energy to sustain our psycho-physio-spiritual functions.

Prana is the subtlest, vital, eternal energy. The sanskrita term prana comes from 'Pra'- which means existed before and Anu which means atom. Hence it is a most delicate electromagnetic energy at sub-atomic and quantum level. Great Yogis and Rishis have known about this subtlest force for thousands of years. To protect this vital force of Prana they always recommended a thick layer of insulation in the form of a straw bed, lion or deerskin, a thick wool or jute blanket should also be used for yoga and meditation sadhana. Otherwise when you meditate or practice yoga sadhana it can be drawn down into the earth, and you will lose all your energy.

This Pranic body just like the electric or magnetic force has positive and negative ions. In Yogic, Vedantic and Tantric traditions they describe that positive prana dominates in men and negative prana predominates in women. Positive and Negative energies are naturally attracted to each other to complete the energy cycle. These positive and negative vital forces determine the way we behave, act, react and think. A yogi seeks to balance these energies to live in serenity or harmony.

This Pranic body holds our body, mind, karma, and soul together. As the soul departs or leaves the body, so does the prana. In most ancient cultures, where they had released this pranic body, they usually prefer to complete the funeral/ceremonies as soon as possible after death, otherwise it is understood that the prana will still feel attracted to our physical body and this can hold the soul from moving on to next life. Energy from the pranic body gets transformed into various life forces by the Chakras and flows outward into different physical parts of our body as well as mental, emotional and spiritual aspects in us. Once we start meditating, this pranic energy will start flowing back into the pranic body or its source.

Our right half of our body is represented by the masculine characters of shiva and the left half of our body is a representation of the feminine characters of shakti. This sun and moon; warm golden and cool silvery; ha and tha, energies are known as loma and viloma respectively. These are also represented by the pranic and apranic energies.

Prana moves down from the top to the bottom in the right half of the body while apana moves up from the bottom to the top in the left half of the body. This is also found in the concept of the polarity of the human body. Energy always flows in a wide oval shape in and outside the body.

The loma and viloma energies are a manifestation of the positive energy and the negative energy from the subtle to the gross body.

The process of human evolution from animal nature to human nature and then to the purest nature of super conscious is from the gross or the physical body. Body awareness and awareness of the loma and viloma energies refines and purifies these energies to their subtle forms to gain the harmony and oneness with the self and our true nature/higher self.

Five gross pranas, apana, vyana, prana, samana and udana flow in various parts of our body and in various directions to keep the physical, mental and emotional processes in health and harmonious functioning. They regulate the normal functioning of the body area they are concerned with.

This Loma Viloma series taught by Dr Swami Gitananda Giriji can help with balancing, nurturing, healing and enhancing the quality of pranic-apanic, loma-viloma, or solar-lunar energies, leading us to complete health and well-being. This will help Sadhakas for preparing for healthy conception and pregnancy.

Loma-Viloma sequence

The Loma-Viloma series helps balancing of the Pranic-Apanic, Loma-Viloma or positive- negative ions of the subtlest life force known as Prana. There are also many physical benefits, and here are just few to mention-

- Help improve mobility of limbs
- Improve strength and flexibility of the back
- Improves strength, flexibility and endurance of abdominal, pelvic and all the muscles associated with the spine
- Stimulates various parts of the brain regulating legs, arms, torso, hips, pelvis and abdomen as you are using all these parts with breath and awareness
- Balances hormones and autonomic system
- Improves sleep and enhances mental clarity
- Balances Chakras and energy flows
- Improves blood circulation in our body

Precautions-

- If you suffer with back problems, you may begin with bent knees in all leg lift movements
- Practice under strict guidance or in modified way if you have had any abdominal or pelvic surgeries in past
- If you have any back or shoulder problems, follow modified variations of Bhujangasana and Dhanurasana under strict guidance.

The Loma-Viloma Hatha Yoga Sequence
The four starting positions:

This sequence has four parts and can be further divided into four 'starting' positions for each movement. As we move though each part the movements become more intense and challenging. The four starting positions are all lying down postures described as follows:

1. Savasana

Lie straight on your back; while keeping the legs straight. Try to keep your feet close with heels touching each other if possible. If you feel uncomfortable you may have a little distance between both the feet. Place your hands along your sides with palms upward at a little distance from the body. This is Savasana and especially used for doing the conscious relaxation. For all the straight lying poses we are going to use this asana.

2. Unmukha Asana

Lie straight on your abdomen in the face prone position. Place both hands close to your buttocks along your side. You may keep your legs a little apart. This is the position for doing all the face prone positions and sometimes it could be used as the relaxation pose during the face prone asanas. The forehead can be on the floor or the chin preferably if its comfortable.

3. Dakshina Dridha Asana

Turn straight on your left side, keeping the right side dominant (in Sanskrit the dominant or active side is described not the side we are lying on) Try to keep the whole body straight like a stick. You may fold the left elbow to place below the head to support. Right hand should be kept straight over the body or place in front to support.

4. Vama Dridha Asana (as above opposite side)
Turn straight on your right side keeping the left side dominant. Try to keep the whole body straight like the stick. You may fold the right elbow to place below the head to support. Left hand should be kept straight over the body.

Part one of the Loma Viloma series:

Eka Pada Uttana Kriya- Single leg lifting
From Shava Asana, lift the right leg up slowly with a 6 count as you breath in and release back down in a controlled way on 6 count with the out breath.

Your leg should be straight during the process. The force for lifting should be used from the abdominal muscles without arching the spine. Repeat with left leg.

Shirsha Uttana Asana - Head lifting In Savasana slowly lift up your head without arching the back. Stretch your neck as much as you can. Slowly release whilst breathing out.

Ardha Shalabha Asana - Half Locust Come to the Unmukha Asana and slowly lift your right leg without bending the knee whilst breathing in and release the pose whilst breathing out. Repeat the same with the left leg. You can place your hands under your thighs for support.

Unmukha Shirsha Uttana – head lift
In Unmukha-Asana slowly lift up your head without arching the back. Stretch your neck as much as you can. Slowly release on an out breath.

Dakshina (right) Dridha Eka Pada Uttana Asana – leg lift
Turn to the Dakshina or Dridha-Asana and slowly lift your right leg straight up as high as you can with the breath. Try to keep the leg straight.

Shirsha Uttana Asana – head lift Now slowly lift your head high while breathing in and lower it on the out breath.

Part two of the Loma Viloma series

Stambham Asana – the pillar
From the Savasana come to the Uttana-Asana, the straight sit up position. Now lift your right leg high and hold the ankle of it with the hands. Without bending the knees try to touch the knee with the nose. Your left leg should remain straight on the ground. Try to balance the whole body straight on the tail bone. This is the stambhama asana. Practice the same with the changed legs.

Ideally we are trying to bring the head and torso close to our leg in the complete pose.

Ardha Dhanur Asana – the half bow
Turn to the Unmukhha-Asana and fold your right leg over the buttocks. Hold the ankle of the right leg with the right hand and stretch up gently as high as you can. Your left leg should remain straight on the ground. Spine should be arched in the half circle. Repeat the same with the changed legs.

Dakshina Dridha Eka Pada Uttanasana Privritti-I – leg lift variation

Turn to the Dakshina- Dridha- Asana and place the left elbow on the ground with keeping the arm straight supporting the head to keep high from the ground (or cradle the head in the hand) Now fold your right leg and hold the ankle. While in breath slowly lift your right leg straight up as high as you can with the support of the hand. Try to reach to the straight leg position.

Part three of the Loma Viloma series

Dvi Pada Uttana Asana – double leg lift

Come to Savasana and lift both the legs straight up to the ninety degree angle with the torso. Keep both the legs straight and don't allow your back to arch. Slowly release the pose while breathing out.

Danda Asana – the stick

Slowly lift your torso up and come to the Uttana-Asana, the straight sit up. Now slowly raise up both the hands in the anjali mudra over the head, clasp them and stretch the palms upward. Try to keep the spine erect and legs straight. This is Danda-Asana.

Shalabha Asana – the locust

Come to the Unmukha-Asana, the face prone position and adjust both the hands below your thighs. Lift both the legs high up while the in breath with keeping the legs straight. Release the pose on an out breath.

Bhujanga Asana – the cobra

In Unmukha-Asana place both the hands close to the shoulders. Stretch your upper back while in breath with the support of the hands. Stretch the neck little backward and look to the sky.

Your legs should be straight and touching each other. Your navel should also keep touching the ground in the final position of the asana. Return to unmukha-asana on the out breath.

Dakshina Dridha Eka Pada Uttanasana Privritti-II – leg lift variation

Turn to the Dakshina- Dridha- Asana and stretch the torso up and place the left hand on the ground close to the buttocks with keeping the hand straight supporting the head and waist to keep high from the ground. Now fold your right leg and hold the ankle. While breathing in and slowly lift your right leg straight up as high
as you can with the support of the hand. Try to reach to the straight leg position.

Vama Dridha Eka Pada Uttanasana Privritti-II

Turn to the Vama- Dridha- Asana and stretch the torso up and place the right hand on the ground close to the buttocks while keeping the hand straight, supporting the head and waist to keep high from the ground.

Now fold your left leg and hold the ankle while breathing in to stretch your leg over to the side and release with the out breath.

Part Four of the Loma Viloma series

Sapurna Vajroli Mudra-II
Come to the Savasana and then perform Uttana-Asana. Now fold both the legs and hold the ankles. Slowly stretch your legs straight and high. Now try to balance the whole body weight on the tailbone. Your body should attain the perfect V-shape in the completed pose.

Dhanura Asana – the bow
Turn to the Unmukha-Asana and fold your legs over the buttocks and hold the ankles of the respective legs with the hands. While breathing in, try to stretch up the body as much as you can. Only your navel and closer part of the abdomen should remain on the ground. Your head and both the legs should be high.
Release the pose during the out breath.

Dakshina Vashishta Tapasya Asana – the posture of sage Vashishta
Turn to the Dakshina Dridha Asana and lift your whole body and try to balance on the left hand and the left foot. Fold the right leg; hold the ankle and stretch the right leg as high as possible. This asana was used by the Rishi Vashishtha to perform his penances and hence known as the Vashishtha Asana.

Vama Vashishta Tapasya Asana
Turn to the Vama-Dridha-Asana and lift your whole body and try to balance on the right hand and the right foot. Fold the left leg; hold the ankle and stretch the left leg as high as possible.

Yogic practices to release trauma

In preparation for children, we must not only consider building the body up into health and fitness but also in some respects the yogic way is to also break it down or clean it up or empty it out of rubbish, toxins, negativity as all these samskaras / negative conditioning can and will affect our babies. In Yoga we have a plethora of practices that deal with internal cleaning our body, mind and 'soul'.

I often reflect back into my days working as a social worker, one of my posts was working in a drug rehabilitation community team. If we met an addict who was desperate and willing to change their life to get away from drugs, at that time it was possible to get funding for residential rehabilitation. I would visit many of these rehabilitation centers in my work and found them to be very similar indeed to spiritual Ashrams! They were very strict on many things, there were curfews, if you did something very wrong you would be thrown out, there was a great deal of discipline but in a positive way, lots of counselling, group discussions and people constantly being asked to look at themselves, their own behaviours and to take ownership and responsibility for themselves. These programs for the drug addicts were a type of cleansing of their lives, in the same way Ashrams work like this, they direct us to 'weed out the trash' in our lives, whether they are people, memories, traumas, places or past events. We have no need to carry the past. What has happened 'happened' but it is not happening right now, therefore if we remember it we are still consciously carrying it. Most of the time we do not have the knowledge of how to get rid of terrible experiences from our body and mind. Thankfully Yoga has so many ways of dealing so directly yet so subtly with events of our past. I do not believe we can deal with everything through 'talking therapies' as these methods do not deal with the stresses that are trapped within our bodies cellular memory, so they will not be as effective as the yogic methods which do exactly this. This is why Emotional Freedom Technique (EFT) has proven so effective in dealing with post-traumatic stress as its method incorporates body movements.

Kaya Kriya

Kaya kriya is aimed for the relaxation of the whole body. According to Swamiji "relaxation could not be attained only by simply lying down. You need to stretch properly before going to relaxation". 'Spanda and Nispanda' is part of the theory behind the kaya kriya. Stretching increases the flow of the blood and energy in the respective areas and then relaxation allows free flow of the toxins out of the muscles and the joints to the excretory organs. Mostly though the Kaya Kriya is a movement that will mimic a body writhing in pain, but in a safe way. Through this practice we can work out pains and psychological or emotional traumas through these simple moments. Many people find this practice quite irritating or 'annoying' at first, because it is rubbing against you. It is starting to peel away or tear away at layers within you. Perhaps you are so used to them being there you no longer realise they are not you; they are just something attached to you that you carry around. Sometimes removing these things can be painful as we imagine they are part of who we are. Then you have to make a choice either to let it go or make it a part of you. Swami Gitananda would say that if this practice is irritating for you then you need to do it many times!

The Kaya Kriya works especially well for psychosomatic disorders, where the mind and the body are no longer communicating well with each other. The Kaya Kriya practice will bring the mind, body and emotions into harmony and balance with each other. It also works on the vibhaga pranayama or complete breathing whilst doing the practice. When we practice the kriya for the lower legs we also breath into the lower lobes of the lungs. The arm movements connect to the mid chest and the head movement to the upper lobes breathing. When we then connect all three parts we breath into all parts equally and fully, so the Kaya kriya is also excellent for breathing patterns and lung function. We are bringing the mind and body together with the breath. We also bring many memories out from our subconscious through this practice that our cells remember, but we may have forgotten. When memories are revealed into the conscious mind we can then release them and let go!

Method:
Lower legs roll inwards with in breath and outwards with the out breath – practice for 3, 6 or 9 rounds
Arms roll outwards with in breath and rotate inwards with the out breath– practice for 3, 6 or 9 rounds
Head rolls to the right side on in breath and the left side on the out breath – practice for 3, 6 or 9 rounds.
For the complete Kaya Kriya and mahat yoga pranayama (complete yogic breath) we connect all the above movements one after another in one breath, in and out. Dr Ananda Bhavanani suggests we can start with 6 count in breath and 6 count out breath and gradually work on increasing the exhale from a 6x6 sukkha pranayama to a 6 in breath and an 18 count out breath when working on all three parts.

It should be done before performing the shavasana or the yoga-nidra. It is done in the position of the shavasana. It can be performed with the vibhaga pranayama/ sectional breathing.

Section-I. Adhama Kaya Kriya
In the position of savasana keep your legs apart so that when you turn them inward, the toes of legs should touch each other. Now while inhaling in the lower lungs rotate your legs inward to touch the toes of both the legs and rotate outward while breathing out. This should be done nine rounds to rounds multiple of the three.

Section-II. Madhyama Kaya Kriya

In the position of savasana keep your legs closer and both hands little apart from the body. Now while inhaling in the middle lungs rotate your hands outward to touch the palms to the ground and rotate inward while breathing out. This should be done nine rounds to rounds multiple of the three.

Section-III. Adhyama Kaya Kriya

In the position of savasana keep your legs close to each other, hands close to the body. Now while inhaling in the upper lungs rotate your neck and head to the right side, and rotate to the left side while breathing out.
This should be done nine rounds to rounds multiple of the three.

Section-IV. Mahat Kaya Kriya

In the position of savasana keep your legs apart so that when you turn them inward, the toes of legs should touch each other. Hands should be little apart from the body. Now while inhaling in the lower lungs rotate your legs inward to touch the toes of both the legs; followed with the hands rotation outward and the neck rotation to the right side with the middle and upper breath. Then rotate legs outward, hands inward and neck to the left side while breathing out. This should be done nine rounds to rounds multiple of the three.

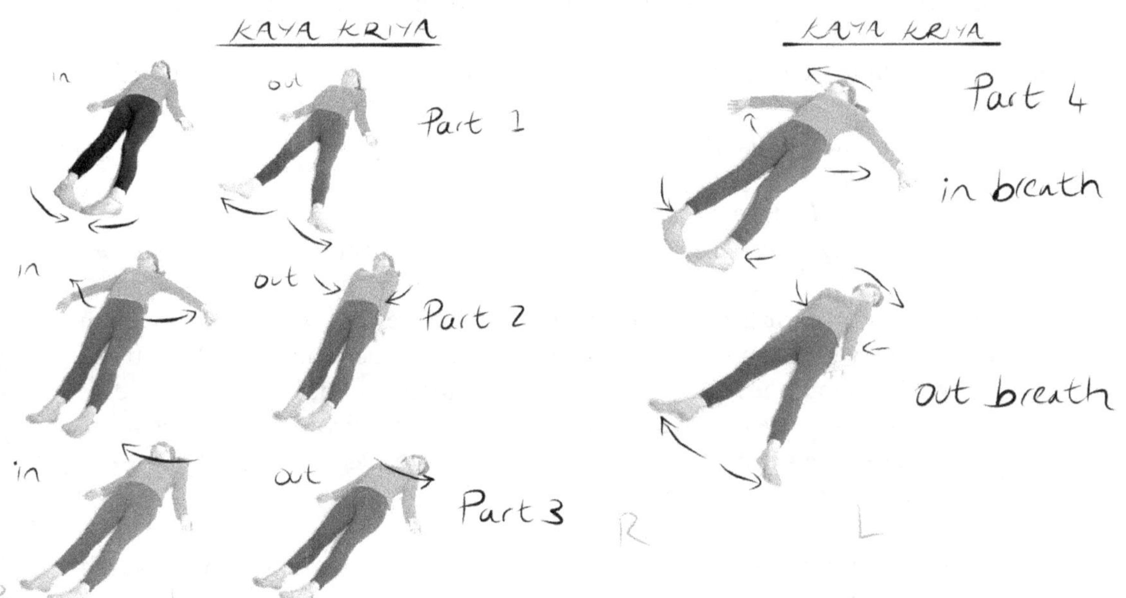

Moksha Kriya
for Freeing us from past and current hurt and anger

We all hold anger and frustration and accumulate it in our subconscious and unconscious minds. Our body naturally likes to relax, rejuvenate and heal. It is the in-built concept of Spanada-Nispanda which means stretch or to give 100% effort and then let go completely, or relax. But our mind has a different conditioning, so it needs to be re-trained. If we hold any tension or emotion in our mind, our body has to constantly respond, act or react to it. The anger we hold in, has constant and chronic effects upon our personality and behaviour patterns. The longer we hold on to anger and frustration creates deeper and more intense negative effects on our body. Anger and fear cause constant disturbances in the hormonal and chemical secretions in our body, which leads to greater health issues.

Some of us might think that getting the anger out or releasing it can help. But actually getting it out can be like putting petrol on a flame, it makes it worst. The best way to deal with it is allowing it to evaporate or dissolve. The following regressive practice is to take you through that journey to help erasing those memories of anger or hurt you are holding in.

Practice- Ideally try to sit straight in a comfortable posture. But if that is too uncomfortable you can follow it in shavasana. While you are following the process, you don't need to look into causes, why, how, or who, or analyse it too much.

Each time we think of an event that effected our life, we should think of these four aspects:

1	*details of the environment*
2	*details about the other person*
3	*details of yourself in that situation*
4	*imagine how you would like to be and feel instead*

❖ Softly focus in your heart and try to look back to yesterday and find any event or incident which caused anger or disturbed your equanimity (1 to 2 minutes). Now think about the first three aspects of the memory and three times release the different aspects by holding it in your hands and throwing it out by lifting the hands to the sky and whooshing it out with the breath. For the last aspect, bring your palms to your heart.

❖ Reflect in back to the whole week and find any event or things which caused anger or disturbed you (1 to 2 minutes). Now think about the first three aspects of the memory and three times release the different aspects by holding it in your hands and throwing it out by lifting the hands to the sky and whooshing it out with the breath. For the last aspect, bring your palms to your heart.

❖   Reflect back to the whole year and find any event or events which caused you anger or disturbed you (1 to 2 minutes). Now think about the first three aspects of the memory and three times release the different aspects by holding it in your hands and throwing it out by lifting the hands to the sky and whooshing it out with the breath. For the last aspect, bring your palms to your heart.

❖   Reflect in back as far as you can in your life and find any event or events that caused anger or disturbed you (1 to 2 minutes). Now think about the first three aspects of the memory and three times release the different aspects by holding it in your hands and throwing it out by lifting the hands to the sky and whooshing it out with the breath. For the last aspect, bring your palms to your heart.

❖   Reflect back to your earliest memories of your childhood and find any event or events which caused anger or disturbed you (1 to 2 minutes). Now think about the first three aspects of the memory and three times release the different aspects by holding it in your hands and throwing it out by lifting the hands to the sky and whooshing it out with the breath. For the last aspect, bring your palms to your heart.

Now it's time to let go or erase. Visualise yourself back in your mother's womb, the most beautiful and safest space for our creative beginning of new life. Here you are free of all the memories, concepts and conceptions or ideas. In yoga we call this as Hiranya- Garbha, the golden womb or divine mother energy. Feel free and safe in this space and let yourself be absorbed in this free space for few minutes.

Finally bring your mind and awareness back, to where you are now and visualise yourself here and now, free from all those memories and anger. Visualise yourself meditating in warm-golden womb or Hiranya-Garbhaya.

Wake up, rubbing your hands and giving a warm touch all over your face, head, neck and shoulders.

Hiranya-Garbhaya.

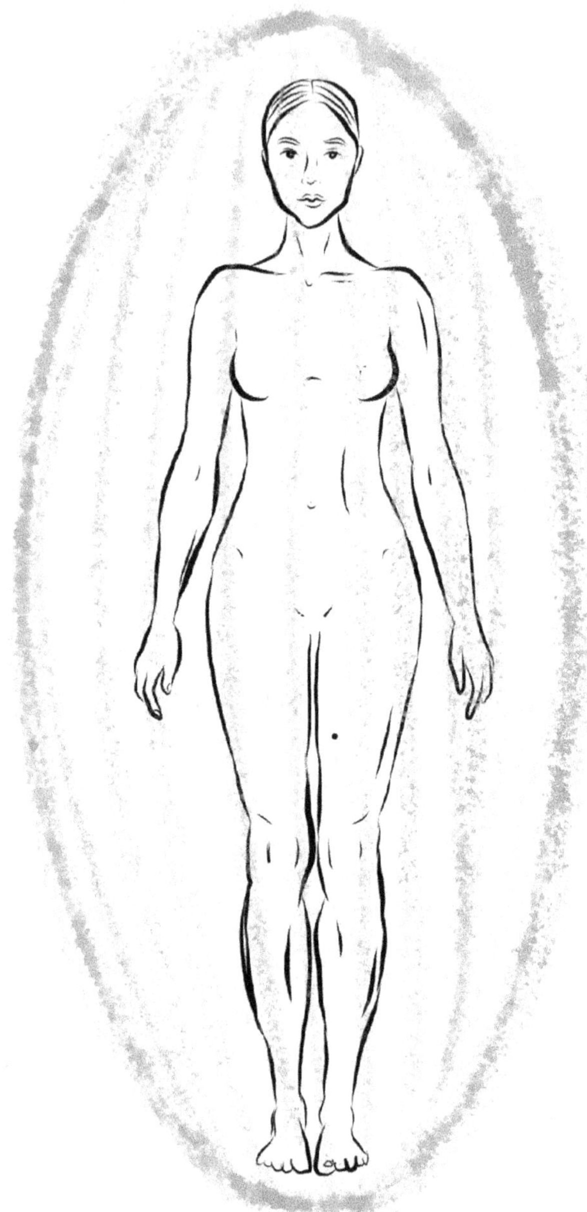

WHAT IS PRANAYAMA?

Pranayama yoga is the 'science of breath', the control of the vital force (prana) present in the air we breath. The Sanskrita term pranayama means: 'Prana' which is the divine universal creative energy or power, and the 'yama' means control or the science of control.

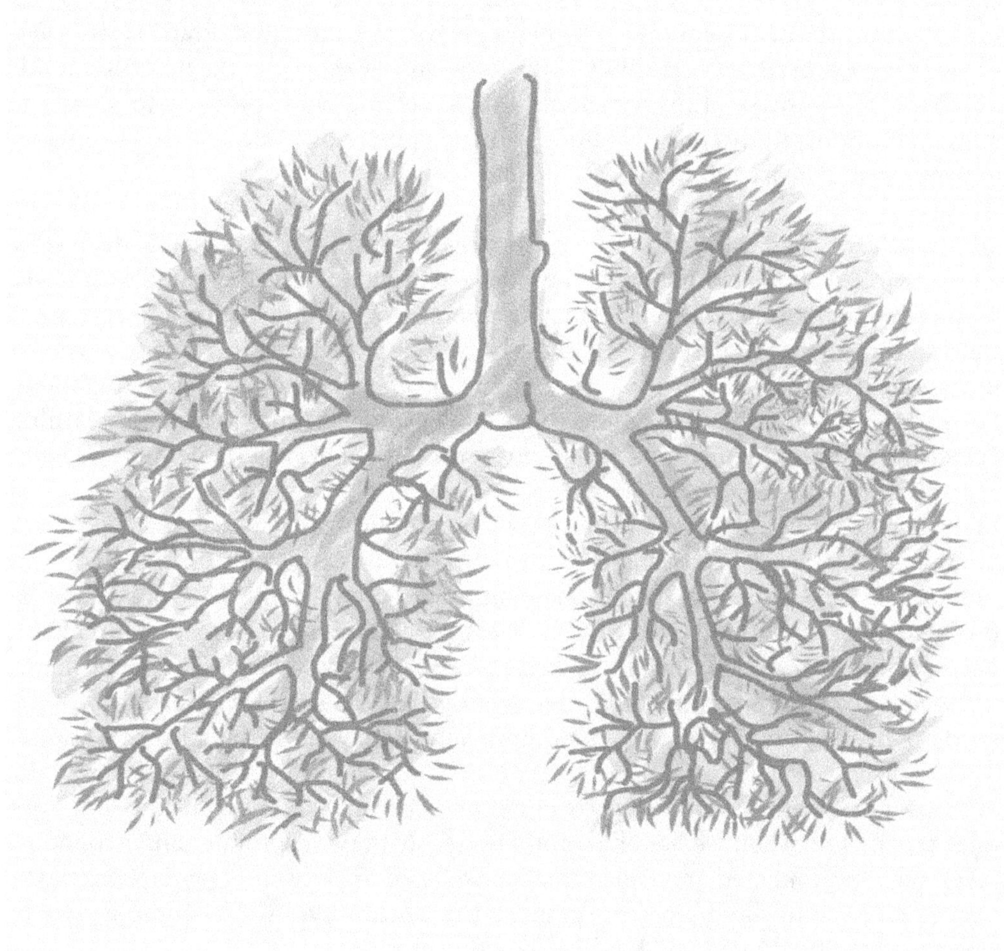

The word 'prana' can be broken further as 'pra' which means to exist independently, or prior to existence. 'Ana' is a shortened term of 'anna' which means a cell, or collectively 'ana'. Thus prana means 'that which existed before any atomic or cellular life came into being'. Such life is termed as the manifestation of the divine.

Behind all the manifestation of creation and life is this divine energy prana. Most of the prana we receive is from the air we inhale. But we also receive it to some extent from food. Some part is also absorbed directly in the skin from the atmosphere.

Remember that prana is not oxygen or the other gases we inhale and not the nutrients we take from food. The truth is that behind using all these nutrients and the gases for breathing this divine energy prana plays the role as the catalyst. Prana is absorbed through the exposed nerve endings of the body and especially in the nostrils, mouth and back of the throat. Thus we should eat slowly and chew properly to allow the release and absorption of prana. Water should be sipped slowly to allow the absorption of prana in the throat and mouth.

We must learn pranayama from the beginning to do Dirgha Pranayama; deep slow and controlled breath. Most of us nowadays are shallow breathers and lacking in prana or enough oxygen for the normal functioning of our body, mind and emotions. Most of the current diseases are caused by improper breathing in Yogic science. All illnesses can be alleviated by practicing pranayama properly and by perfecting them. For a yogi breathing should be under their total awareness. This conscious breathing brings the autonomic functions under the control of the nervous system or the will.

Improper breathing, dyspnoea or laboured breathing is not only a recent problem for mankind, now it has become more prominent because of a stressful life and the adverse environmental conditions making it worse. Even Yogi Gorakshanatha travelled the whole of India and gave the message - "O men and women of India! You have defaulted from good health by being the shallow breathers". He stated that in his age people were breathing only one-eight of their capacity. He cured many of the modern diseases only by teaching predominately pranayamas and only a few asanas.

When we breath in a shallow way, the nerve receptors sited deep in the lungs are unaffected. Only when we breath in and out deeply these inspiratory and expiratory receptors are stimulated and called for their desired activity. This sends the reflexogenic feed-back to the brain. This governs the control over the in and out breath, along with the holding in and holding out of breath.

Breath is also related to our life and spirit, or the soul. Even it is said that there is life in the body, if there is breath in the body. In Sanskrita the word Brahman is used for the breath. The in-taking of the breath is termed as inspiration derived from Greek, which comes from 'in-spiro' means being in tune with the spirit or God. While expiration is originated from the 'ex-piro' means to be out of the spirit. In India if someone dies, it is said that 'the prana has left the body' people do not use the word 'death' or 'died'.

The yogis performed the pranayamas and found that they can fulfil the need of prana purely by getting it through the air. They don't need to eat food and are known as the breatharians. Still there are yogis in various parts of the world who live without depending upon food and even some without water! This lifestyle would be for the very few on this Earth who have been able to create the right circumstances required to live in this way.

Benefits of Pranayama?
Pranayama can help us improve our general health and well-being as well as lead us to Pratyahra (sensory withdrawl), Dharna (concentration) and Dhyana (meditation).

Here are key benefits of Pranayama-
❖   The enhance quality and quantity of vital life forces, leading to lightness and vitality of body and mind
❖   They stimulate and rejuvenate various parts of the brain and hence improve mental clarity and thought processes
❖   They improve blood circulation and remove all the blockages
❖   They improve body immunity
❖   They balance hormones
❖   They balance the autonomic nervous system
❖   They improve concentration and memory
❖   They improve sleep and emotional well-being

Please understand that Pranayama is much more than a mere breathing exercise, it is a way of enhancing our intake of Prana (life-force) by bringing our mind, body and emotions together. This method is a much more powerful practice. 'Where the mind goes the Prana flows'.

Pranayama and Mental Purification
The word, prana, can also be broken down into 'pra', meaning to bring forth;
while 'na' means vibration. Prana is the underlying energy of all existence as well as consciousness. As such it is the animating principle of the Spirit as it manifests in the body. The law of existence is that where the mind's attention goes, so does one's energy or prana. Taken as a unit, this is called the cit-prana. So, by controlling the outflow of the prana and regulating that, then the citta or mind is stabilised, clarified, and prepared to deal with all the changes and challenges. This works with the underlying energy behind negative thought patterns and allows us to release them. Pranayama helps us to purify and enhance the quality of this subtle and vital life force.

Exhalation is associated with release and can be consciously used to release negative energy, thoughts, and emotions which interrupt the Divine mind-stream.

Inhalation is related to our intake of basic vital energy to sustain all life processes. Thus, with conscious inhalation we can improve the quantity and quality of energy we take and absorb. So, if we can inhale and exhale consciously, deeply in rhythm, this will bring freshness and clarification to the mind.

In a practical way as in meditation in daily life, we can keep coming back to the breath as a gross and subtle way of redirecting our awareness from outward flows of prana and sense objects (vishaya) or external events (visayanam). This will help reduce or prevent all the mood swings and mental changes and bring joyfulness and divine experiences. Thus, in pranayama with breath and awareness we release the negative thought with the exhalation (pracchardana) and hold it outside gently (vidharanabhyam). This refers to the emphasis on exhalation to release negative thoughts or attachment in general, so it gently dissolves into a subtle external release into emptiness. This is similar to the well-known Buddhist practice called anapana-sati in which sadhaka observes the breath. In Laya yoga, visualisation of blackish air to the exhalation and whitish air to the inhalation, sounds and so forth, are added. This develops heightened balance, equipoise and a self-supporting mutual steadiness, symmetry, synchronicity, synergy, and continuity permeating the body, breath, energy, and mind with the higher mental states and awareness.

Prana, Thoughts and Emotions
Try to remember a situation when you were very happy and cheerful; how did you feel about your body and about yourself at that time? You may feel very light, energetic and willing to do everything at that moment. What is behind all this?
Now remember a situation when you are sad, unhappy and in a bad mood; how do you feel about your body and yourself? You may feel very heavy, tired, exhausted, lacking interest and will. What is behind all this?

Our physical, mental and emotional processes are carried on through the energy of prana. So, our mental and emotional states directly affect the levels of prana in us. All the negative thoughts, and negative emotions block the refinement of prana and flow of prana in the nadis (energy channels). They consumed a high amount of the prana because negative thoughts create the situation of emergency. Our autonomic nervous system and the endocrine system have to prepare for the fight-flight response. This consumes a lot of prana, preparing for nothing. So be careful about what you think and feel!

Patanjali describes that in all the adverse mental and emotional processes, use the opposite thought or emotion to get rid of the negativity (prati-paksha-bhavanam). It is also stated in the Upanishads that your prana goes where your awareness goes. So the more distracted your thoughts and emotions are the more your prana is scattered or poor.

In the Bhagavad Gita, the Lord Krishna states that the mind is the vehicle of our prana. Thus, your awareness goes where your thought goes. Your mind goes where your awareness goes and there goes the prana. Thus, the mind or the thoughts and emotions need prana, or the conscious, to travel in and out. Those who do mental work, at the end of the day feel more tired in comparison of the person doing only physical work, why? Because our mental and emotional processes consume more prana than the physical process. So be careful and aware of what you think and what you feel. You need to be aware of the mental and emotional processes and to check and remove them.

Pranayama Practices -
Some of these practices are suitable for Preconception only and others for both Pregnancy & Postnatally

Sukha Pranayama
(Suitable for all stages)

Pranayamas are particularly important in preconception, pregnancy and postnatal yoga because they teach a woman how to focus on her breath, which helps her relax. Importantly they are also a good practice for breathing techniques that will help during labour and delivery.

Sukha Pranayama is one of the unique practices of the Rishiculture group of Dr. Swami Gitananda Giri. Pranayama is the process of refinement of the gross prana to the subtle prana and this is enhanced positively with the intensity of the awareness of breath. To practice any pranayama without your conscious awareness is nothing other than a breathing exercise. Pranayama is not a breathing exercise, but the process of refinement of prana into subtler and subtler forms.

Various rhythms of Sukha-Purvaka Pranayamas are also used as the higher practices of dharanas in mandala dharanas (visual auspicious images or aids for meditation) Thus perfection of the Sukha-Purvaka Pranayama is compulsory for the serious sadhakas of yogic evolution.

These rhythms are related to the five-elements (earth, water, air, fire, space or ether) of our physical structure called the pancha-mahabhutas. These all align the pranic flow in various chakras concerned with the pancha-mahabhutas. These rhythms help to get rid of all kinds of problems associated with the imbalance of the pancha-mahabhutas in our body. For example we may not have the right balance of water in our body or earth elements (solids) or digestive energy (fire) or lack energy (fire) or air with breathing disorders or arthritis (space) joint misalignment are some examples.

Sukha Purvaka Pranayama could be practiced with various rhythms, in beginning one could start 4 count breathing in and a 4 count out breath rhythm, if the person has a low breath capacity. The rhythm means the time or the counts of the inhaling and exhaling breath. The count of inhaling and exhaling should be always equal.

Method-
- ❖   *Part 1*: 4 counts in x 4 count out breath
- ❖   *Part 2*: 4 counts in x 4 count hold
- ❖   *Part 3*: 4 counts in x 4 count out x 4 count hold
- ❖   *Part 4*: 4 counts in x 4 count hold x 4 count out x 4 count hold

Repeat each part 3 times then move onto the next part.

Swasha Prasawasha Pranayama- This simple in breath and out breath pranayama was taught to Arjuna by Lord Krishna hence also known as Gita Pranayama. This includes inhaling and exhaling in the equal counts or timings with deep awareness. For physical, mental and emotional harmony one can practice the 6X6 rhythm. For physical health one can practice 8x8 rhythm. Gradually you can practice the higher rhythms like 10x10 or 12x12.

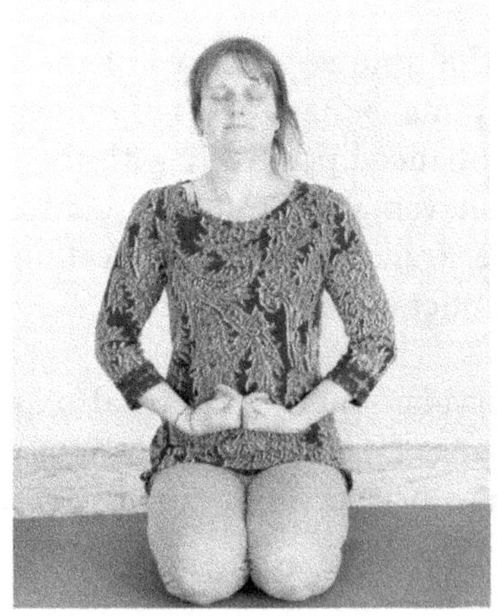

Breath in
count 4

Breath out
count 4

Savitri Pranayama
(Suitable for all stages)

Savitri means rhythm or harmony, thus savitri pranayama is rhythmical breathing. It brings one-ness and harmony between entire system of your body, mind, emotions and spirit. Many other terms are used in Sanskrit for this pranayama - Tulaa, mayadeyaha, shesha-avashesha, and all in some way represents the harmony.
This pranayama is practiced in various timings and counts. The breath has four parts:

- ❖ Inhaling, breath in known as Puraka
- ❖ Holding in known as Kumbhaka
- ❖ Exhaling known as Rechaka;
- ❖ Holding out known as the Bahir Kumbhaka (or Shunyaka)

We use the ration 2:1 for the Savitri rythym: you have to inhale and exhale in equal timings while holding in and out for half of that count. This count is known as the Tala. If you are practicing a four Tala, it becomes 8x4 x 8x4, this means inhale and exhale in eight counts and hold in and out for four counts. All the talas have their own effects, like 3 tala balances the emotions, 4 strengthens and stabilises the body, 5 tala increases the metabolism. The 6 tala increases the oxygen supply to brain, 7 tala promotes serenity and peace, and 8 is for rejuvenation. More than 8 tala represents the senior or the higher practices of the pranayama.

You can practice any of the comfortable rhythms and gradually can increase the talas. Twenty minutes of savitri pranayama is said to be equal to a rest of eight hours sleep. This could be practiced in any of the classical sitting postures, like sukhasana, vajrasana, padmasana, siddhasana, or may be even in resting asanas like savasana, makarasana, etc.

In preconception and pregnancy the 3 tala 6x3 x 6x3 is the most appropriate, as it works more on our emotional health and activates the parasympathetic nervous system.

Savitri Rhythm

Then sitting in Vajra asana continue on to practice the Savitri rhythm:

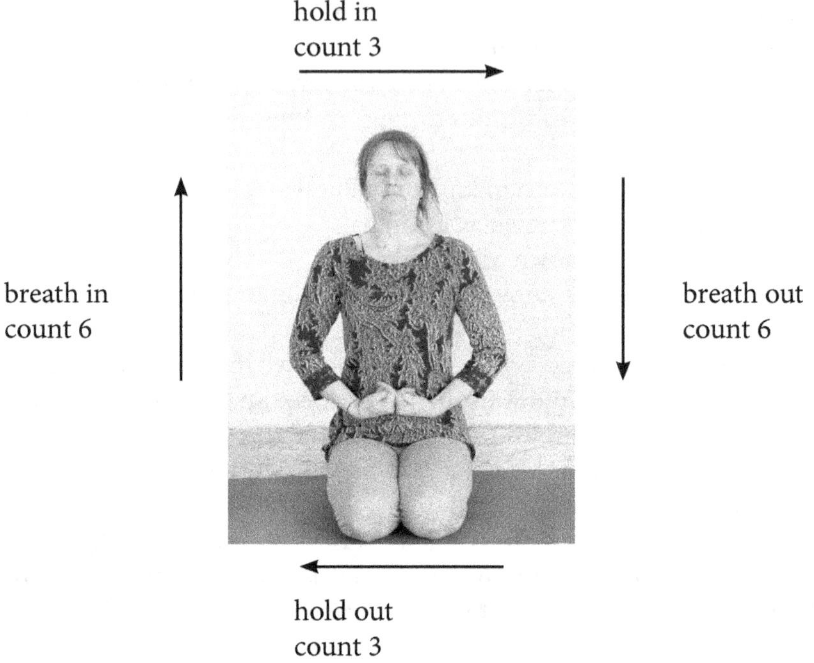

The rhythm will work on our parasympathetic nervous system, bringing back into a normal healthy balanced state.

Mukha Bhastrika for cleansing
(Not suitable during pregnancy, only preconception and postnatal)
There are nine types of bhastrika pranayamas and Nasarga-mukha bhastrika is recommended for cleansing abdominal and pelvic area along with lungs and gradually refines the blood and brings vitality.

Method-

❖ Sit straight in Vajra asana and fill the lungs with a big in breath
❖ Blast the breath out the mouth with the mouth into Kaki mudra (crows beak gesture) whilst bringing the body down finally reaching the head to the floor

Technical points: We repeatedly blast the breath out whilst pulling back with our abdominal muscles. We do not breath in until we are ready to come up from the floor. Keep the chin extended on our out breath and lift and extend the chin first before coming up. We can continue this at least 3 times.

**Alternate nostril breathing for all phases
(pre-conception, pregnancy and post natal)**
The intricate balance between the two
energies—Loma (with the flow) and Viloma
(against the flow)—and their importance
in creating mental and physical harmony
is described in the scripture the Shiva
Swarodha. The concepts of loma and viloma
are integral to the rich tapestry of yoga,
underpinning our understanding of the
energetic flows that govern our existence.
Loma, meaning "with the flow," represents
the natural and harmonious progression of
energy, while viloma, denoted by the prefix
"vi" which can signify a superlative or the
opposite, refers to the act of moving against
this flow.

When these two opposing forces are united,
they create a delicate balance, akin to the
ebb and flow of the tides or the dynamic
interplay of anions and cations within our
cells. This balance is not only a hallmark of yogic practice but also a fundamental
principle that permeates the very fabric of life itself.

In the Indian tradition, where the understanding of these energetic flows has been
deeply ingrained, the maintenance of electrolyte balance is of paramount importance,
particularly for the elderly. This concept extends beyond the physical realm, as the
ancient yogis recognized the need for a harmonious balance between the various
energies that govern our existence. The idea of moksha, or liberation, is intimately
tied to this understanding of balance, as every atom in the universe is said to be
constantly striving for a state of equilibrium in its outermost orbit.

The practice of alternating nostril breathing, commonly known as nadi shuddhi or
nadi shodhana, although in the Gitananda tradtiton this names refers to another
practice Loma and Viloma. While the common approach is to begin on the left side,
*the Gitananda tradition emphasizes the dynamic balance achieved by starting on the
right, creating a passive and active approach to this practice.*

The practice involves controlling the breath in a specific pattern: inhaling through
the right nostril to stimulate pranic energy and exhaling through the left to promote
relaxation. Additionally, the alternate nostril breathing technique (Aloma Viloma)

creates a dynamic balance between the two hemispheres of the brain. The starting nostril in this practice significantly impacts its effects; for instance, starting with the right nostril initiates a more activating and cleansing process, while the left nostril provides a tranquilizing effect. This balancing of prana and apana is central to achieving equilibrium within the body and mind.

1. Loma Pranayama

The steps for Loma Pranayama are as follows:

Steps:

1. **Preparation:** Sit in a comfortable meditative posture (e.g., vajarasana, Sukhasana or Padmasana) with erect spine and relaxed body.
2. **Inhale through the Right Nostril**
   - Close the left nostril gently with your ring finger (in nasagra mudra or Vishnu Mudra) and inhale deeply through the right nostril.
   - Focus on activating the pranic energy.
3. **Hold for Half the Duration of the Inhalation:**
   - After inhaling, hold the breath for half the time of the inhalation.
4. **Exhale through the Left Nostril:**
   - Keep the right nostril closed and exhale through the left nostril.
   - Focus on releasing energy smoothly and maintaining an even breath.
5. **Hold After Exhalation**
   - After exhaling fully, hold the breath for the same duration as after the inhalation.

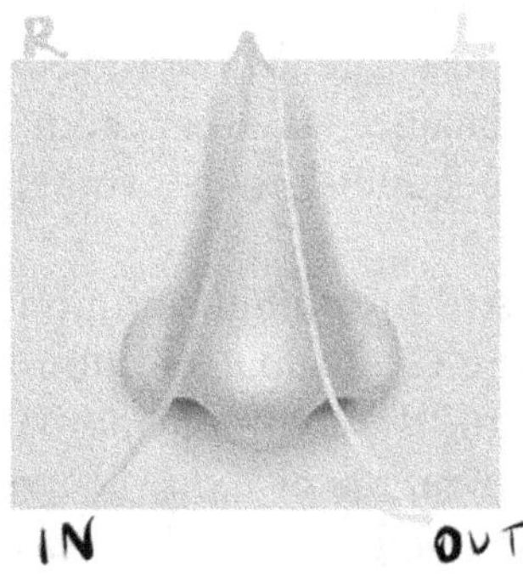

**2.	Viloma Pranayama**

The steps for Viloma Pranayama are as follows:

Steps:

1.	**Preparation:** Sit in a comfortable meditative posture (e.g., vajarasana, Sukhasana or Padmasana) with erect spine and relaxed body.
2.	**Inhale through the Left Nostril**
	❖ Close the left nostril gently with your ring finger (in nasagra mudra or Vishnu Mudra) and inhale deeply through the right nostril.
	❖ Focus on activating the pranic energy.
3.	**Hold for Half the Duration of the Inhalation:**
	a. After inhaling, hold the breath for half the time of the inhalation.
4.	**Exhale through the Right Nostril:**
	a. Keep the right nostril closed and exhale through the left nostril.
	b. Focus on releasing energy smoothly and maintaining an even breath.
5.	**Hold After Exhalation**
	a. After exhaling fully, hold the breath for the same duration as after the inhalation.

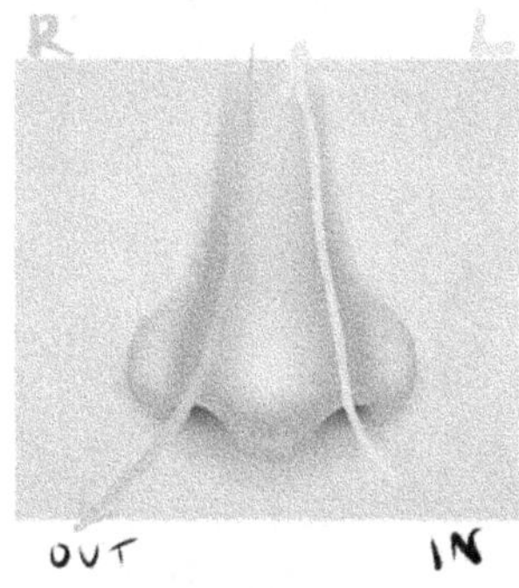

1. Aloma Viloma

The steps for Aloma Viloma Pranayama are as follows:

Steps:

1.	**Preparation:** Sit in a comfortable position with your spine straight and shoulders relaxed. Close your eyes and focus on your breath.
2.	**Inhale through the Right Nostril :**

❖ Close the left nostril using your ring finger (in nasagra mudra or Vishnu Mudra) and inhale deeply through the right nostril.

❖ As you inhale, focus on activating the prana in the body and hold the breath for some time.

3.   **Exhale through the Left Nostril :**
   ❖ right nostril is closed and slowly exhaled through the left nostril.
   ❖ As you exhale, focus on releasing and calming the prana within the body and again hold the breath.

4.   **Inhale through the Left Nostril:**
   ❖ Inhale through the left nostril and hold the breath.

5.   **Exhale through the Right Nostril :**
   ❖ Exhale through the right nostril and hold.

6.   **Alternate Nostril Breathing:**
   ❖ After exhaling through the right nostril, switch and repeat the process, inhaling through the right and exhaling through the left and vice versa.

7.   **Rhythm:** The duration of inhalation and exhalation should be equal or in a comfortable rhythm, keeping a steady pace.

ALOMA – VILOMA

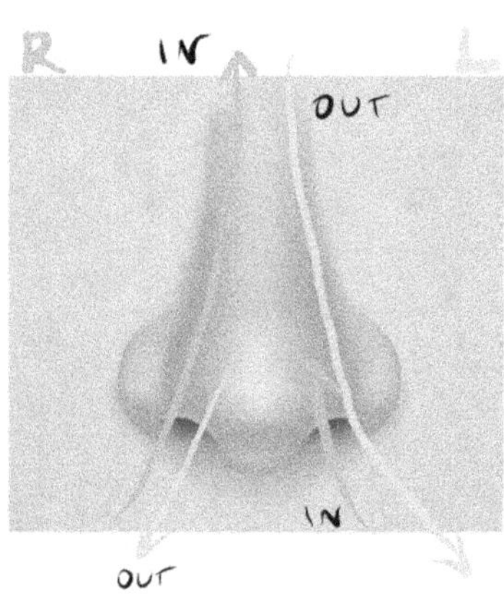

From 'Yoga-Step-by-Step' by Swami Gitananda Giri Guru Maharaj

Swamiji said that the balancing Pranayama benefit a lot in conditions such as neurasthenia and psychasthenia which are conditions related to the nerves and your mind. There are a few symptoms that are getting alleviated, like irritation, irritability or emotionality and sleeplessness, dyspepsia, dizziness, inertia, laziness, dullness. So many other things that are related to this. So, it's basically our nerves are getting calm because the Vishnu Mudra that we use, the slight pressure on the Bhrumadhya, which is a direct connectivity with the HP axis, the hypothalamopituitary Axis, the Bindu here. So, direct relativity which is balancing and controlling the autonomic tone. So the sympathetic and the parasympathetic branches of the autonomic nervous system. So you have a stability, a balancing ability with these Pranayama practices. The hypothalamopituitary axis is being activated or stimulated with this Mudra and hence one finds a direct relativity with the adjustment of the autonomic tone. So, it's a normalizing activity that we find in these.

We have an energy bank, a power bank, a reservoir of energy at the base of the spine which is called the Kanda. Which is an egg-shaped body situated at the base of the spine. The direction of flow of energy from the Kanda depends on the activity that we are doing; the process, the pattern of movement that we are doing. So, that is where the Loma-Viloma comes in.

So Loma, in the practices, the Loma flow, you know, like from the Kanda the energy flows upwards. Or the energy flows downwards towards the Kanda. So, these are two energy sequences here. From the Kanda, from the base of the spine, to the top of the head, to the cranium. Or from the cranium to the base of the spine. The earlier one, from the base of the spine to top of the head, is the upward movement. And the other one, from the cranium to the base of the spine, is the down- ward movement. So, Loma promotes the upward movement and Viloma promotes the downward movement.

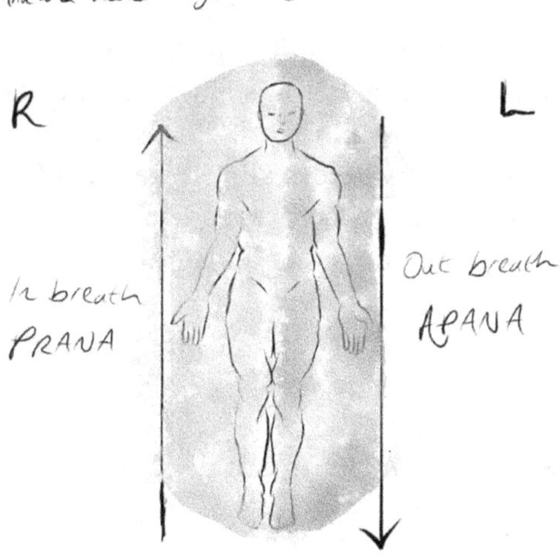

Science of Nasal Cycle and Lunar Cycle, and Yoga

The nasal cycle (NC) is the spontaneous congestion and decongestion of the nasal mucosa during the day. In this cycle, congestion of one side is accompanied by reciprocal decongestion of the contralateral side. It is based on the expansion and contraction of the venous cavernous tissue in the submucosa of the turbinates and septum, as well as the ethmoid sinuses (Pendolino et al., 2018).

The nasal cycle is dependent upon the tonic activity of the limbic autonomic nervous system, levels of circulating catecholamines, and other neuro-hormones (Bhavanani, A.B). This Nasal cycle is directly related to the Moon or Lunar cycle. In all this, our nostrils play very vital roles. As it may seem that the nostrils are ordinary empty spaces divided by a septum but it's not. The two nostrils are of great significance according to yoga. The left nostril is called ida (Chandra nadi) and the right nostril is called pingla (Surya nadi). The dominance of either nostril at different times is responsible for various changes in our body and mind, which is ultimately responsible for our actions.

(Shiva Swarodaya, verse 374)
Ida nadi is known as Ganga, pingala as Yamuna, and the central nadi (sushumna) as Saraswati, and the place of their confluence is known as Prayag.
- (Shiva Swarodaya, verse 374)

Ida pathway
The Shiva Swarodaya likens its nature to the energy created by the moon; therefore, it is also known as the Chandra or lunar nadi. Ida is associated with the parasympathetic nervous system (PNS), which sends impulses to the visceral organs to stimulate internal processes. This creates a general state of relaxation in the superficial muscles, thus lowering the outer body temperature. Therefore, it is said that ida is cooling, relaxing, and introverting.

Pingala pathway
Pingala is the transmitter of prana shakti. It is also known as the surya or solar nadi because its energy is as invigorating as the sun's rays. Pingala energy activates the physical body and externalizes awareness. It is associated with the sympathetic nervous system (SNS), which releases adrenaline to stimulate the superficial muscles. The SNS prepares the body to cope with stress and external activity. To control Pingala the breath in the right nostril is manipulated.

In every Lunar cycle, the dominance of ida or pingla at different phases could be observed.

The eight Moon phases of a lunar month are divided into four primary and four

intermediate (waxing and waning) Moon phases:
1. *New Moon*
2. *Waxing Crescent Moon*
3. *First Quarter Moon*
4. *Waxing Gibbous Moon*
5. *Full Moon*
6. *Waning Gibbous Moon*
7. *Third Quarter Moon*
8. *Waning Crescent Moon*

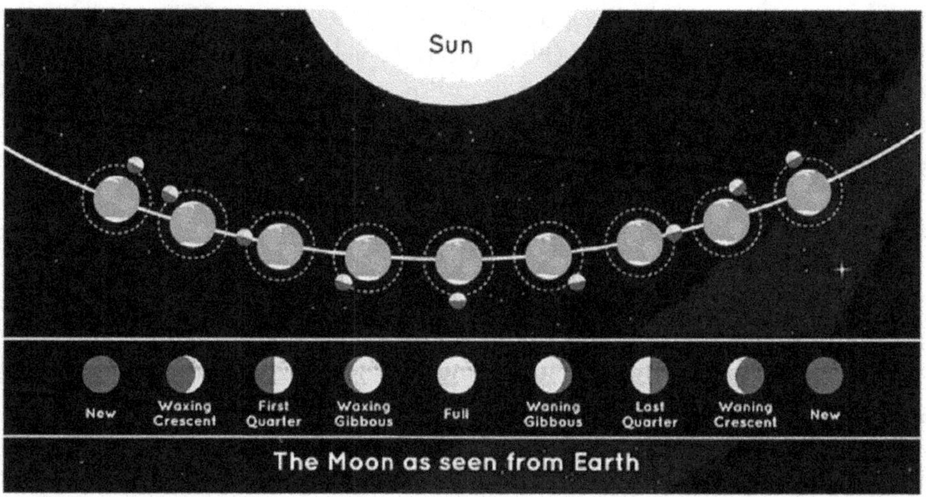

Fig. The position of the Moon and the Sun during Each of the Moon's phases and the Moon as it appears from Earth during each phase. Credit: NASA/JPL-Caltech

We already know that the bright, lit side of the moon is facing away from us. Only the dark, unlit side is facing toward us. Everyday, the moon rises around 50 minutes later than the day before. A few days after **New Moon**, it rises a few hours after the Sun. The moon is only visible as a crescent when the Sun sets. A few days later, it rises around midday and is visible in blue afternoon sky and exactly half of its face is illuminated. This is the **First Quarter Moon**. About two weeks after **New Moon**, it's rising at sunset. The **Full Moon** is the only phase where the moon is up for the whole night. This time the moon is on the opposite side of the earth to the Sun, and the side facing us is completely lit up. About a week after Full Moon, the **Third Quarter Moon** is rising around midnight. As before, half of the Moon's face is illuminated. But it's the other way round to the First Quarter Moon two weeks ago. A few days after Half Moon, it shrinks away again, rising as a thin crescent just before sunrise, and once more, it's lost in the glare of the Sun. As the Moon passes between the Earth and the Sun, we are back at New Moon again. It's been just four weeks since the last New Moon and the lunar cycle begins again.

One must be familiar with the moon phases in order to determine the timing that ida, pingla, or both become active. The Shiva swarodaya describes a definite pattern of breathing in a healthy person on each day of the month at sunrise. It is said that on days 1,2,3,7,8,9,13,14,15 of the bright fortnight or Shukla paksha (begins on the Shukla Amavasya (New Moon) day and culminates on Purnima (Full Moon) day), the breath is to flow predominantly in the left nostril (Chandra nadi or ida nadi) at sunrise and on days 4,5,6,10,11,12 it is to flow in the right nostril (surya nadi and pingla nadi) at sunrise. Similarly, on days 1,2,3,7,8,9,13,14,15 of the dark fortnight or Krishna paksha (begins on the (Full Moon) day (Purnima), culminating on (New Moon) day (Amavasya).), the breath is to flow predominantly in the right nostril (Surya Nadi or Pingla) at sunrise and on days 4,5,6,10,11,12 it is to flow in the left nostril (Chandra nadi or ida)at sunrise.

The moon phases are interesting to contemplate and corollate with a woman's menstrual cycle, of course not all women have such a cycle but personally it was typical to bleed around the full moon, my period was always like clockwork! When a cycle so predictable and stable the calendar method if contraception should be safe to use, plotting the cycle and ovulation time. This method should be studied first in depth before following.

The Shiva Swarodha also indicates that the sex of the child will depend upon the predominant nostril the male and the female are breathing through at the time of conception! This is something that is virtually impossible to scientifically study, nevertheless it is something to consider if we follow the yogic lifestyle! The scripture states that if the man is right nostril breathing and women is left nostril breathing they will conceive a male child. If it's the opposite a female child. If they are breathing through both nostrils they will not conceive.

Bhramari and Bhramara Pranayama

Bhramari and bhramara pranayamas are related to the sound of male and female bees. These are also cleansing pranayamas. Both cleanse our whole nervous system, brain, mental and emotional processes. These pranayamas are also described as the tools of dharana for meditation and Samadhi. Especially Swami Dayananda Saraswati used to practice the bhramari pranayama for hours during the night time to attain the Samadhi and wisdom. Bhramari pranayama directs the flow of the warm golden prana towards the head and with the sound of the female bee the vibrations are produced to open and cleanse the nadis in the upper region. While the bhramara pranayama directs the upward flow, the silvery apana balances the right and left hemispheres of the brain.

These both are extremely good for any neuronal, mental and emotional disorders. Regular practice increases concentration and memory power. Small kids enjoy doing this and it is very helpful for their mental growth. This nourishes the brain. These pranayama are good to heal and rebuild the brain. It is also good for cleansing out the throat area, so is helpful in conditions including sinusitis, coughs, asthma, bronchitis and nasal allergies. Importantly it balances the autonomic nervous system and thus is very good for the heart and blood pressure. Mental deterioration and related problems can be managed by regular practice.

One can attain the purity of mind and emotions by practicing these two jointly with in and out breath for a minimum of 20 minutes daily for one month.

Method-
- ❖ Sit in any of the meditative poses and place both hands in any of the comfortable mudras. Inhale deeply and whilst breathing out produce the humming sound of the female bee by using the upper plates and concentrating at the top of the head. Inhale and exhale ratio should be 4 x 8. This is the bhramari pranayama.
- ❖ Try to produce the humming sound of the male bee on the in breath for four counts and the female bee humming sound for 8 counts whilst on the out breath. This is bhramara pranayama.
- ❖ Practice the bhramar pranayama with the yoni mudra.
- ❖ Practice the bhramar pranayama with the sanmukhi mudra.

Mayuri Mudra- This is a great Kriya or Mudra to maintain health and flexibility of the neck as well as improving thyroid function.

Method-
- ❖ Sit straight in any comfortable posture. With inhalation move your chin forward stretching your neck and creating a gentle pressure for also muscles connecting your neck to head and upper spine.
- ❖ With exhalation draw your chin down to press it against your upper chest. You

can move your chin forward and down in all directions from centre to right and left at various points.

Brahma Mudra Kriyas for The Neck and The Unconscious Mind

Brahma mudra kriyas in Rishiculture Gitananda yoga, includes the bija mantras or root sounds to vibrate the prana or vital energy in the neck, shoulders and head areas. This relates to the physical, mental, emotional and energetic levels as in the pancha-koshas and it symbolises the four heads of Lord Brahma.

The base of the head and neck areas are the points where we carry our unconscious memories and traumas. They gradually create blockages and manifest in the form of pain, discomfort and behaviour disorders. Also our negative or ego-driven self-centred attitudes can cause stiffness in the neck. Many people hold themselves too uptight and never allow time to relax. Also many of us never allow others to explain their point of views or their side of the story, which causes tension in our relations with other people. To understand every event in life, we need to be able to see or perceive the events from many angles. Bhrama mudras can help us to widen our vision and understanding in life. Our vital energy moves in various directions, in their certain energy channels all around our pancha-kosha. Blockages are caused in this energy circulation due to the physical, mental, emotional or spiritual issues, stress and trauma. To be healthy, feel ease and also to allow vital energy to flow freely, we need to use our breath, sounds or vibrations and awareness in those areas, Brahma Mudra Kriyas with 6x6 breathing and bija sounds are powerful practice for the areas of the neck, shoulders, and head.

Method-
- Sit straight on your heels (Vajrasana) or in cross-legged posture with an erect spine. If it's too uncomfortable to be on the floor during pregnancy, you can sit comfortably on a chair too. The hands are clasped, fingers are interlaced in Dhyana Mudra (gesture of meditation) or Ushas Mudra(gesture or day or light). Place hands on your thighs in mudra.
- Slowly turn the head to the right with in breath in 6 counts. Bring the head to the centre on a count of 6, with the sound "AAA" with the out breath.
- Turn the head to the left, with the in breath on a count of 6. Return the head to the centre to the count of 6, sound "OOOU " while exhaling the breath out.
- Lift the chin upward to the ceiling, on a count of 6. Bring the head to the centre on a count of 6, with the sound "EEE" while breathing out.
- Move the chin down to the chest, on a count of 6 with the in breath. Bring the head to the centre on a count of 6, with the humming sound "MMM" while breathing out.

Practice 3-6 rounds at each side.

Brahma-Mudra Kriyas (Neck Exercises and Sound Healing) (Suitable for all stages) Many people hold tension in their necks and shoulders, leading to stiffness, bad posture, and tension headaches.

Yoga practice can ease tension, increase flexibility, and tone the muscles. Learn some Neck Exercises in this section. We breath in with the movement and make the sounds described on the exhale bringing the head back. On a psychic level this helps us to open up our perceptivity and outlook.

EEEEEEE

3

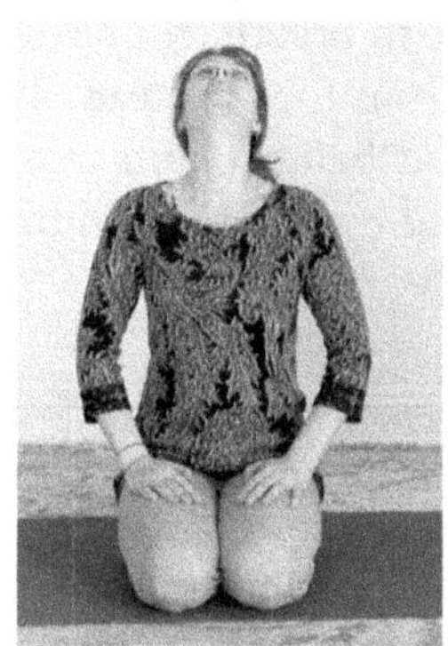

1

AAAAAA

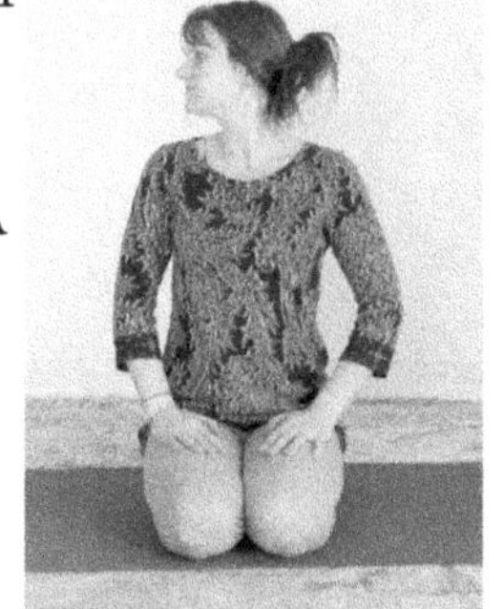

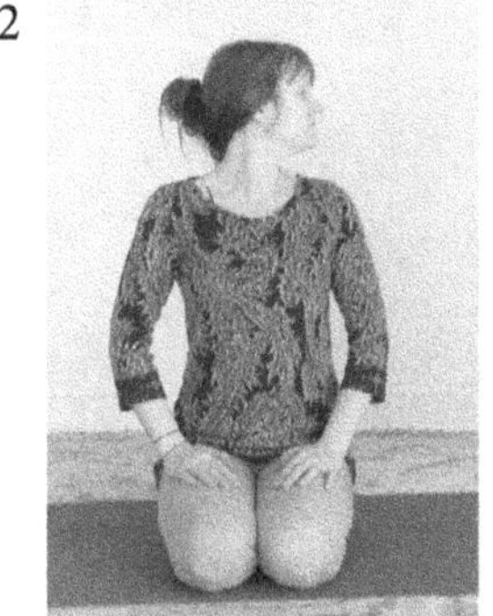

2

OOOOOO

4

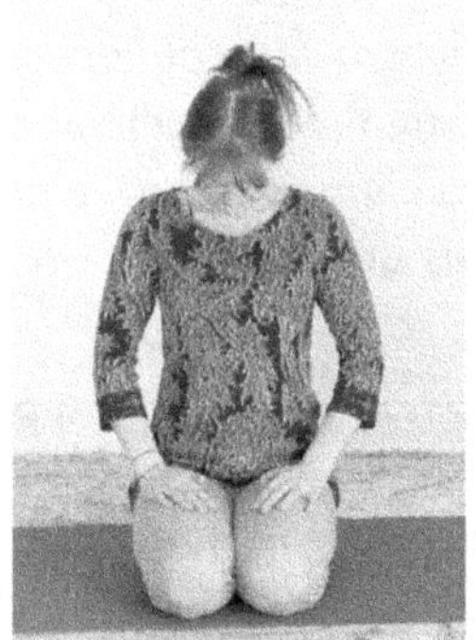

MMMMMM

Shavasana Relaxation practices:

These practices are supportive to women during this time and can support the woman in coping with pre-conception, pregnancy, birth and postnatally. They help with balancing the nervous system and allowing the body to function in an optimal way. A relaxed mother leads to a relaxed baby as we know that stress hormones in pregnancy can cross over to the baby; so supporting mothers to learn how to relax at this time is very beneficial.

Anuloma Viloma Kriya – In this kriya we start by visualizing a pranic golden healing flow down the body on the in breath from head to toes and an apanic silvery releasing flow on the out breath from toes to head. This works well after the loma-viloma sequence to harmonise and balance and works along the same concept as Loma Viloma which was described earlier. Remember all pre-conception practices are for both men and women.

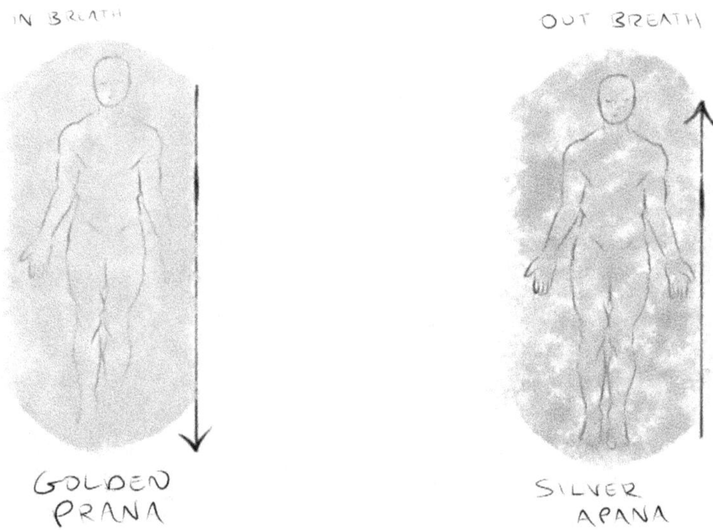

Anuloma Viloma Kriya – visualizing a pranic golden healing flow down the body on the in breath from head to toes and an apanic silvery releasing flow on the out breath from toes to head. This works well after the loma-viloma sequence to harmonise and balance and works along the same concept as Loma Viloma which was described earlier.

Nadi Jnana Kriya

Nadi Jnana Kriya – In this kriya we visualize a pipe around the body and then choose a dirty substance (rocks, oil, waste) that flows down through the pipe from top to bottom. Feeling the run off pouring out of the bottom of the pipe removing all your toxins, until it runs clear. This is a psychic cleaning technique, where the substance chosen is the symbolic image of our psychic 'rubbish' we need to get rid of!

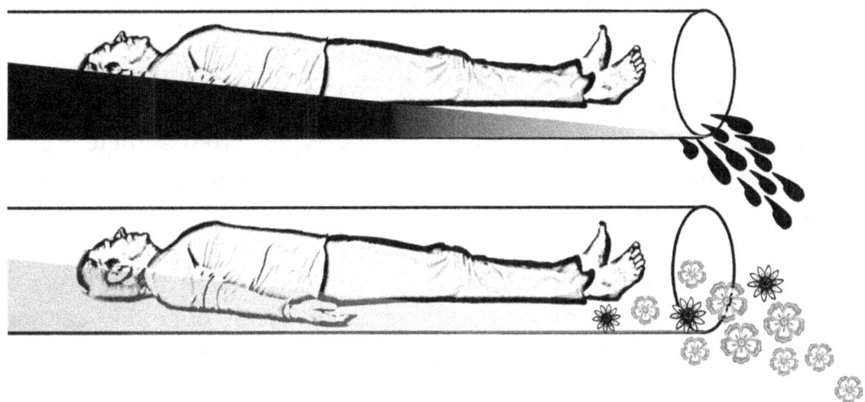

Jnana Yoga Kriyas and Detoxing of the body, nadis and subtle forces

Jnana yoga kriyas we are going to introduce here are one of the unique teachings of Rishiculture Parampara of Swami Gitananda Giri Ji. Jnana yoga kriyas are a very important part of direct teachings from Guru to Chela as relaxation, pratyahara, dharana and polarity practices. These are basically aimed to release stress, polarise the body, and develop the awareness and sensory withdrawal for higher yogic practices.

As we have already discussed the polarity of energy, in loma-viloma vidya. Our physical body contains blood vessels which circulate the nutrients to all parts of the body, and waste products for excretion. Over accumulation of toxins in blood vessels and joints creates various problems. These can be easily prevented and cured by practicing some purifying jnana yoga kriyas.

These kriyas refine your whole nadi system and refine gross prana to the subtle prana. This process of purification releases physical, mental, and emotional stress. These are especially designed for serous seekers to perfect the pratyahara or sensory withdrawal.

These are also found in Kashmir Bhairava Tantra as higher practices of dharanas to attain the meditative stage. The concept of the jnana yoga kriyas is developing awareness of body, mind and emotions to attain the awareness of pranic flow. Yoga is the union of shiva and shakti; loma and viloma energies; masculine and feminine energies; and sun and moon energies. Jnana yoga kriyas are aimed to attain this stage of union.

These refine your mental and emotional traumas seated deeply in your unconscious mind. Past traumas, depression, stress, anxiety, phobias, and other personality disorders related to any negative past experiences can be eradicated easily by practicing these jnana yoga kriyas seriously.

Body-Mind Toxicity and their effect on health and well-being?

Any form of toxins in our body and mind will cause obstruction in the health and balanced flow of energy in the respective areas, causing dis-ease or health problems. The toxicity can be classified in many ways and types. From a Yogic and spiritual perspective we have: the body or physical toxins; the mind or thought toxins; emotional toxins; karmic toxins; and spiritual toxins.

Dahika or Bodily Toxins - We can add or accumulate toxins in our body through unhealthy foods, drinks, junk or processed foods, foods our body cannot digest or eliminate, drugs, alcohol, smoking etc. Toxicity in the body can also be caused by dehydration as in situation of not having enough water in our body, it can start absorbing water back from the kidneys or it reduces the amount of urine elimination which results in an increased amount of toxins in the blood and cells. Constipation and improper blood supply can also result in the accumulation of toxins in our body.

Mansika or Mental Toxins - These are all the negative thoughts, and information we feed into our mind and brain. This can be through material we read, watch or listen to, or activities we take part in etc. Remember whatever goes on in our mind, or our body also responds to that by producing many hormones, and chemicals to create that experience. So mental toxins also cause physical toxins.

Emotional Toxins - All the negative emotions, desires and drive forces we carry or hold in our system are a simple form of emotional toxicity. Emotions like anger, guilt, frustration, and hatred are causing chronic physical disturbances and produce physical and mental toxins as a result. These emotions also affect our day-to-day behaviour and our ability to make choices.

Adhyatmic or Spiritual Toxins - In many ways Adhyatmic, religious and spiritual toxicity cause more trouble for human life and our society than anything else. Many types of violence, and hatred is caused by religious and spiritual conflict.

The Importance of Cleansing practices or Saucha in Pregnancy?

From conception to pregnancy all that goes in to our body, mind and soul will be also carried down to the baby growing inside the womb. Hence to grow a healthy child, we need to certainly work on cleaning or purifying our body, mind, emotions and lifestyle. We should try our best to abstain from all unhealthy food, junk and processed diets, toxic drinks, alcohol, drugs and smoking, to supply healthy energy to the baby growing inside.

A peaceful, calm and positive environment can not only keep you and your partner happy but, will also supply an abundance or positive vibes and energy to your child. Emotions of love, compassion, kindness and acceptance will bring harmony, and all those feel-good hormones will be supplied to your baby inside the womb.

Shata-Karmas (Six Cleansing Practices)

Yoga gives great importance to cleansing. Various physical and mental cleansing practices are described in Hatha-yoga-pradipika, Gheranda-samhita, Yoga-chudamani-upanishada, Kashmir-Bhairon Tantra and other rich sources of yoga. For us to grow on the path of yogic evolution, we need to be purified and strong enough. If your body, mind and emotions are full of impurities and negativity you cannot practice serious yogic practices. Although it is to be remembered by all serious yoga sadhakas that you should undergo all these cleansing practices under strict guidance of a guru. I am giving all this information here only to give you detailed insight into the shat-karmas.

Three types of doshas- vata, pitta, and kapha are removed by these cleansing sadhanas. One who practices all these sat-karmas under guidance of their guru, attains immortality. She/he gets rid of all physical, mental, emotional and spiritual problems.

For details one can undergo Hatha-Yoga-Pradipika and Gheranda-Samhita-

❖ By removing the impurities, the air can be restrained, according to one's wish and the appetite is increased, the divine sound is awakened, and the body becomes healthy. H.Y.P. Sutra-20.
❖ If there be excess of fat or phlegm in the body, the six kinds of kriyas (duties) should be performed first. But others, not suffering from the excess of these, should not perform them. H.Y.P. Sutra-21.
❖ The six kinds of duties are: Dhauti, Basti, Neti, Trataka, Nauti and Kapala Bhati. These are called the six actions. H.Y.P. Sutra-22.
❖ These six kinds of actions which cleanse the body should be kept secret. They produce extraordinary attributes and are performed with earnestness by the best Yogis. H.Y.P. Sutra-23.

Pregnancy and healthy Ahara Vihar

Ahara is what we feed to body and mind and Vihar is how we live. Eating healthy and nutritional fresh food can bring health and vitality to your body. It will improve body immunity. Vihara means lifestyle or things we do in day-to-day life. Being around positive people, keeping positive in work, going out for walks in nature, regular exercise, good relaxation and proper sleep, all these are part of Vihara. All these can boost our health and well-being.

Yogic Cleansing Practices for Preconception

Cleansing practices can be quite an alien thing to us, especially coming from a western culture. We tend to think on a '2d' level of washing our clothes, or having a shower and we are done, all clean! Not so in Yoga. Yoga and Eastern thought in general has a deeper level of insight. In Yoga we consider many more factors, we think about what we consume and what we have consumed in the past. If we have eaten a lot of red meat in the past which is known not to digest easily and sit in our intestines for perhaps decades, then we really need to have a good clear out. Laxatives, herbal or otherwise are not the answer unfortunately these will just scratch the surface so to speak. Instead we use other internal cleansing methods which are perfectly safe but would always be done under the expert guidance of a teacher who knows the methods well. Therefore I will not describe these methods in depth but I would encourage the reader to seek out an authentic and classically trained teacher to guide you through them.

Yogic Cleansing techniques:

❖ Jala neti – keeping out nostrils and head clear to allow us to practice pranayamas properly and keeping our head cavities clean and clear.

❖ Digestion – we can clear out our entire tract through the shanka prakshalana (Caution: only practice under proper guidance).

❖ Eka dasi pranayama – a powerful psychic cleansing that takes 11 days to complete. (A regression practice) This must be done under guidance in a safe yogic environment ie. Ashram.

❖ We become what we think and we are what we eat! In other words, mind your thoughts and mind what you put into your mouth as well as comes out of your mouth! All these things are basic awareness of self-practices.

❖ Drink plenty of water to keep flushing out toxins.

❖ Cleanse you pancha kosha (5 energy layers) through the sun salutations conscious work and loma-viloma sequence balancing left and right, male and female aspects. Release/throw out toxins whenever you can, do not hold onto them. Try the whooshing out exercise throwing out above the head with a bhastrika breath.

❖ Yamas and Niyamas – our moral and ethical approach to life: Having a child is taking on a huge responsibility for the rest of your life. Seeing the reality of the situation.

The Yamas and Niyamas are really the foundation of our Yoga life. They will be the foundation of a happy and healthy parenthood experience. The Yamas and Niyamas come from our Yoga sutras on ancient yogic scripture of 196 verses divided into four 'Padas chapters'. The Yoga sutras were codified by Maharishi Patanjali. The exact date of the Yoga Sutras is greatly debated from anywhere around 2500 to 5000 years plus. Patanjali says that in order to attain a higher state we must perfect the Yamas and Niyamas first:

Yamas – controlling our lower animal desires-

- ❖ Ahimsa – non-harm
- ❖ Satya – truthfulness
- ❖ Asteya – non-stealing
- ❖ Bhramachariya – control on our creative energies
- ❖ Aparigraha – Non-attachement / possession

Niyamas – observances to evolve into a humane (and spiritual) being. We can also apply the principle of actions in thoughts, words & deeds to almost all of these-

- ❖ Saucha – purity
- ❖ Santosha – Contentment
- ❖ Tapas – discipline of practice
- ❖ Swadhyaya – Self-study/enquiry
- ❖ Iswara Pranidhana – Surrendering to the Divine (trust in the Universe)

Our Indian History is full of amazing stories that try to teach us about good and bad decision making if you like that in turn leads to either good or bad outcomes. The Yamas and Niyamas are simple universal laws to follow if you want to live a healthy happy life.

A story from Mahabharata from Great Epic History of India:

In Hastinapur, King Vichitravirya died at a young age, leaving his two wives Ambika and Ambalika childless. Satyavati, mother of the late king was worried and anxious to ensure the continuation of the royal lineage. Satyavati called upon her other son, the ascetic great Rishi Vyasa (born through Sage Parashara), to bestow motherhood upon the two widowed queens, (like a surrogate father).

Vyasa, as a hermit was practising severe austerities, and was unpleasant and even fearsome in appearance, he asked his mother to wait for a while so that he could change his appearance. However Satyavati was so anxious and she could not wait, so she ordered Vyasa to impregnate her daughter-in-laws and her son Vyasa had to obey her wishes.

Vyasa went to Ambika, but she was so scared and fearsome of his appearance that she shut her eyes tight throughout the experience Vyasa saw immediately through his psychic powers that she would bare a son who would be born blind. He was known as Dhritarashtra who later became the famous blind king. Knowing this Satyavati send Vyasa to her sister Ambalika. She was also scared and went pale with fear. As a result, the sons she bore was the sickly albino Pandu. Due to health issues neither of them at this time were assumed fit enough to become kings.

Thereafter, Satyavati asked Vyasa to grant a son to Ambika once again, to ensure that at least one of the boys born would be eligible in all respects. However, this time Ambika too terrified to repeat the experience sent her maid to Vyasa instead. The maid was not terrified and felt honoured to meet the great sage, resulting the birth of Vidura. The maid had a normal healthy son born to her. Thus the wise Vidura was born. He was raised and educated by Bhishma as the half-brother of Dhritarashtra and Pandu. A very long epic story unravels which will not be told here.

This story simply illustrates how even the conception experience has a major influence on the baby itself. It is something difficult to prove as there are no studies! But we can reflect perhaps in our own lives and the behaviours/ weaknesses and/or strengths of our parents and how we have been influenced in our own lives. Relationships, Responsibility and Morality (Yamas and Niyamas), we can reflect on this in terms of our behaviour, living in a clear and responsible way when planning a family.

The story of Abhimanyu - Learning in the womb
The following story is about Abhimanyu, the courageous son of the great Arjuna. Arjuna was married to Krishna's sister, Subhadra, and this story begins just before Abhimanyu was born. When Abhimanyu was in his mother's womb, Sri Krishna used to take Subhadra on excursions. To humour her, Krishna used to relate many of his adventures to the pregnant Subhadra. On one such excursion Krishna was narrating his experience with the technique of Chakra-vyuha and how step-by-step the various circles could be penetrated. Chakra-vyuha was a military formation which was an effective form of defence. The army would be arranged in the form of a circular grid and would then challenge the enemy to break that grid. Nonetheless, it seems that Subhadra did not find this topic interesting and she soon fell asleep. However, someone else was interested in Sri Krishna's narration – the yet to be born Abhimanyu.

While Subhadra dozed off, Abhimanyu continued to carefully follow Sri Krishna's narrative of the Chakra-vyuha. But, after talking for some time and not receiving any response from Subhadra, Sri Krishna realised that she was savouring a sweet nap. Sri Krishna, who had at that time come up to the seventh step of the Chakra-vyuha, gave up his narration and returned with Subhadra to the palace. The unfortunate Abhimanyu could never obtain the technique of breaking all the circles in the chakra-vyuha, but whatever he had heard Sri Krishna say, he carefully preserved in his memory. He grew up to be a brave, handsome young man. Many years later, during the Mahabharata war at Kurukshetra, the Kauravas set up a Chakra-vyuha and challenged the Pandavas to come forward and break it. However, only Arjuna (who was fighting elsewhere) knew the technique of doing so. At that stage, to save the honour of the Pandavas, Abhimanyu came forward and offered his services for the task of breaking the chakra-vyuha. Despite his incomplete knowledge of the technique he entered the grid and overcame one circle after another until he came to the seventh one, the breaking of which he had no knowledge. Brave and ambitious as he was, he fought valiantly in the unequal struggle but in vain. His strength and bravery proved no match against the skillfully laid out maze of warriors, upon fighting whom, he met his end.

This story highlights the importance of the first 3 sanskaras and how the healthy mental growth of a child begins even before it is born, while still in its mother's womb. Scientific findings have shown that babies can indeed hear from inside their mother.

Detoxing

Ideally before becoming pregnant mum-to-be (and fathers should be actively involved in this too) should have a detox of the physical body. There are many different types and levels of detox. In yoga we have many ancient yogic cleansing techniques, however these may not be for the general public who do not practice yoga on a regular basis as they may be too intense and strong an experience, also the body may not cope well if it is very toxic as so many modern men/women have high levels of alcohol, drug and tobacco use in the population, not to mention, most have a large amount of meat in the weekly diet. However! It is probable (though unfortunate in some ways that so many will miss out!) that the type of people coming to yoga will probably be drawn to it as they have refined their lifestyle to some level.

So again it will come down to the individual on what type of cleansing methods they can take during the preconception period, the more cleansing the better! If someone is at a good level - physically and mentally strong, they will be able to cope with the full yogic cleansing shanka-prakshalana method of cleansing the entire gastro intestinal tract. This is hugely beneficial to the body and will remove so many toxins that get stuck in our gut. This practice is very intense however and must be learnt by a qualified classical yoga teacher who is well versed to the practice!

There are other physical practices then that can be done, less intense on a sliding scale depending on the student's experience, physical health and level. They can simply follow an aurevedic diet, do some other cleansing techniques such as jala neti for the sinuses along with some good physical yoga workouts to build up their core strength and abdominal area in preparation for the baby and after! Alongside any cleansing of the physical body we should take the opportunity to clean up on other levels of our being!

The changes for most women (and men) from a single or married life without dependents, to suddenly having child/ren will be life changing for most! Leading a mature and responsible life and evolving as we embrace family life.

Swamiji said that being a mother is the ultimate yoga sadhana – the attainment of motherhood is the height of ego-less-ness, which is the goal of all spirituality.

This is true and can be experienced if you have the correct attitude and foundation. It is important that women planning pregnancy or going through pregnancy are changing their life already in a positive way. If they have negative habits, friends or family with negative lifestyles etc. these should be avoided if possible. The same goes for the places you take your body, we pick up from our environment around us on many levels and are affected by it, again think carefully where you want to go and why or where you need to go. Once pregnant it is not just your body you are taking care of and there is plenty of evidence to suggest that the fetus is affected by the mother's condition – again on all levels.

In Yoga we have not only the 5 senses but also many other ways of experiencing the world, the pancha-kosha for example refers to the 5 energy layers that surround our body, similar to the idea of an aura. We should try to keep it as clean as possible through yogic cleansing methods described earlier.

The condition of our mind we have talked about a little, but it is important to realise that our mind is a powerful tool, that can create things – physically, mentally and emotionally! Through yogic practices we can use some methods of pranayama and relaxation to purify the mind.

All these Yoga practices will help create and maintain a healthy happy and balanced individual! Because the union is so deep and so close, what happens to one will happen to the other. If the mother is unhappy, restless, and agitated she can expect that her child, when born will be unhappy, restless and agitated. Everything the mother thinks, feels, does, eats even the way she breathes will vitally affect the child.

Four Dharmas or Ashrams

The Yogic and Vedic lifestyle provides us with a scientific approach as well as a practical framework to live our life in a way to fulfil all the Dharmas or Duties we are supposed to live in this lifetime. This gives us full opportunity to experience every aspect of our life and to bring out the best in us. Yoga and the Vedas divide our life into four different phases. These are:

❖ Brahmachariya- This is first phase of life from birth to 27 years. This phase is for education and Sadhana, to learn and grow. This gives us full opportunity to work on developing the skills or potential abilities we are born with.

❖ Grihastha- This is second phase between 28 to 54 years. In this phase we can use all our skills and abilities to work, earn a living, make a family, have kids and help our families and society by all the means we can. You could say this is a testing phase of all your skills and abilities that you have learned and acquired in first phase.

❖ Sanyasa- This is the third phase, from 54 to 81 years. In this phase you can renounce from your household life and live with family or in society to help the younger generations by sharing your knowledge and experience as well as supporting young families in many ways.

❖ Vaanprastha- This is the fourth and last phase from 82 years onwards. In this phase you can completely renounce and leave your family or society. You can live in solitude in an ashram, monastery, or retreat to nature, a forest to devote your life to attain self-realisation.

Importance of Pregnancy in this Chatur-Ashram system

Every life has its own ways of conception and reproduction to keep their species alive. Every form of life has to adhere to it, so does the human life. It is part of our dharma or duty to reproduce new life to keep the human race in existence. Many Vedic and Hindu scriptures describe that conception, pregnancy, birth and growing a healthy virtuous soul is one of the highest Yajna -spiritual rituals, and Sadhana- practices to grow spiritually. This gives us full opportunity to experience all the potentials we all are born with in human life.

Conception or Pregnancy is not only about giving birth to a child, but it is creating a whole new opportunity to live our life as a mother or father. To look after, care, educate, create and provide opportunities for the child to reach their own true potentiality.

Diet

Yoga, Health and Diet.

In my view total health cannot be attained only by practicing yoga poses, pranayama, and relaxation techniques. There must be proper consideration given to a balanced diet too or whatever you take into the body.

Purification of the body from the toxins, through shankha-prakshalana, sutra- neti, jalaneti, kunjar, etc. and pranayama are not so beneficial until you can find the source of the toxins, where the waste materials are coming from and how they can be avoided. Then we need to consider how can we rebuild body tissues and organs damaged by all these toxins and impurities?

A complete yoga health program includes harmony of the following things-

- ❖ Techniques useful for cleansing the toxins from the body.
- ❖ Supply of proper dietary supplements for growth and dynamic energy.
- ❖ Practice of physical activity, such as asanas and pranayama.
- ❖ Living as natural life as possible.
- ❖ Consumption of fresh air and sun light.
- ❖ Proper rest, relaxation and sleep for repair of the whole body.
- ❖ Motivation to develop a positive attitude and healthy mental state.

When the connective tissue of the body, bone and cells wear out, they take out materials present in the system to replace themselves. This is the automatic and perfect process, if they have the good material required to repair and rebuild. If your blood stream is full of toxins, nicotine, alcohol, opiates, caffeine, protein or carbohydrate poisoning, or waste products, then the cells cannot undertake the perfect replacement, repair, and reconstruction as in the healthy condition. A person with toxic material and a toxic system is poisoning themselves and are developing a faulty unhealthy micro-structure, instead of a healthy and clean body.

'Health begets health; disease is the mother of death.'

If you are seeking good health, you must ensure that your body is getting all the nutrients and food elements necessary for health, energy, cellular replacement and defence against disease. Your regular diet should have all the nutrients in balanced amounts to balance the functions of all the body's systems. It must be supported with sun light, fresh air, exercise, rest and relaxation. Too little or too much of anything is dangerous. You must find the balance for your own good.

Our mental attitude is also a most important ingredient of our healthy diet. The environment during food preparation, eating and afterward should be pleasant, peaceful, cheerful and relaxed. Any stress or tension and emotional negativity during these times, will contribute toward producing negative effects on your health. Your positive attitude and cheerfulness helps in digesting food properly and fast. So take care of your health. Only a healthy person can enjoy all of the aspects of life. Nothing is of value if you are unhealthy. There is no pleasure greater than the pleasure of health.

Yoga Diet
Simply, a yogic diet refers to the pure vegetarian diet. Our Indian yogis are the best examples of health through the vegetarian diet. They could stay in the high mountains, both hot and cool places without having enough resources, where the normal person like us cannot even think. Their diet is very simple; free of meat, fowl, fish and other animal products and even sometimes they cease the by-products of animals.

Non-vegetarian people say that they could not survive without these animal products, because these are the richest sources of the proteins. This is a totally false concept and it is proven by a large number of healthy vegetarians. Even Hindus in large number are vegetarian to fulfil the Yama of 'non-killing', or 'ahimsa'. All of the natural food we eat, possess a large number of proteins. A simple question you can answer is- where does a cow get its protein from? Why would we want to get this second hand then?

A Yoga Diet means a total balance of nutritious healthy vegetarian food. Your daily intake of food should possess the desired amounts of proteins, fats, carbohydrates, minerals, vitamins, and resins. Then clean and cool water, fresh air, natural living, exposure to sun light, and physical exercises are a very essential part of the complete yoga diet.

There should be balance between your action, energy and rest. Only you can find these balancing measures for you. Do self study with awareness and then make a balance chart for yourself. Balance of action, energy and rest is very important to be understood. How much and which type of physical and mental work you do have to do? Is it balancing for all aspects of your body, mind and emotions? If not, then try to balance it through selecting and practicing a group of the hatha-yoga practices.

Then try to find out the energy requirements of your body according to your work, body build up and environmental conditions. You should eat the food grown in the area you are living, this will make your body homeostatic with the surroundings and you will enjoy your health better with nature. Finally rest, a sound sleep makes you fresh and energetic. So enjoy your sleep, not too little and not an excess. Lord Krishna states the middle path for a yogi as to do everything in the balanced way.

Important Diet Rules for Natural Health

1. Include at least 40% raw, fresh foods in your diet, concentrating on seasonal fruits and vegetables. You can improve your natural health by following nature and by eating seasonal food, vegetables and fruits, sourced from your local area. Nature has its own cycle and produces the food, fruits and vegetables as per the requirement of the area. So don't avoid this if you are seeking good health.

2. In the 60% cooked food, consider whole grains to maintain the balance of acid-alkaline ratio in the body. Never over cook food this will save the essential nutritional elements of the food. Try to use the water used for boiling the vegetables which contain the most essential ingredients of the vegetables.

3. The skin of the fruits is rich source of the alkaline contents, so don't throw them. Wash the fruits and vegetables properly under the tap water and use them fully with their skin. Don't throw away your health producing food with the peelings.

4. The use of animal fats in cooking even ghee, increase the amount of acid in the food. Poly-unsaturated, cold pressed vegetable oils are the most satisfactory for the maintenance of smooth working body processes and nerve tone.

5. Adding white and refined sugar to the fresh fruits and juices makes them highly acid; if you need to sweeten them then add natural sweeteners like honey or jaggery.

6. Avoid any unnatural, junk, processed and long stored foods. They are rich in calories but having no nutrients. The producers may claim there are proteins and vitamins in them and can be proved in the laboratory testing. But are they chemical or inorganic in nature and can they be assimilated by the body? This should be verified. You should avoid preservatives and artificial additives used in all these type of food in any condition.

7. Be aware of the psychological causes creating the feelings of unnatural appetite. Many negative emotions, thoughts, feelings and situations may create this appetite. Remember that appetite is mental, while hunger is a body process.

8. Eat to satisfy hunger and fulfil the bodily needs of all the nutrients and not to satisfy the appetite or to satisfy the sensory pleasure.

Dr Swami Gitananda Giri, founder of Ananda Ashram, Pondicherry, India has said that the yogic diet is-

- ❖ Lacto vegetarian diet
- ❖ 40% raw, fresh foods, natural seasonal foods and local
- ❖ 60% cooked food -whole grain products
- ❖ Don't overcook
- ❖ Save the vegetable cooking water for sambar, soups and sauces
- ❖ The skin of the Veg /fruits is healthy because it is alkaline
- ❖ Use poly unsaturated oils
- ❖ Avoid refined food items
- ❖ Avoid unnatural / produced items
- ❖ EAT to satisfy hunger and not psychological disturbance
- ❖ Beware of bad habits – appetite
- ❖ Don't misuse salt or spices
- ❖ Balance diet in calorie needs with adequate vitamins and minerals

Vegetarianism in Hinduism

The Yogic living to adhere to with the Yama Ahimsa or non-harm, requests that we take a vegetarian diet. It is impossible to live a life of complete non-harm, we have bacteria's living on us, we kill insects accidently etc. but we should at least try to move our life in this direction. It can be challenging for people who are used to a meat-based diet to change to a vegetarian or vegan one, and often guidance may be needed to make sure a balanced diet giving us all the right nutrients are there. During Pregnancy is an especially physically demanding time, so care must be taken, and I would not advise making major changes in diet during this time, you will have enough on your plate so to speak! It is better to start to gradually reduce your meat intake, rather than not attempt it, or try to make a sudden change where your body could have a negative reaction which could cause you to give up. So, without judgment start to explore, maybe twice a week to replace meat with vegetarian meals and try to increase this, as and when you can. 'Mitahara' means the habit of moderate food, we aim to eat a moderate amount of food, only what your body can easily digest, and with sufficient nutrients.

Those trained in Vedic knowledge, however, never adopted a meat-oriented diet, and the pious Hindu still observes vegetarian principles as a matter of religious duty.

That vegetarianism has always been widespread in India is clear from the earliest Vedic texts. This was observed by the ancient traveler Megasthenes and also by Fahsien, a Chinese Buddhist monk who, in the fifth century, travelled to India in order to obtain authentic copies of the scriptures.

Hindu scriptures unambiguously support the meatless way of life. In the Mahabharata, for instance, the great warrior Bhishma explains to Yudhishtira, eldest of the Pandava princes, that the meat of animals is like the flesh of one's own son, and that the foolish person who eats meat must be considered the vilest of human beings [Anu. 114.11]. The eating of 'dirty' food, it warns, is not as terrible as the eating of flesh [Shanti. 141.88] (it must be remembered that the Brahmanas of ancient India exalted cleanliness as a divine principle).

Similarly, the Manusmriti declares that one should "refrain from eating all kinds of meat", for such eating involves killing and leads to karmic binding (bandha) [5.49]. Elsewhere in the Vedic literature, the last of the great Vedic kings, Maharajah Parikshit, is quoted as saying that "The animal-killer cannot relish the message of the Absolute Truth" [Shrimad Bhagavatam 10.1.4].

Hindu Religious Leaders on Non-Injury

The great teachers have imparted their wisdom to guide us on this aspect of our lives:

The greatness of a nation and its moral progress can be measured by the way in which its animals are treated. Mahatma Gandhi

As long as human society continues to allow cows to be regularly killed in slaughterhouses, there cannot be any question of peace and prosperity.
A.C. Bhaktivedanta Swami Prabhupada

Refrain from killing knowingly even the trifling insects like a mouse, a bug or a mosquito. Use no violence even to gain possession of a woman, wealth or kingdom. Never kill any animals even for the purpose of sacrifice. Non-violence is the greatest of all religions. Swami Sahajanand

O lover of meditation, become pure and clean. Observe nonviolence in mind, speech and body. Never break another's heart. Avoid wounding another's feelings. Harm no one. Help all. Neither be afraid nor frighten others. Swami Muktananda

Someone who believes in violence and continues causing injury to others can never be peaceful himself. Swami Satchidananda

To be free from violence is the duty of every man. No thought of revenge, hatred or ill will should arise in our minds. Injuring others gives rise to hatred. Swami Sivananda

By ahimsa, Patanjali meant the removal of the desire to kill. All forms of life have an equal right to the air of maya. The saint who uncovers the secret of creation will be in harmony with Nature's countless bewildering expressions. All men may understand this truth by overcoming the passion for destruction. Sri Yukteswar to Paramahansa Yogananda

If you plant aubergine, you can pluck aubergine. If you sow goodness, you can reap goodness. If you sow evil, you will reap evil. Do good to all. God is there, within you. Don't kill. Don't harbour anger. Sage Yogaswami

The test of ahimsa is the absence of jealousy. The man whose heart never cherishes even the thought of injury to anyone, who rejoices at the prosperity of even his greatest enemy, that man is the bhakta, he is the yogi, he is the guru of all. Swami Vivekananda

Strictly speaking, no activity and no industry is possible without a certain amount of violence, no matter how little. Even the very process of living is impossible without a certain amount of violence. What we have to do is to minimize it to the greatest extent possible. Mahatma Gandhi, My Socialism, 34-35.

Lifestyle

In our modern-day busy lives, most of us have an over stimulated nervous system, with advancing technology we spend a lot of time in front of computers, or sitting at a desk in work often experiencing the fight/flight responses on a subtle level (work stress, family stress, financial stress etc.) without moving our body very much! By developing a regular Yoga routine, we can again address the balance in our body, particularly after some conscious physical stretching our relaxation will be deeper and more healing to the body and mind. Swamiji would say that 50% of our yoga work is doing the postures and the other 50% is conscious relaxing (Shavasana) and observing and absorbing the benefits.

Generally we find that most people are run down, worn out, over busy and need to slow down! Particularly if they want to grow a healthy family 'mum' needs to be as calm and relaxed as possible, yet also have some energy. To be relaxed or calm doesn't mean to suddenly stop doing anything or just lie down on the sofa all day! It means that when we are relaxing we should fully with 100% awareness relax and let go all of the tension in our body parts, then our mind. The greatest problem for people is to be able to relax properly. It would be better to relax properly for a few minutes every day than to sit in a distracted state of mind for hours in a day! This would usually have the opposite effect creating further anxiety.

So for the general public, the best place to start with a pregnant woman is definitely to get her to learn to relax properly through developing awareness and evolving the conscious level of the individual. Pranayama is a powerful tool for cleansing the body and mind as well as increasing our awareness. Most of us know by now that the slowing down of the breath naturally causes a slowing down of the mind. It is only through slowing the mind down we can then look at our thoughts and choose what to do with them! As a teacher you don't have to worry about the task of increasing an individual's awareness or consciousness level; the practices will automatically do this after some time. This is the power of yoga, as Swamiji said, Yoga is the Mother of all Sciences!

When planning pregnancy we should be aware of balance in all parts of our life, or work, rest and play/fun! All things in moderation. When we work, we should work and try to do this with our full intention, but we shouldn't be working 24/7! When we rest, we should so this in a healthy way, using the time to practice relaxation techniques to ensure that we get proper rest; and when we play, have fun in a good healthy way! When we eat, we don't stuff ourselves silly, we should have an awareness of how much our body needs to eat rather than how much it wants to eat. The common saying that 'we are eating for two' when pregnant does not mean two full grown adults, does it?

Mum however will be doing a full-time job in growing a baby from day 1 and in an ideal world she will be getting enough rest and rejuvenation time as well as good healthy meals. In our modern age, most women go out to work during pregnancy: I feel it has become far harder to manage for a woman, who at the same time, up until just a week or two before the due date still has to hold down a full-time job. This is not in balance with what the mother's body and the growing baby's needs, not only physically but mentally and emotionally too.

Needless to say, there is little that can be done about it, as it is what has become usual in the world, and there are pros and cons. The best we can do in the situation is optimise our relaxation time and time away from work, spending this time wisely and not wasting our energy or taking our body to undesirable places. The mother's body is the baby's home and we need to keep it comfortable for baby or we risk the baby wanting to come out early. In yoga we say the body is a Temple! There are many cases where a Mum has gone into premature labour due to too much physical exertion; this is an example of how women today need to get more in touch with their bodies to prevent such a tragedy. Though it's not always the woman's fault, my own mother had to spend three months in hospital prior to my brother's birth as she worked so hard on the farm and was simply not able to rest enough, until she had no option, as she kept going into premature labour and was admitted into hospital to rest, otherwise her body was going into labour. This brings me to one of our famous Yogic sayings from the Yoga Sutras:

Heyam dukham-anāgatam
Avoid miseries yet to come
'Patanjali'

Why attend a Pregnancy Yoga class?

Specialist Pregnancy Yoga classes have so much to offer for a woman. The pace of the class will be better suited to her condition and the practices tailored all around pregnancy. I would always urge women to attend an Antenatal Yoga Class rather than a general class where the instructor may not be trained and therefore not insured, and not be able to give any special attention to the pregnant woman. They meet other new mums, or second/third etc. time mums. Growing a support network is really important and being able to talk to others who share many of the same challenges is hugely beneficial.

Some useful questions Mum may be asked by the Yoga Teacher:

❖ How she's coping generally? What week/trimester is she in?
❖ Is this her first pregnancy?
❖ If not how did the other/s go? (without being too intrusive)
❖ Are things going well (midwife or consultant lead care)?
❖ Is there any complication you need to be aware of? (Does she need to check with the midwife is Yoga suitable or not?)
❖ What is her yoga experience? (A regular practitioner or complete beginner?)
❖ What does she want out of the sessions? (relaxation, birthing and breathing techniques, flexibility)

For Yoga Teachers
As already qualified yoga teachers you will have developed many teaching skills. When teaching pregnant women just as you would have concerns or keep an extra eye on someone who comes to class with a specific health need for example, so you will treat the pregnant woman with a little extra TLC! And meditations and visualisations will be made around keeping the baby bump clearance / space.

It is essential you know about any previous or current complications, such as miscarriages in the past and is this a potential current risk? If so this mum-to-be will probably need much less physical work and more breath and relaxation work so as not to put any stress (which would normally be a healthy stretching type of stress) on her body. Every woman is different but as a teacher its better play it safe and air on the side of caution.

The most common times for a woman to miscarry are at 8 weeks and at around 12 weeks when the fetus is undergoing huge growth spurts/changes. It may be advisable to avoid practice in these times particularly if there is a history of miscarriage. Remembering our Yoga practice time is essentially a time for women to get some quality rest and relaxation and check in with themselves and connect with baby.

Personally, I would find it very difficult to believe that Yoga practice in this gentle way could ever cause a miscarriage, that said if a woman is going to miscarry and this is natures plan, it is likely to happen around these times (8 weeks and 12 weeks) and rather than risking being a potential point of blame, just skip class around this time. To be completely safe only accept Pregnant women over 12 weeks (this tends to be the policy of more insurance companies now).

On the other hand then you may have students whose bodies are well trained and used to yoga or other similar activities and providing there are no complications or concerning history they may prefer a more active class, as with any non-pregnant student it is often the case that some physical work is required to allow some people to relax better and balance out their energy, especially if they have a desk job, or are generally quite mentally over active personalities, they need to move around a bit for their own general health as well as babies. Some women are able to do their usual Yoga practice right up to the last few days! It's all very individual. For the purpose of your own classes though you will need to pitch at the level of the beginner, as your classes are likely to be a mixed group of experience. Besides every sincere student of Yoga knows that there is not really a beginner's class as such – more of a beginners mind set or state of consciousness! Even the most simple posture work used with breath and awareness can be deeply profound.

It is a good opportunity to give out additional information (eg. leaflets) with your initial 1:1 session or discussion on complimentary or natural remedies/tips, support groups etc. in the area. You can network with other health professionals and other local specialist working with pregnancy eg. National childbirth trust, doulas, hypno-birthing etc., and in this way promote each other.

It is also a good time to give any general info about upcoming motherhood and healthy lifestyles so I would put a leaflet together and other handouts regarding support for mum (maybe from other sources too, eg. breast feeding support which depending on your area, services etc. their own midwife may not give this info, or students may prefer to talk to you).

Then give some general guided jattis and kriyas and pranayama as well as a good relaxation at the end. Give them something they can practice at home. Remember you won't know everyone's personal circumstances; they may not even get a chance to come back again so give them something they can use at home and something positive to read over at home, if you can prepare a handout and a daily practice. Try to give them a breathing technique and a relaxation they can use throughout the pregnancy.

Strong advice - Keep all class sessions positive around the topic of birth, do not allow others to share negative experiences in the class space, this can be particularly frightening to new mums! Hold the sacred space for the mother and baby.

We read in the Christian Scriptures "As a man thinketh

in his heart, so he becomes" So it is also true that as a mother

thinks during Pregnancy she so shapes her child.

- Ammaji Meenakshi Devi
(Quoted in Yoga for Expectant Mothers and Others).

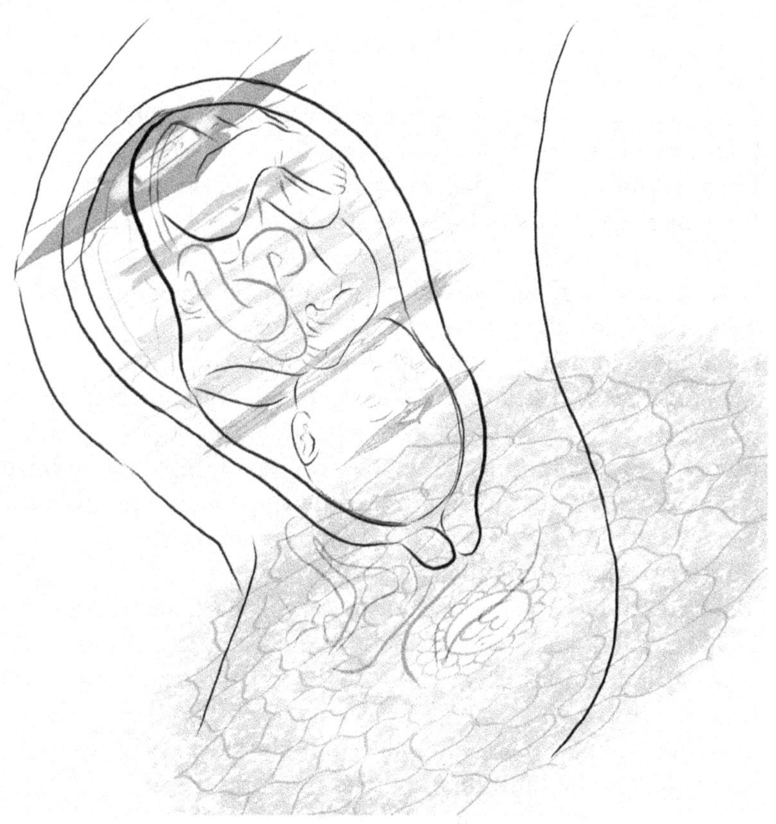

Jattis (warm ups for all stages of pregnancy)

Jattis- are unstructured jiggling and shaking movements of body parts and joints. The hissing out to release all the stress and toxins from physical as well as the mental body are also called jattis. One can use jattis as part of yogic healing/therapy. We tend to accumulate many toxins in the form of acidic crystals around our joints and muscles associated with them. Gradually these toxins cause trouble in the movement of those joints and muscles which can lead into pain and arthritis. Jattis can help us removing those toxins and crystals. Jattis also stimulate deep-rooted nerve endings in our muscles and tissues improving neuromuscular health.

Make adjustments when necessary to avoid larger baby bumps.

Jattis – warm ups
Generally, start from the lower body working toward the upper body – moving from the lower to the higher.

From seated position:
1. Wiggling toes
2. Flexing feet back and forth
3. Circling feet in both directions
4. Alternating flexing feet back and forth
5. Bounce knees
6. Open legs and work on one leg at a time – circling, flexing, wiggling toes, bouncing knee, rolling leg in and out
7. Then rolling both legs in and out toes together on in breath
8. Bouncing legs in and out to wide stretch
9. Catch knee and circle foot, flex foot, shake leg - both sides
10. Catch under thigh and stretch the leg out and open and close moving the leg in back and forth sideways (opening hip also)
11. Circling leg into knee joint both sides
12. Legs together and straight, breath in stretch both feet back towards body and on out breath push forwards
13. Bend knee bring foot inside thigh or on top of thigh and bounce knee
14. Catch foot and knee, on an out breath bring knee in towards chest (Janu shirsha kriya) (will modify with growing bump, knee to side)
15. Circle into hip holding the knee
16. 'Baby cradle' holding knee and foot rocking back and forth
17. Hold right foot and swing leg open and back, hip opening
18. Fold leg, hold into belly, then breath in stretch to front and breath out bring back to the body
19. Then breath in leg out to the side x 3 or alternate if you wish
20. Feet together bhaddha kona (binded) bounce forward
21. Cross legged, start working on fingers, moving, stretching or circling

22. Move into wrists, elbows
23. Shoulders, circle both directions individually then together
24. Head, circling both directions
25. Chin forward on in breath and down to chest on out breath (Mayuri mudra)
26. Circling both shoulders holding onto top of shoulders with the hands
27. Shake hands
28. Tapping with hands, down arm, up front of arm, sides of arms and sweep away
29. Draw shoulder up to ears on in breath and whooooosh releasing breath out
30. Circling from cross legged, moving the hips
31. Legs to front, right foot into thigh bouncing down to leg
32. Free right hand and stretch back on the in breath and release back to the foot on out breath – both sides (janu shirsha kriya paravritti)
33. Alternate legs bringing them to chest (or to sides depending on bump space)
34. Bounce over both legs and then pause into pastimottana asana - (open leg variation)
35. Pedal knees, go side to side
36. Fold knees bounce forward in between the knees elbows down if possible
37. Catch feet and breath in as you stretch feet forwards and come back to bent knees on the out breath
38. Walk back and forth on buttocks on the mat
39. Circling shoulders holding onto them with the hands, circle down towards legs on the in breath and circle back upwards on the out breath (you can reverse the circle as you come up if you like)
40. Circle the head whilst resting on the hands behind the back
41. Sitting up stretch out one arm and twist it back on an in breath and twist in forward on an out breath dropping the head down, both sides
42. Repeat both arms together either both together twisting back and forth or alternating the arms
43. Drop the right forearm to the right side and stretch over with the left arm and keep alternating sides with the breath
44. Lift up right arm with the breath above head left hand remains behind supporting on the floor, repeat both sides moving with the breath
45. Right hand onto back, use left hand to push the elbow down more, repeat other side
46. Counter balance push elbow across the front of the body, hand will go beyond the shoulder
47. Arms in front and stretch palms up and down with the breath
48. Repeat with the elbow joints
49. Hands onto shoulders breath in, lift the elbows breath out, release down
50. Always take time to relax back down onto the floor have spaces
51. Relax forwards, then to the right side, the left side
52. Extend to a gentle side stretch elbow bent touch floor stretch other arm overhead
53. Circling the waist

54. Open the legs out wide and tap down the inside of the leg and up the outside of the leg
55. Bounce over the right leg and move in a semi - circle from one to the other foot
56. In the centre bring the elbows into the middle and rest chin in hands
57. Hold feet breath in lift and breath out release down
58. Free left hand and breath in stretch in out behind and alternate sides
59. Bounce to each side bringing the free arm overhead towards the foot and hand
60. Gomukha paravritti– counterbalance, fold the knees and sit so they are parallel to each other, then breath in sit up and breath out release the chin down towards the chest, repeat both sides

From lying on (either) side:
1. Lift dominant (active) leg up and down with the breath
2. Flexing foot
3. Circling foot of lifted leg
4. Bend knee on in breath and straighten leg on out breath
5. Breath in straighten the leg forwards and up to 900 angle and release on an out breath
6. Open hip lifting knee up towards ceiling on in breath and release down on out breath
7. Lift arm up and back opening chest if you can reach floor behind on in breath
8. Lift arm up sideways beyond the top of the head on the in breath and release back onto the body on the out breath
9. Hands behind head elbows to front, breath in open elbow out and up towards ceiling and breath out release back

From lying on the back / shava asana (only suitable during early pregnancy)
1. Circling feet
2. Flexing
3. Roll toes together on in breath and roll out on out breath
4. Bring hands under the head and roll onto one hip twisting slightly on the in breath and release flop back down on the out breath
5. Roll head side to side
6. Bring the elbows together in front of the face on the in breath and release back on out breath
7. Palms onto abdomen and breath in lift chest up and breath out roll shoulders together
8. Fold right leg and circle the knee moving into the hip, both directions, both legs
9. Knee up and drop it out to the side on the in breath and back up on out breath
10. Extend this to roll the knee right over to the floor on the in breath whilst twisting the head to look the opposite way, both sides
11. Knees together feet to buttocks, breath in drop knees out to sides and breathing out knees back together

12. Setu kriya gentle version – knees together breath in lift the pelvis up release on out breath lifting heels up
13. As above but try not to lift the heels
14. Release knees from the floor and circle the knees massaging the back
15. Hold the ankles and try to circle the hips
16. Hold the knees and rock back and forth to sitting and back down
17. Kicking the buttocks with the heels

When teaching women yoga who will be not only at different stages of pregnancy but also at different levels of yoga experience you will need a selection of warmups that will be safe to use which the individual can always vary to their own level.

A note on Relaxin hormone: During pregnancy (and after, whilst breast feeding the body produces a hormone called relaxin which softens the ligaments, cartilage and cervix to allow for the delivery to take place. Women may notice they feel more flexible. Please request the pregnant ladies to use some awareness and discernment not to try and overstretch into new territories in their body, the main aim of the class is not about flexibility.

Pregnancy Kriyas

A note on posture and names: the The Asana Sanskrit names used are from the Gitanda or Rishiculture Ashtanga tradition. This is an old tradition with an unbroken lineage back to the ancient Rishis of India. Many of the names may not be the common names used, however, this text will stay true to tradition as it believes in a great importance and of using the correct names and Sanskrit sounds rather than the most popular and well known in the modern yoga world.

VAJRA ASANA (Thunderbolt)

Sitting on the heels in this position give the lungs and rib cage the maximum capacity to breathe. This position however may not be comfortable for many beginners to Yoga for very long! Use supports, cushions under the ankles and if it's not comfortable take a crossed legged position. We use this sitting posture to begin classes with some simple breathing techniques before we begin our physical practices. Practice a few rounds of Sukkha or savitri rythym pranayama (as described in the Pranayama section)

SHASHA ASANA (rabbit pose)

This posture assists us to breath primarily into our lower lung area and is a nice position to rest our breathing apparatus in, it should feel quite comfortable. We make a variation in the leg position by opening the knees out to allow room for baby between the knees. We keep the head and chin up and take in a few deep breaths in and out using the 6x6 sukkha rhythm. It will be normal to feel a little constricted in our breathing during the later stages of pregnancy when the baby is often taking up space and pushing into the lower lung area.

PURNA SHASHA (the hare)

This posture assists us to primarily breath into the mid section of our lungs. We make the usual variation in the leg position by opening the knees out to allow room for baby between the knees. We keep the head and chin up and take in a few deep breaths in and out using the 6x6 sukkha rhythm.

DHARMIKA ASANA (devotional pose)

(sequence follows)

PARI-PURNA SHASHA ASANA (completed rabbit)

This kriya (movement with the body and breath) we start from vajra asana breathing in. As we breath out we bring our head down to the mat (opening the knees unless we are in very early stages of pregnancy), then as we breath in we lift up our hips and roll up onto the top of the head. Breathing out coming back down to sit on the heels and breathing in lifting back up into vajra asana. We can repeat this 3 times. This will aid the flow of air to primarily enter the upper most section of our lungs the clavicle region under the collar bone.

We try to work on the lungs regularly in this way as mother and baby need plenty of oxygen and this will help both mum and baby in labour and after as our breath is so connected to our energy levels.

CHATUS PADUS KRIYA (crawling on all fours movement)
Balancing up on your hands dropping down under shoulders and knees under hips is Chatus-padasana. Try to crawl around your yoga space in four footed-pose loosening up your hips and shoulders and putting stimulating pressure on your knees. This type of movement is probably the number one most beneficial movement for getting the baby into the optimum birthing position!

If you think of the baby lying in a hammock (which is effectively the shape, we have created during pregnancy) the baby will position itself most comfortably lying on its back (as we all would) in a hammock.
Therefore the baby will be in the anterior position, head down towards the cervix and its spine lying along mums 'belly'.
Note: babies can move into this with lots of crawling by mum if they are back-to-back especially. I have had several students who have experienced this.

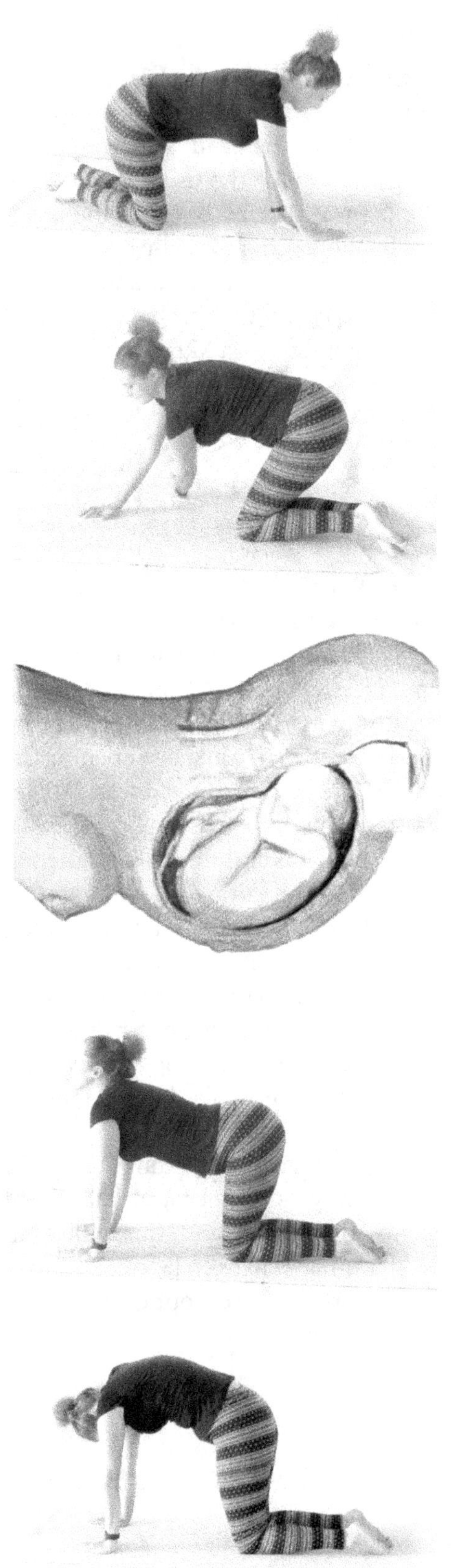

VYAGRAHA pranayama (Tiger breathing)
Palms below the shoulders and knees below the hips, on the inhale dip the spine and lift up with the chin, on the exhale arch the spine up chin in towards the chest. This is a beautiful movement for the spine, as well as an excellent way to get the deep inhale into all sections of the lungs and on the exhale to fully empty the lungs, particularly the stale air that tends to stay in the clavicular area of the lungs if we are not able to fully exchange the gases in the lungs through deep breathing.
Remember that if your own body is well oxygenated then babies will be too!

SHASHANGA ASANA (Baby Rabbit)
Relaxing down into Shashanga, arms outstretched and opening the knees depending on the size of the 'baby bump' a nice stretch for the spine here and a restful position.

DHARMIKA ASANA (the devotional pose) Bringing the head in towards the knees and reaching back to hold onto the feet.

CHIRI KRIYA (cricket action)
From four footed / chatusa-pada-asana, lift right leg up above your back as far as you comfortably can and bring your leg and knee back down on floor with the out breath. Repeat 3 to 5 five times with each leg.

Then repeat but add with the out breath bringing the knee to the forehead.

In later pregnancy you will only do the first half, lifting the leg up over your back, with in breath and bringing your knee back down on floor with out breath.

BALA ASANA (Baby)or NIKUNJA ASANA (flower bower)
Coming forward to rest the arms and upper chest on the mat, lifting up with the hips. Turning the head to one side for a few breaths then opposite side.

Especially good if mum is suffering from sciatica / back pain or sciatica! It relieves the pressure on the lower spine.

MERU ASANA

Push up with the arms lifting the hips up coming into the mountain pose. Its best to loosen up the backs of the knees a little first by doing a gentle movement back and forth with the knees. When ready you can push the heels towards the floor. With all the asanas in Pregnancy we do not hold for too long.

MERU ASANA

from here walk the hands back, bend the knees and slowly uncurl upwards into standing

It is important to keep in mind that our bodies must work pretty well, for their wouldn't be so many humans on the planet.

Ina May Gaskin - Ina May's Guide to Childbirth

Meru Asana (mountain posture) IN STANDING – Swinging right leg forward and backwards,
-swinging the leg in front of the body, opening out the hip-repeat on left side
-circling the knees
-hips rotations in both directions, which is another good one for pregnancy!
-circle the waist
-circle the arms backwards then forwards (separately then together)
-circle the arms in opposite directions
-circle the neck and head
-shake the head, body, legs
-shake all over to clean up our pancha-kosha- levels of energy in and around us.

KONA KRIYA – both arms or single arm variation.

Start from samastithi (equal footed standing pose) and lift up the arms on an in breath to Anjali mudra (palms together above the head). On an out breath bend sideways to the right. On an in breath straighten up.

On and out breath bend sideways to the left, on the in breath straighten up again. Repeat 3 times each side.

This movement is excellent for spinal health allowing all the capillaries between the vertebras to get a fresh oxygenated supply of blood. The spine is supporting our weight and the babies therefore it is really important to take care of the spine and keep it strong and healthy to prevent or ease back ache which is common in pregnancy.

KONA KRIYA - double arm variation
Moving side to side with the breath

UTITHA BHUJANGA- Standing Cobra

Stand straight in samasthiti and join your hands and interlock fingers behind your back. With in breath stretch your arms down towards buttocks with pulling your shoulders and upper chest back.

TRIKONA ASANA - Triangle.
Stand up straight and open legs to your own comfort.
Lift arms up to shoulders and try to turn to left side and reach to hold your left knee with right hand, keeping your left arm up if you can otherwise keep it to your side to support. Repeat the same to other side.

VEERA ASANA - Heroine
The Warrior Pose stretches and strengthens the arms and legs, increases stamina, improves balance and concentration, and can also relieve backaches.
If you are suffering from diarrhoea, high blood pressure or neck problems, you should take extra caution practicing this pose.

PARSHVA KONA ASANA - Side angle pose

Starting with legs wide but comfortable stance, open arms out at shoulder level.

Bend the right knee and bring the right forearm down just above the knee.

Stretch up and over with the left arm and hold for not more than 3 breaths, or you can also do this as a slow kriya work moving in and out of the posture with the breath.

Always balance practices by doing the same number of rounds to each side, or alternating equally.

VRIKSHASANA OR TREE POSE

This helps strengthen your thighs, calves, ankles and back. It can also increase the flexibility of your hips and groin. Your balance and concentration can also be improved with constant practice. This Yoga Pose is recommended for people who have sciatica and flat feet.

Stand straight with balancing on one leg and try to place the other foot in one of the positions as in photos below and join your hands together in namaskar or Anjali mudra.

MALA KRIYA

Stand straight with legs open to hip width or more. Hold to your arms and elbows together in front of chest. With the out breath bend from knees and come down to squatting and with the in breath come back up to standing position. Repeat it several times.

RAJA KAPOTA (early pregnancy only)

Sequence to come into Rajakapotasana

Come to chatuspadasana and push back on your feet to stretch your legs and arms straight in merua-asana.

Bend from knees and look forward. Slowly and carefully bring your right leg forward and turn it so the knee points to right hand and foot to left hand as close as you can.

Now slowly come down from hips, and buttocks as far as you can stretching from thighs, knees, lower back and pushing on arms and shoulders.

Summary of medical research study of Pranava Aum in pregnant ladies

This is an extract from a research study completed by Dr Vasundhara VR at Sri Balaji Vidyapeeth, Yoga Therapy Department at Mahatma Gandhi Medical University Hospital, Puducherry, Tamil Nadu, India.

Summary

The present study evaluated the immediate effect of Pranava Pranayama on maternal and fetal cardiovascular parameters.

Yogic intervention included listening to OM chanting using headphone and performing pranava pranayama along with breath awareness were carefully selected by conducting a detailed literature review.

Pregnant women who satisfied the inclusion criteria and exclusive criteria were selected for the study and the sample size was taken by convenience sampling. Three interventions (Breath Awareness, Listening to OM and Performing Pranava Pranayama) were randomized and sequenced by 3 ways 3 periods cross study design. The techniques were given to pregnant women in the IP ward on three consecutive days for 10 minutes each day. Out of 71 pregnant women 11 pregnant women dropped out and a total of 60 pregnant women were successfully followed up.

The following parameters were studied pre and post each intervention:

- Fetal Heart Rate (FHR)
- Maternal Heart Rate (MHR)
- Systolic pressure (SP)
- Diastolic pressure (DP)
- Mean pressure (MP)
- Pulse pressure (PP)
- Rate pressure product (RPP)
- Double product (DoP)

Thus the study was designed to examine the effect of pranava pranayama, listening to OM on pregnant women's and fetal heart rate over breath awareness.

The main findings of this study are

- Yoga practice offers many benefits to pregnant women and the fetus.
- There were significant changes in MHR and FHR immediately after single session of Breath, OM and Pranava and this attribute to an overall normalization of autonomic cardiovascular rhythms.
- The cardiovascular response with regards to RPP and DoP were more significant immediately after single session of Breath, OM and Pranava.
- There was no significance both in systolic pressure and diastolic pressure; whereas the OM group shows close to significance denoting that if the study had been done in more number of subjects for a longer duration, the value may become significant.
- The MP decrease significantly following OM. The fall in SP and MHR in OM attribute to this fall.
- The plot of delta % changes during pranava showed greater fall in MHR compared to OM and Breath. In OM group delta % changes were greater in both FHR and MHR.
- The response regarding FHR was more significant while listening to OM and Pranava pranayama. On listening to OM, mothers experienced more fetal activity especially during the chanting of Makara phase (Mmm...) during Pranava Pranayama.
- Pregnant women felt more relaxed and comfortable while listening to OM.

Conclusion

It is concluded from the present study that yoga has therapeutic effect during prenatal period. It reduces physical difficulties such as leg pain, sleep disturbance, breathing difficulty due to gravid uterus. While performing pranava pranayama pregnant women were able to regulate the breath at their comfortable level, thereby it was noted after 10 minutes of practice they felt more relaxed and was able to feel the bonding with the fetus.

As positive significance was evident in MHR, FHR, RPP and DoP, the practice of yoga as therapy is said to enhance the physiological strength and feeling of wellbeing of pregnant women.

Yoga as therapy is cost effective, relatively simple and carries minimal risk and hence could be advocated as an adjunct, complimentary therapy in integrated system of medicine for producing health and wellbeing for all.

Shoulder and Arm Kriyas

During pregnancy, every woman experiences something new, different and extraordinary on a daily basis. These experiences are different for each woman. Along with the joy and anticipation for the new baby, there are also chances of one or other type of pain and discomfort during pregnancy and child birth. Along with the common discomforts most woman go through like weight gain, nausea, oedema, constipation and stretch marks; a pregnant woman may also suffer with several types of pain.

These pains include, back pain, shoulder pain and neck pain. A combination of severe shoulder and neck pain in pregnancy is also one of the common complaints of women according to Health Organisations. Shoulder and neck pain can be classified in various types, on account of their severity level and the time of occurrence. For instance, some women suffer from a higher degree of shoulder pain but more frequent neck pain. On the other hand, some women suffer with severe neck pain which is sometimes accompanied with shoulder pain. The causes of neck and shoulder pain may vary depending on their nature. Similarly back pain can also be of various levels, degrees and in differing parts of spine. There can be various causes for different women, depending on their body structure, exercise and pre-existing health issues.

There is significant postural changes for pregnant women. As the baby grows in womb, it makes changes in the posture of the backbone, hips, pelvis and all the muscles around them. It also takes over much of the space in belly and diaphragm area too.

As we know, the human backbone is in a curved shape which works perfectly for normal conditions. But when a woman is carrying the extra weight of the baby in her womb, it puts pressure on the lower back region. Body parts like shoulder and neck, that are located at the upper back regions try to relieve the pressure and get strained. This entire process causes neck and shoulder pain.

There are also other physical changes. Along with change in the posture of the backbone, certain other organs like breasts, pelvis and stomach increase in size. The added weight of the baby and organs like breasts and stomach stretch the shoulder and neck forward, which may also cause discomfort or pain during pregnancy.

While as the baby grows, many women find it difficult to do exercise which can exacerbate these factors. Additionally as the baby grows, it puts pressure on the lower back, and the abdominal and pelvic muscles get stretched, which can cause further tension and pain in the lower back.

Poor posture and lack of exercise is a very common cause of pain in the neck, shoulders or back, during pregnancy. Poor posture during walking, standing, sitting, shifting position or getting up, puts stress on the back, neck and shoulder muscles,

Shoulder Kriyas
working slowly with the breath

Rolling shoulders
Circling with the
breath opening
out expanding
the chest with
the breath

causing pain and discomfort. A wrong sleeping posture can also cause a significant amount of stress to the muscles in the back and the neck causing pain.

As soon as they come to know about their pregnancy, many women quit their regular exercise routine due to all the changes, fatigue, and early pregnancy symptoms.

We carry lots of stress and injuries in our shoulders and it effects our posture and sense of well-being as well as day-to-day life tasks. Shoulder pain or injuries can be due to physical reasons like improper postures, heavy weight lifting, sleeping positions, sitting jobs for long hours, driving etc. Mental or emotional states also influence our shoulders as we carry our responsibilities and strengths in our shoulders. People with low-self esteem, and depression tend to have crunched shoulders. Stronger, healthy and happy people will generally have wide open shoulders. Aggressive, irritative and angry people will have very tight, and tensed shoulders. There are also some sports injuries we carry due to excessive over exertion in certain sports and exercises.

Back and shoulder practice method: Sitting straight with cross legged or legs stretched in front or this can even be done sitting straight on a chair if the woman finds it difficult during the pregnancy.

1. Join your hands together in front of your chest. With the in breath open and stretch out your arms and shoulders back and bring your hands back together with the out breath.

2. Interlock your fingers close to heart, turn your palms inside out and stretch to front with in breath and bring back to heart with the out breath.

3. Keep your hands to the side and raise them over your head in a circle with in breath and bring them back down to sides with the out breath.

4. Interlock your hands on top of head and with the in breath turn your palms inside out and stretch over your head and bring them back down with the out breath.

5. Place your hands on your shoulders with elbows joined together. With the in breath open then backward and bring back together with the out breath.

6. From above circling your elbows clockwise and anti-clockwise with deep breathing.

7. Raise one shoulder up and other one down with in the breath and release with the out breath.

8. Keeping your hands on your knees or at the side, raise both your shoulders up towards ears with the in breath and drop them with the out breath, using a hissing sound.

9. Place your one elbow behind and over your head with hand pointing back to the shoulder. Use other hand to gently stretch your right elbow to left side with in the breath and let go with the out breath.

10. Place both hands behind your shoulders with elbows pointing over your head, try to bring them close together with in the breath and release with the out breath.

11. Sit straight and stretch your arms to both sides. Now place right hand under left arm and left arm over the right arm, giving a nice hug of arms to chest and hold it for few breaths.

12. Bring both your hands to front and place the right arm on left and twine your arms to each other in Garuda Mudra. With the in breath raise your Mudra upward in front of your face and with the out breath draw it back down. Repeat it several times and follow the same with changed hands.

13. Place your right hand on floor behind your body and then raise your left arm over and stretch back. Hold it for few breaths and repeat the same with switched arms.

14. From Sukhasana come down to left side and place your left arm and elbow on floor with raising your right arm over your head with creating a nice stretch in your arm, shoulder and side muscles. Repeat the same with switched sides.

stretching arms up with the in breath

opening arms back down on the out breath

stretching arm forwards on in breath

back to the heart on the out breath

After lots of shoulder loosening work sit in your most comfortable seated posture and practice some deeper shoulder stretches to help release tension from the upper back and shoulders.

HAMSA MUDRA

Sit straight in vajrasana or sukhasana. Bring your hands behind your back and join your palms together with fingers pointing up in reverse namaskar mudra.

GOMUKHA ASANA

Come to vajrasana and place your right elbow behind and over your head and fingers pointing down.
Bring your left hand from behind and down to reach to hold to right hand or touch to fingers. Repeat the same with swapped arms

ANJALI MUDRA FROM VAJRA VEERA ASANA

Tucking under with the toes to stimulate the cranial nerves associated in foot reflexology, stretching up into Anjalir Mudra, saluting to the Divine!

NAMASKAR MUDRA FROM VEERA ASANA

Bringing the palms down to the heart this is a nice place or pause for a few deep breaths.

PARIGHASANA - GATE POSE (below image)

From kneeling down toes tucked under position stretch your right leg to right side. Keep your left hand to left leg to support, stretch right arm straight to over head and then try to stretch towards left side as much as you can as the picture. Repeat the same with other side. Legs

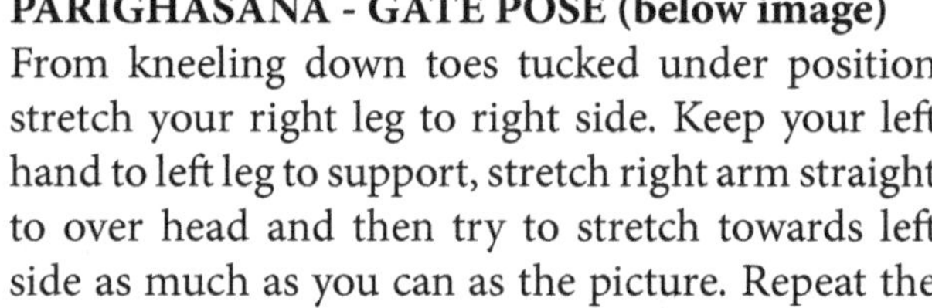

Whilst seated practice some more side stretching and gentle back bending, always moving with the breath - the kriya - moving with the breath work is what will really help the pregnant woman to tune into her breath easily and automatically when the birthing process begins!
Remember breath work is one of the greatest pain management techniques!

BADDHA KONA KRIYA

In sitting position bring both your feet together close to groin as much as you can. Pushing your feet against each other and allowing knees to come down to floor if possible, will help strengthening and loosening of the hips as well as correct the blood circulation in thighs and legs. If you are comfortable, try to also practice the butterfly- bouncing the knees to the sides gently. But be aware that the hormone relaxin, that is released during pregnancy can make us feel more flexible than we actually are so just be aware of over stretching.

Hand Variations for energy work-
1. Holding to big toes with index fingers and thumbs.
2. Holding to both feet together wrapping hands around toes.
3. Holding to ankles with cross hands.
4. Placing hands on shoulders with crossed arms.
5. Holding to ears with crossed arms.

MAYURI MUDRA - The Peacock gesture

Sitting straight, breath in and stretch the chin forward and as you breath out pull the head back and bring the chin to the chest.

SAPURNA VAKRASANA-SITTING TWIST

Bend right knee and twist to the right so to gently lengthen the spine and breath deep, release after 2-3 breaths. (repeat on left side)

DANDA ASANA

Stretching your arms over your head with palms turned inside out.
Lift and lengthen through the spine, shoulders, arms and hands.

MODIFIED PASCHIMOTTANA ASANA

Gently reach forward without compressing your baby bump.

PARSHVA EKA PADA PRASARA KRIYA HIP OPENING / SWINGING

Keep the back lengthened up and catch hold of either foot (bend the knee initially) swing the leg open, back and forth. You can also hold the leg in different places and take a few deep breaths.

UPAVISTA KONASANA

From upavista asana keep holding to your right foot or toe with right hand and slowly lift your left hand over to ceiling from left side with creating a nice twist from upper back, chest and shoulder area, but not forcing much in pelvic area and hips. Repeat the same to right side.

Easier variation is doing it with one leg bent from knee and foot pointing to other thigh as in picture.

GENTLE TWIST

There are many simple twist variations that can be used here, the legs can be outstretched, or one leg crossed over the other, or crossed legged as in the picture.

Lengthen up the spine and twist the spine looking beyond the shoulder of whichever side we are twisting to.

Take a few deep breaths and release on an out breath.

Repeat on the opposite side.

ASWINI MUDRA and MOOLA BANDHA (modified) pelvic floor exercises.

Sapurna Vakra Asana- Sit straight with left leg extended in front while the right foot is placed against the thigh of left leg. Reach with your left hand to catch hold on to right knee and place your right hand behind to support the gentle twist of your spine.

Modified Paschimottanasana- Keep your legs extended to the front with space between your legs to allow space for your baby-bump. Now try reach forward to catch hold on to your legs, ankles or feet to give a gentle stretch to back, arms and muscles or ligaments in legs.

VAJRA ASANA

Take a few relaxing breaths in Vajra asana, always taking some time to observe the body, feel inside and tune into baby!

EKA PADA PAVANA MUKHTA ASANA (hip opening variation)
Lying down on your back with a pillow under your head. With the in breath pull your knees up and out to the side opening the hip and bring your head towards knee as in picture. Keep your other legs relaxed and knee slightly bend to support the baby bump.

NOTE: lying on the back can be uncomfortable, particularly in the third trimester, so most of these can also be practised on the side.

SUPTA BADDHA KONA KRIYA
Lie down on your back, a pillow can be used head (definitely after 24 weeks to be safe) or lower and mid back if needed. Now bring both the soles together close towards tail bone or bottom as far as one can with allowing both the knees to fall out to each side without forcing them.

Kriya- You can try to alternatively roll side to side on your lower back aiming to touch alternative knee on floor, will provide an easing and stimulating benefit around lower back, hips and pelvic muscles. You can also simply rock the pelvis back and forth from lower back rolling the pelvis forward onto the coccyx and back again.

Relax back in SHAVA ASANA for a few breaths.

SETU KRIYA - BRIDGE ACTION

Variations 1 From back lying pose-shavasana, lift your knees up bringing your heels close to bottom and hands straight down towards feet. Now lift up your bottom as much as you can.

Variation 2. From shavasana put your hands under your head, keep both elbows down on floor to sides if you can. Lift up your bottom and spine as much as you can.

From Setu, you can also shake the hips side-to-side which is known to help release the sciatic nerve.

Also try opening and closing the knees with the breath, also useful for sciatica.

EKA PADA UTTANA ASANA - Single leg lifting

Lifting one leg up with in breath and bringing it down with the out breath. Repeat with both legs several times. You can keep other leg straight or knee bend on the lift.

DWI PADA UTTANA ASANA - Double leg lifting.

Using the sukkha 6 x 6 rhythm again to lift the leg on the in breath and release the leg down on the out breath. Most women will need to bend the knees first then lift-up the legs and straighten when they get the feet up in the air, this is much gentler on the lower back.

SHIRSHA UTTANA KRIYA - lifting the head with the breath.

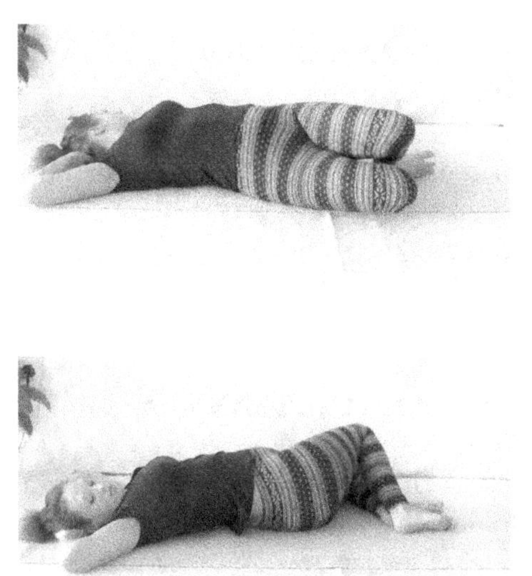

KATI CHAKRA ASANA - Gentle side twisting kriya

From shava asana bend the knees bringing the heels to the buttocks. Bring the hands behind the head and drop the elbows out to the side.

Breath in! On an out breath drop the knees to the right side and turn the head to the left looking towards the elbow. On the in breath straighten back up. Keep alternating sides like this on the in and out breaths.

DRIDHA ASANA OR SIDE LEG LIFTING -

Often women who have sciatica during pregnancy may not like this, so they can opt to do some side leg lifting instead in the same way.

On the in breath lift the leg up and down on the out breath

On the in breath stretch the leg forward and back down on the out breath

On the in breath stretch the leg behind and back down on the out breath

On the in breath lift the head up and down on the out breath

PELVIC PAIN LOCATION DURING PREGNANCY

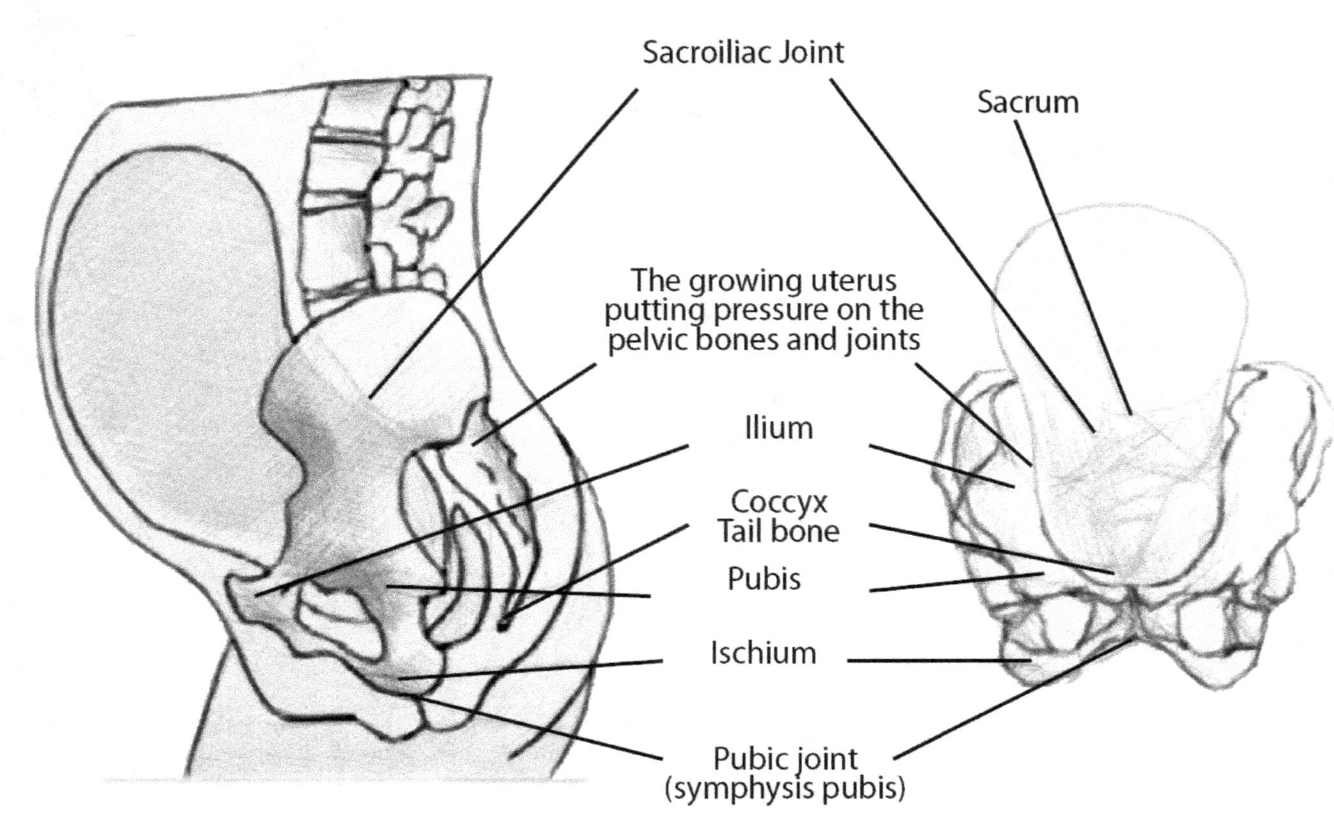

SHAVA ASANA OR SIDE LYING VARIATION

In this tradition Shava asana is a very specific posture ideally, but when you are pregnant you really need to be comfortable too and keep the head elevated! Ideally we will have our head towards the North, hands alongside the hips palms facing up, heels together and toes dropped out to the sides. Use a blanket to stay nice and warm. If its uncomfortable adjust the body until you are, or many women prefer to lie on the side particularly in later stages of pregnancy.

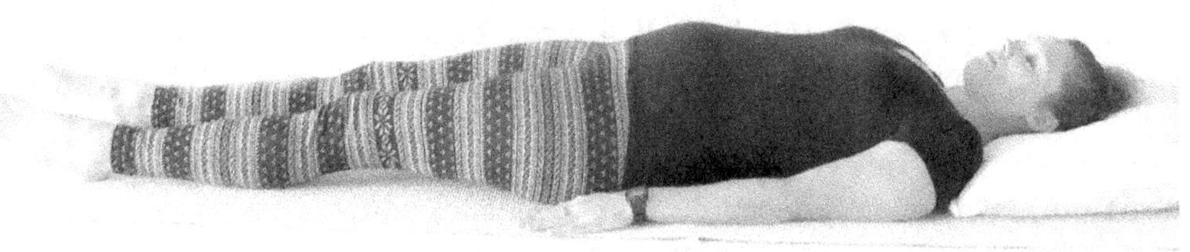

*The Practice of Pranayama during Pregnancy
ensures upmost health, cleansing and calming
the nervous system and concentrating the mind.
As any Obstetrician will tell you, the greatest
enemy in the delivery room is tension, and it is this
tension which can make childbirth a long,
drawn out and painful affair.*
Ammaji - Meenakshi Devi
Yoga for Expectant mothers and Others.

Some reasons you should sleep on your left side

In Pregnancy due to the position of the heart, to avoid fainting or dizziness which can happen when a woman is heavily pregnant, lie on the left side only. This should not be an issue in early pregnancy, but in the last weeks there is a slight risk the womb can collapse back onto the Vena Cava causing the blood circulation to be affected and causing dizziness. Also keep the head elevated, with a pillow under it.

Heart Changes: In the pregnancy period the size and the position of the heart changes. The heart is pushed upwards to the chest cavity by the diaphragm due to the expansion of the uterus, and this will also change the heart functionality. The actual size of the heart increases by 12% during pregnancy.

Cardiac Output: This generally refers to the amount of blood pumped out of the heart during pregnancy. According to pregnancyzone.com the amount of blood pumped to the body is 6.7 litres per day and it increases to 8.7 litres per day during pregnancy and thus the heart works very hard with increased heart risks. The amount of cardiac output will increase the heart rate among pregnant women.

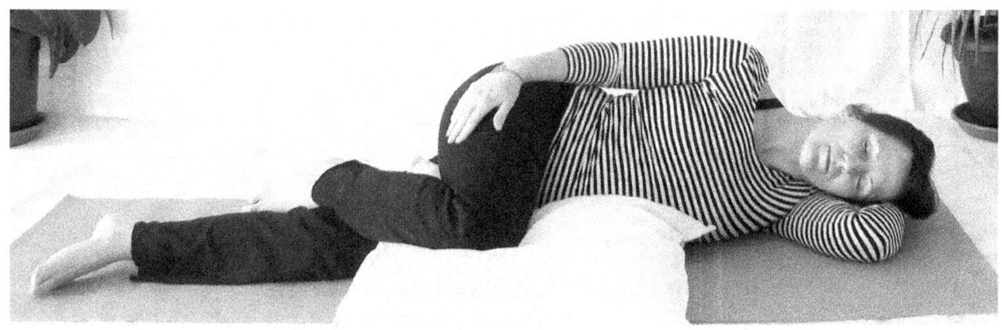

Better Lymphatic Drainage

Back Pain Relief

Heartburn Reduction

Better Sleep During Pregnancy

Better Elimination of Waste Products

Ashwini Mudra and Moola Bandha

The pelvic floor is placed under a lot of pressure during delivery of baby and perineal tears or the need for an episiotomy is quite a common occurrence so it is important to try to prepare the pelvic floor for birthing by practicing Ashwini Mudra and Moolha bandha (in a light way) and for post-natal yoga it is even more crucial to bring the pelvic floor back to a healthy condition to avoid common problems such a stress incontinence.

ASHWINI MUDRA: Helps avoid stress incontinence
Ashwini Mudra, the horse gesture is a simple and effective practice that has a wide range of physical, psychological as well as spiritual benefits. This Mudra can be performed from any sitting position and is done by imposing an anal restraint called Moola Bandha on the external sphincter muscles of the anus and rapidly tensing sand releasing the restraint, like the defecating action of a horse (Ashva).

This Ashwini Mudra energizes the entire nervous system and is an excellent preventive and curative practice for haemorrhoids as well as disorders of the rectum, gonads and perineum. It is useful before, during and after pregnancy and child-birth.

Method: Imagine you're 'lifting' in an elevator with 10 floors, with your muscles rapidly squeeze, tighten and lift the anus muscles several times lifting as high and firmly as you can to the '10th floor'! repeat the practice 3 times or more. This helps avoid stress incontinence.

MOOLA BANDHA: Helps core muscles and posture
The restraint at the root base of the alimentary canal is accomplished as follows. After the breath is held in or out in a Kumbhaka, the rectal muscles are tensed so that the sphincters of the anus are tightened in an exaggerated manner. Moola Bandha balances the autonomic nervous system in a positive manner, thereby reducing tension. Healthy pelvic tone can be developed by the regular practice of Ashwini Mudra and Moola Bandha.

Method: Imagine now you only lift to the 3rd floor of the elevator, using the same muscles but in a slow and controlled way with the breath. Breath in lift and hold...2,3,4,5,6 seconds - release on your out breath relax. Repeat several times. This helps condition our core strength and tone, keeping our back posture strong.

The state of relaxation of the mouth and jaw is directly correlated to the ability of the cervix, the vagina, and the anus to open to full capacity.

Ina May Gaskin - Ina May's Guide to Childbirth

MUSCLES OF THE PELVIC FLOOR
INFERIOR VIEW, FEMALE

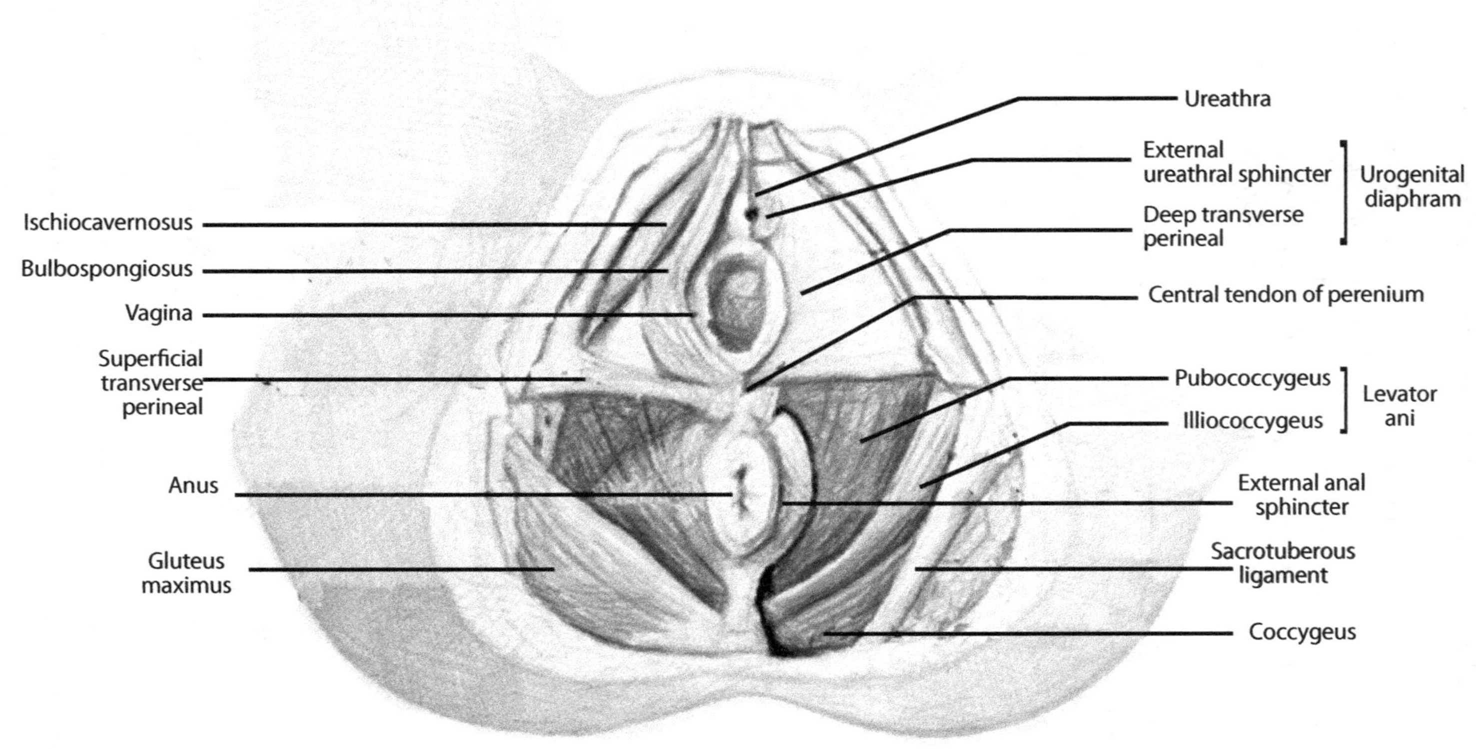

KUKKRIYA PRANAYAMA - DOG PANT BREATH

This is a great pranayama for two main reasons, one it gives us a burst of energy. Secondly and perhaps more importantly using this panting breath should help us to slow down the natural pushing we feel during contractions in labour. We want to do this momentarily whilst the baby's head is crowing, that is when the baby's head has reached the cervix and to deliver the head and at the same time not risk a perineal tear to the mother, we can use this panting breath to slow down that bearing down and pushing at that crucial moment.

Method: In yoga practice we usually do this from the vajra asana seated posture, of course who knows what position you will be in during birth, but for the sake of the yogic practice we would sit in vajra asana (adjust the knees apart as required to accommodate baby) and bring the wrists to the knees, straight arms.

Now drop the head on the exhale. Inhale and raise the head. Start panting high chest breath like a dog would pant. Then release the head down to complete your exhale. Repeat 3 times.

It may help to mention to your midwife please ask me to pant when babies head is crowing. They may have their own techniques or unfortunately may not say anything at that moment so if you are prepared with this practice it can only help!

OTHER PRANAYAMAS TO USE DURING A PREGNANCY CLASS:
In a class this would be a good time to also practice any other choice of recommended pranayamas:
Pranava AUM
Brahmari and Brahmara
Brahma mudra head and neck kriyas
Sukha Pranayama
Savitri Pranayama
Lomaviloma Pranayama

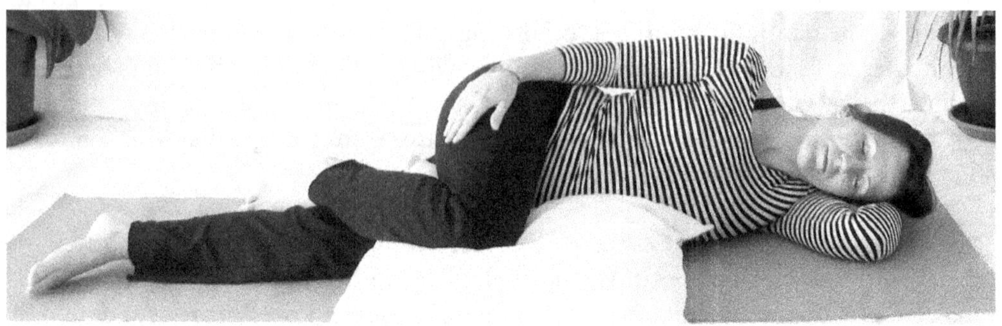

JNANA SURYA KRIYA

Imagine as you lie down a large sun like orb is floating above your Solar Plexus and baby's body. This ball of Prana, Sun with every breath you waft up close too and allow your body to absorb whatever energy it needs from this sun energy. Your body can feel as though it will lift up completely into the sun and stay there until you naturally feel to release out of it.

BREATH OF LIFE

In Yoga and Tantra it is explained that our inhalation or Puraka is represented by an inner flow of life force known as Shakti as in 'Inspiration or Inspiro' (inhaling the spirit of life). The outer flow or exhalation is associated with evolutionary force of Shiva which leads our individual spirit to reunite with the higher or cosmic spirit as in 'expiration or expiro' (exhaling the individual self).

With the inhalation or puraka, the golden solar or loma, the creative force of universe enters in from above the crown or Sahashrara Chakra and flows through the body sustaining all the life process. During exhalation or rechaka, the silvery villoma energy enters from soles of our feet and flow outward from the crown of our head. These two energies of loma-viloma, positive-negative, solar-lunar, prana-apana, shiva-shakti are continuously flowing in two opposite directions, which creates a strong electro-magnetic force or polarity in and around out body.

This healthy and optimum polarity symbolises health and well-being. When this polarity is out of harmony, we suffer with physical, mental, emotional and spiritual health issues. Total loss of this polarity means death. According Tantra and various Yoga therapy concepts, we lose this polarity due to various stress and strains, health issues, lifestyle, dietary habits, electromagnetic toxicity of mobiles, Wi-Fi, and all sorts of electronic appliances. This plays an adverse effect on our nervous system and hormonal secretions.

During the labour and child-birth process a mother can go through an immense amount of tension, fear and pain which many times can cause adverse effects of the birthing process affecting anatomical and physiological changes a mother needs to go through. This stress and strain effects our breathing process too. Our calm, deep, rhythmic breathing is regulated by our Parasympathetic nervous system which also empowers our relaxation response. While the short, and stressful breathing stimulates our sympathetic nervous system which causes the stress response.

To enhance the polarity, and stimulate parasympathetic or relaxation response deep rhythmic breathing is highly recommended. To further increase the benefits of deep breathing we can add our loma-viloma or shiva-shakti visualisation with deep breathing. With conscious inhalation through the nostrils visualise a the golden solar or loma energy entering in at top of your head and recharging your body, mind and spirit. Slowly exhale your breath out through your mouth with gentle hiss sound and visualise cool silvery villoma energy flowing out with releasing all sorts of tension and negative energy.

If you need to rest during labour, you may lay down on your side and follow this loma-viloma visualisation for deep relaxation, enhancing the required physical, and hormonal changes during the birthing process.

LOMA-VILOMA VARIATION FOR BABY
With the in-breath the Pranic, sun-like, healing, revitalising energy moves down through the top of the head and circles and envelops baby with healing light and energy. The light continues out beyond the top of the feet.

With the out breath the Apanic, silvery, moon like, relaxing and releasing energy flows up through the feet surrounding baby, bringing a peaceful and relaxed state to baby and the energy continues to flow up and out beyond the top of mothers head. Continue this visualisation for as long as you consciously can.

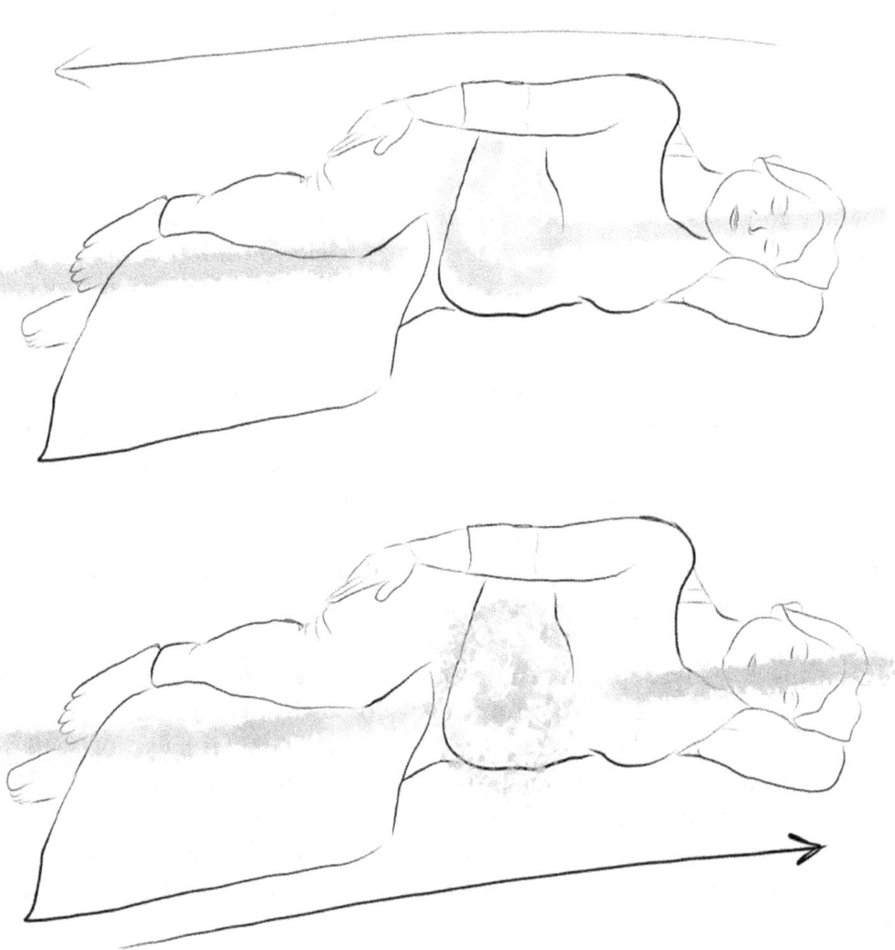

MARMANASTHANAM KRIYA - To fully relax mother and baby
Remember mother and baby are so connected that there emotions and feeling are like one entity! This simple but effective technique helps to consciously relax 22 body parts specifically practiced in the Gitananda Tradition.
Begin with some 6x6 sukkha rhythm or 6 x 3 x 6 x 3 Savitri rhythm.
Describe slowly each of the following body parts relaxing, releasing, softening letting go SUGGESTING RELAXATION:

1	Toes	12	Hands
2	Feet	13	Lower arms and Elbows
3	Lower leg to Knees	14	Upper Arms to shoulders
4	Upper leg to Hips	15	Throat
5	Buttocks	16	Mouth and Chin
6	Base of Spine	17	Nose and cheeks
7	Pelvis area	18	Eyes
8	Abdomen	19	Around the ears
9	Chest	20	Back of the Head
10	Shoulders	21	Top of the Head
11	Fingers	22	Cavernous Plexus - middle of the Forehead

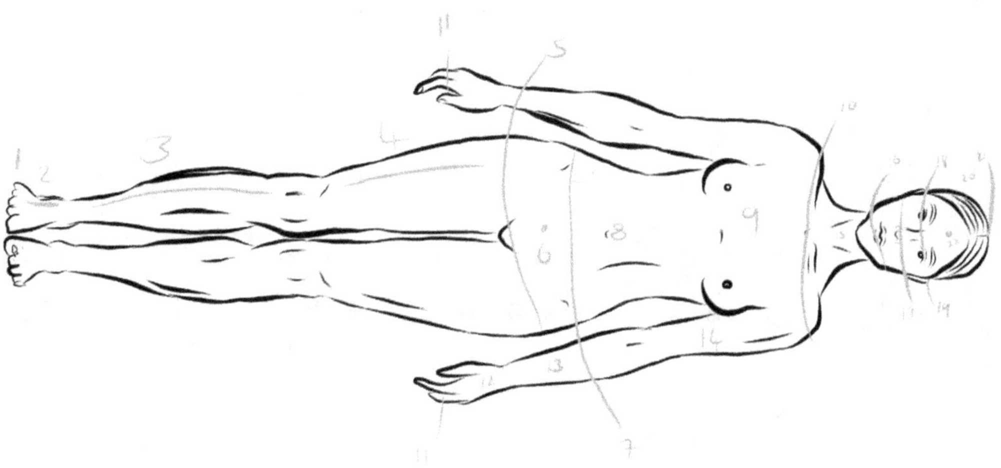

Typical class sequence for all stages of Pregnancy

The Labour breath or birthing breath

This breath is designed to almost mimic the birthing process and prepare mum for her delivery with a good focus on the breath which will help the whole process move along smoothly.

Part 1
We can use the Sukkha 6x6 rhythm to prepare for this. Then we simply start to extend the out breath...

IN BREATH X 6 COUNT

OUT BREATH .... LONG (blowing the air out through the mouth)

Increase 10 or 12 count

Part 2
We can use a light Moola bandha also to help prepare alongside the breath for a few rounds only:

IN BREATH X 6 count

HOLD THE BREATH WITH LIGHT MOOLA BANDHA X 6 count (no more than this)

OUT BREATH - Blow the air out fully relax and let go the Moola bandha feel an opening and releasing and relaxing of the birth canal and visualise an easy birth. (some hypnotherapy techniques can be used here).

Part 3
Adding a visualisation during the birthing breath can help the mother stay focused on the breath so the body can do what it should be able to do naturally without interference from our mental states:

IN BREATH - visualise golden light coming in through the head

OUT BREATH - imagine silver relaxing light blowing out with the breath through the mouth

Try keeping the mind lifted up by focusing on the Bindu point between the eyebrows

We can practice this birthing breath technique either sitting down comfortably or lying down for part of the relaxation at the end of class.

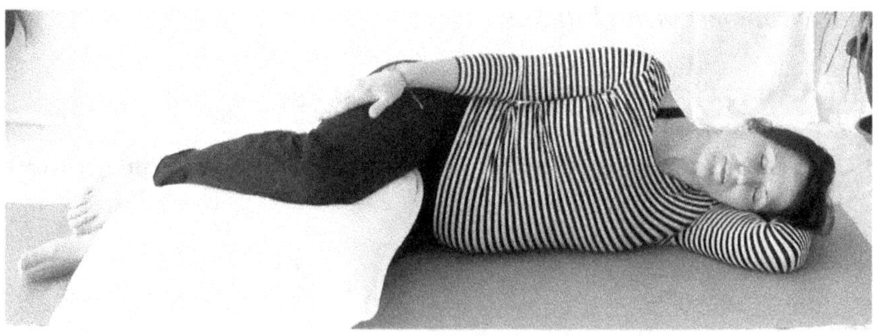

Hatha-Yoga Heart, Spine and Pelvis

A suggested Set of Practices for early pregnancy and post-natal yoga

This series of Kriyas or movement is to work through our whole body from toes to head is designed for loosening up every joint and muscles to free them from accumulated stress, burden, injuries and traumas. There are some kriyas and postures taking us a bit deeper in areas of hips, pelvis, heart/chest and shoulders. This series will help stimulating spine and make it strong and flexible. It will help ease and relax groin area and tightness of hamstrings too. These are a good option if you are already a regular Yoga Practitioner, your body will enjoy the deeper work.

Kriya 1- This part of Kriyas are also good for digestive system, will improve our pelvic health and strengthen your abdominal and pelvic muscles. All these set are recommended kriyas for back, hips and shoulders if one can lye on the back with folded knees. Follow some basic jattis of warm up here for few minutes before you begin.

1. SAPURN EKA-PADA UTTANA-KRIYA - Lye down on your back with knees folded and feet on floor close to buttocks.

Now raise your one leg straight over to ceiling with the in breath and fold it back down with out breath. Repeat with each legs three times.

2. SAPURNA EKA-HASTA UTTANA KRIYA- As above now raise your one hand straight over to ceiling with in breath and place it back down with the out breath. Repeat three times with each side.

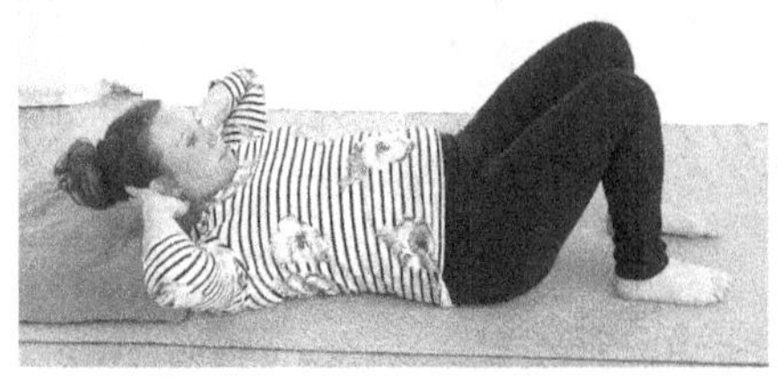

3. SAPURNA SHIRSHA UTTANA KRIYA-
As above raise your head up with in breath and place it back on floor with out breath.

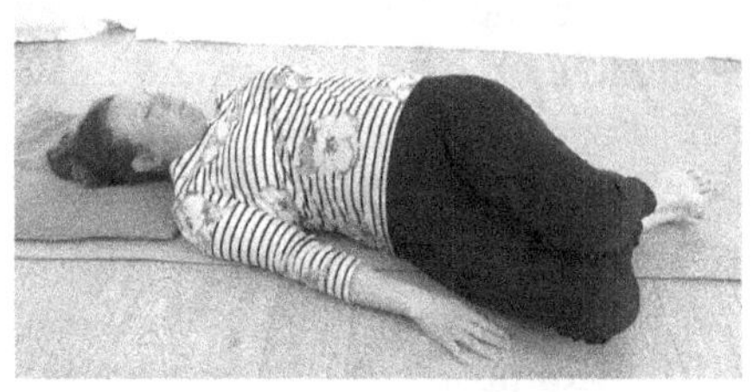

4. KATI CHAKRA KRIYA 1- In position as above bring your knees to floor with creating twist in hips and lower back to right side and head to left with in breath.

Return back to middle with out breath and repeat the same to other side. Repeat three times to each side.

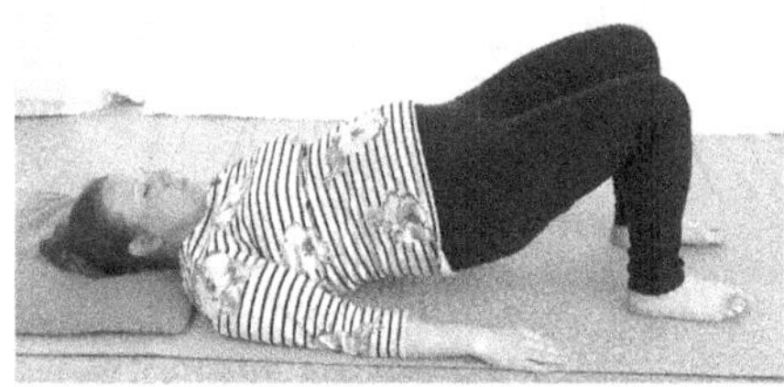

5. SETU KRIYA OR SETU PRANAYAMA 1- As above position raise your buttocks and spine up with in breath reaching into Setu-Asana or Bridge Pose.

6. EKA PADA KATI CHAKRA KRIYA- Now stretch your right leg straight on floor with keeping the left knee bend and arms stretched along side to shoulders. Roll on your right side with aiming to bring your left knee on floor over the right side.

You might like to place your right hand on left knee to get into more deeper twist and stretch. Repeat three times to each side.

7. DVI PADA KATI CHAKRA KRIYA- Draw both your knees towards chest (not compressing baby bump in anyway).

Now with in breath roll on your back towards right side with allowing your knees to reach to your armpit and return to middle with out breath. Repeat three times to each side.

8. SAPURN DVI PADA UTTANA KRIYA- Keep your knees bend with heels close to bottom on floor. With in breath raise your legs over to ceiling and fold them back with out breath.

Repeat three to five times.

9. DVI PADA PAVAN MUKTA KRIYA- With out breath draw your knees to chest, wrap your both arms around them and bring your head to knees. Place your hands and feet back down on floor with out breath.

10. SUPTA BADDHA-PADASANA- From shavasana join both your souls together close to your tale bone and allow knees to open out to each side with aim to touch place them on floor and hold for few breaths. You can keep your hands on floor or on thighs.

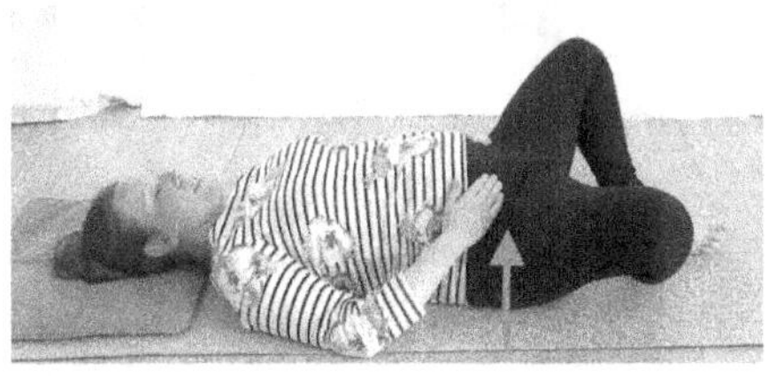

11. SUPTA BADDHA PADASANA UTHITA- From above posture now raise your buttocks and lower back up as high as you can and hold for few breaths.

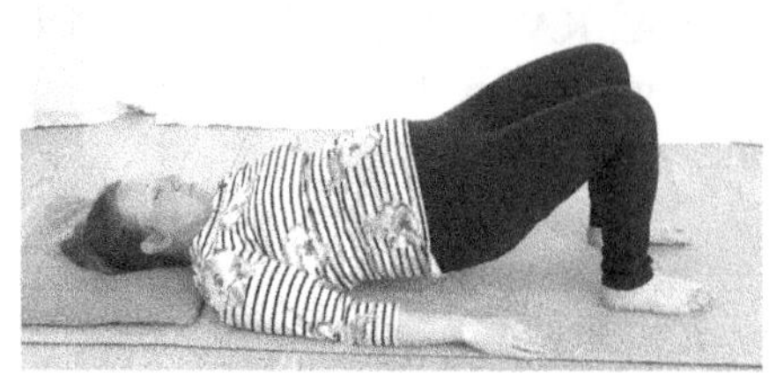

12. SETU BANDHA ASANA - Lie on your back with the knees folded and heels close to the buttocks. Raise your buttocks and back up as high as you can and hold for few breaths whilst keeping your knees hip width. Now bring your hands under, interlace your fingers, stretch your arms away as far as you can and hold the pose for a few breaths.

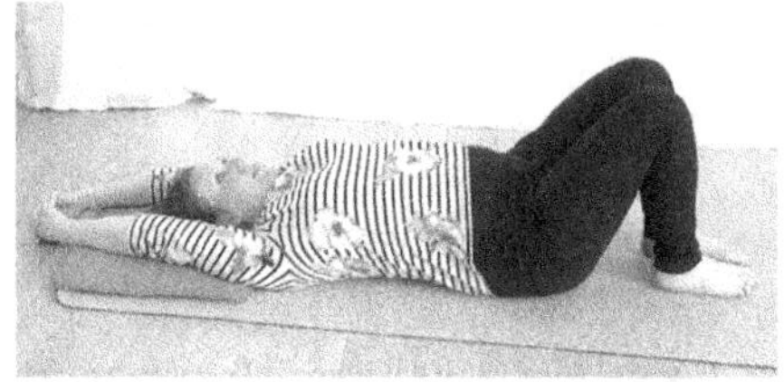

13. DWI HASTA UTTANA Breath in, stretch arms over head and breath out and back down.

14. HUNG-SAH KRIYA -   1.   A powerful psychic cleansing technique, the hung-sah Kriya using the sounds hung on the inhale and sah on the exhale. These sounds are internally chanted you do not need to vocalise them out loud. The sounds actually mimic the natural sounds of your breath with you inhale and exhale.

Technique: Relax in Shava asana or on the side if it's more comfortable. Start with 9 rounds of the sukkha breath 6 count in and 6 count out. Then chant the sound OM in your mind as you breath in and out a few more times. Visualise this Om vibration being drawn down your body (head to feet) on the in- breath and then up the body on the out-breath. Then on an exhale imagine the sound 'hung' focused on the left hip or just beyond it. Then on your inhale the sound sah flows or sweeps to the right hip. Then keep sweeping back and forth to left hip exhale huang and right hip inhale and hear or imagine the sound sah.

After practicing this for several minutes you should start out feel a deep sense of relaxation. This practice is said to remove genetic samskaras we are carrying form our ancestors, it is a very powerful practice which will still continue to work throughout your life,

Wake up in a gradual process when you are ready.

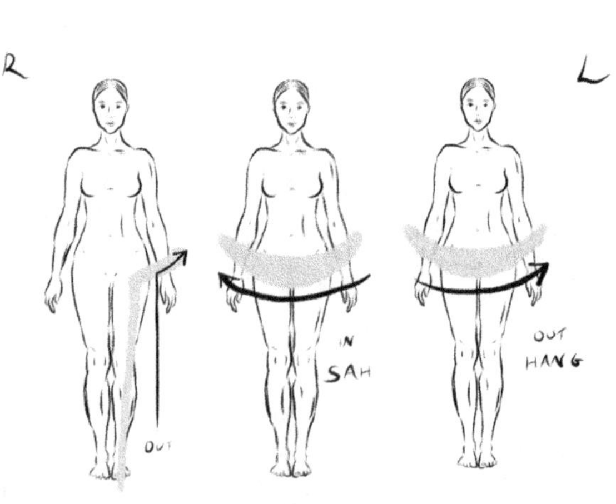

What is Partner Yoga

Partner Yoga is a modified or extended aspect of Hatha Yoga and Yoga therapy. Here you can help or get help to perform certain postures or kriyas which you might find difficult to practice otherwise due to various reasons.

During pregnancy it can be a very helpful tool to help a pregnant woman to perform some postures, to improve strength and flexibility as well as improve blood circulation and pranic energy flow. These kriyas or yoga therapy work can also be very relaxing and healing.

There is so much tension or stress that builds around shoulders, neck and back during pregnancy which tend to not allow many women to even try some basic postures or kriyas. If you can assist someone in simple kriyas like leg lifts, arm stretches, shoulder movements, back lengthening, etc., this can be tremendously helpful.

It is important for fathers to get involved- Ideally partner or assisted yoga provides a perfect way to get fathers or partners to get involved in pregnancy. In many cases the man tends to find themselves left out in this most amazing journey and it can cause change in their life and relationships. This gives them the perfect opportunity to help their partner to feel better.

Partner Pregnancy Yoga

If you can get your partner involved, this has huge benefits, ideally both practice yoga together. Here are some suggested practices.

Assisted Side Stretch

The partner is gently leaning to support in to support mum-to-be and lifting up the arms, taking a few deep breaths here then releasing, and repeating on the opposite side.

Assisted back bend

The partner allows mum-to-be to lean back on them, and stretch the arms over her head. The partner supports the arms on the shoulders and supports the back with the hands. Again breathing deep, not holding these postures for too long in the later stages of pregnancy.

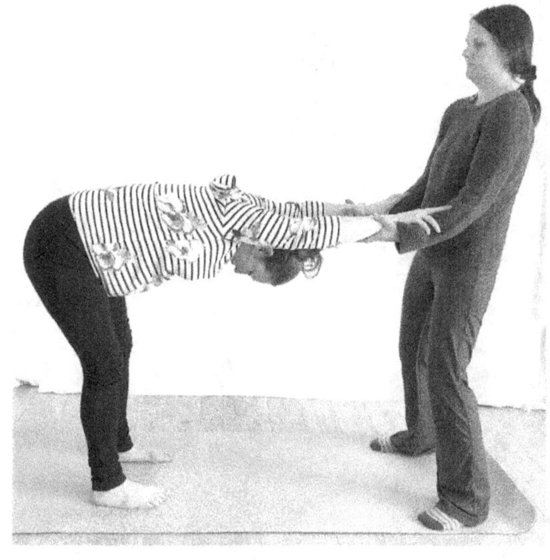

Assisted Forward stretch

A wonderful forward stretch to lengthen and release the spine, the partner stretched out their arms to support mum-to-be as they hold onto the arms and trying to keep the body at a 90 degree angle, take 3-4 deep breaths, it can be repeated.

Assisted squat

Mum-to-be hold onto the arms and squats down, opening the hips, keeping the spine straight as possible. This squat can be deepened, this is a good posture for preparing for birth or even giving birth in!

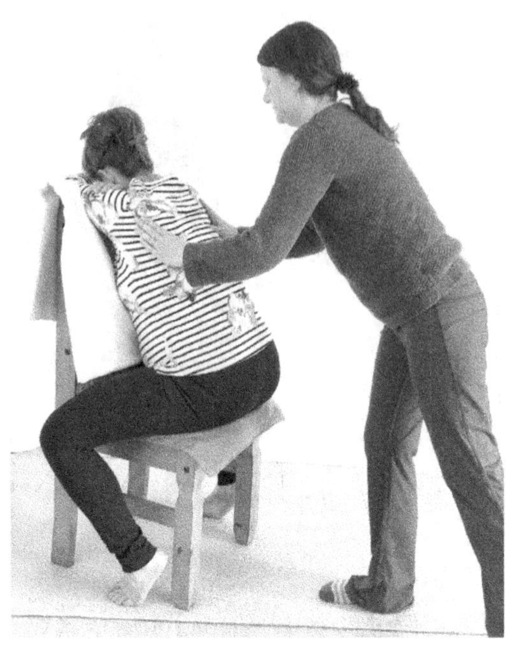

Chair prop for back massage!

Mum-to-be straddles over the chair, use a cushion under the head and rest onto the folded arms. This is a lovely position to be comfortable in whilst the partner can practice some massage of the back, and work through some of the main Nadi/meridian lines.

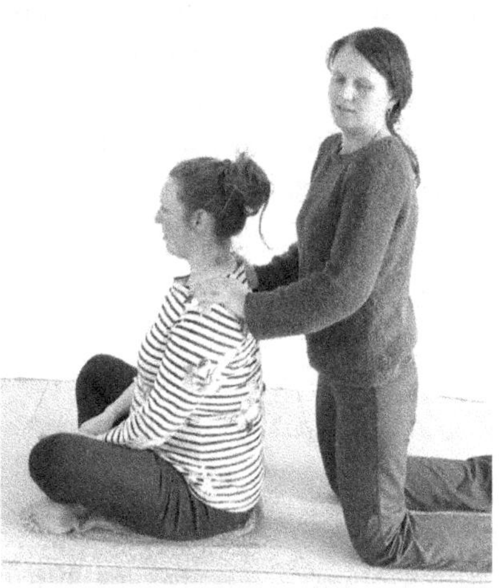

Shoulder massage

This can be done in several different positions, such as remaining in a chair or simply from sitting crossed legged on the floor the partner supports mum-to-be from behind and massages the shoulder, arms, lifting arms arm and down with the breath releasing tension from neck and shoulders.

Circling using the thumbs, or use the sides of the hands, or knocking technique. Repeat three times.

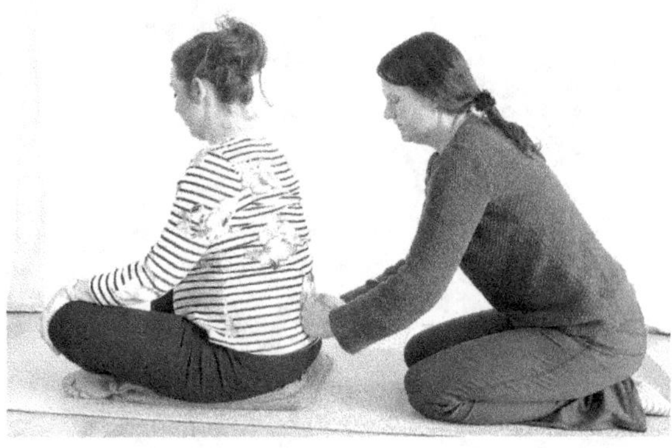

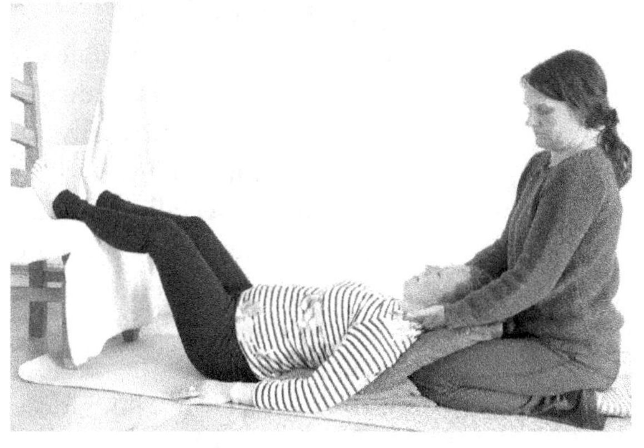

Massage with elevated leges
This is particularly comfortable if you can get the right position relieving the weight from the legs and very relaxing for mum-to-be, being supported from the back with the partner and cushions/pillows.

Again several different massages can be done on the shoulders, back of the neck, also this position is good for the head, temples and around parts of the face.

With any massage work you must make sure that mum-to-be is comfortable with the partner doing this!

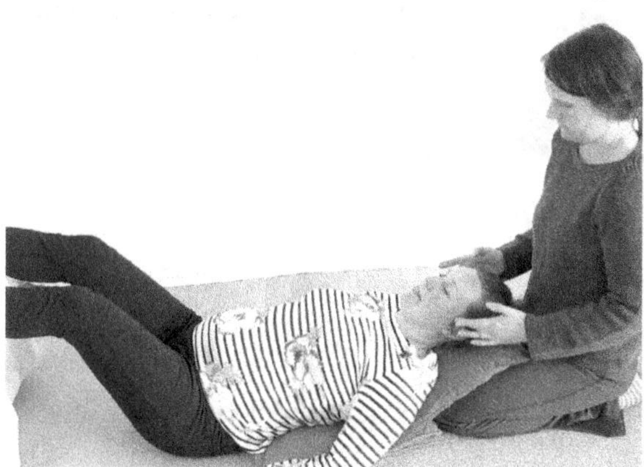

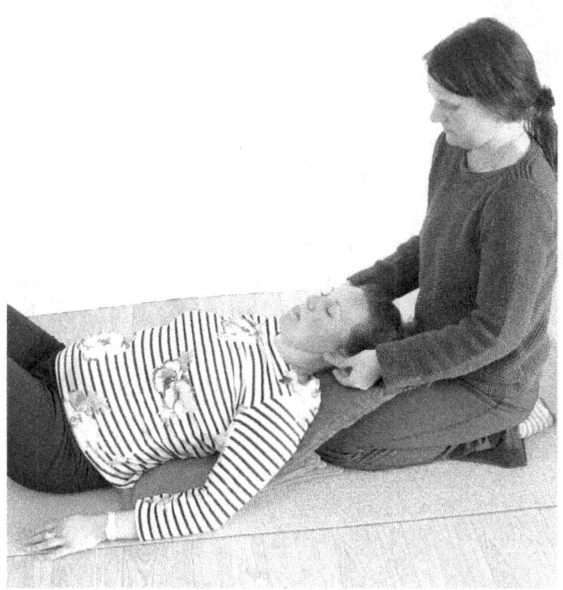

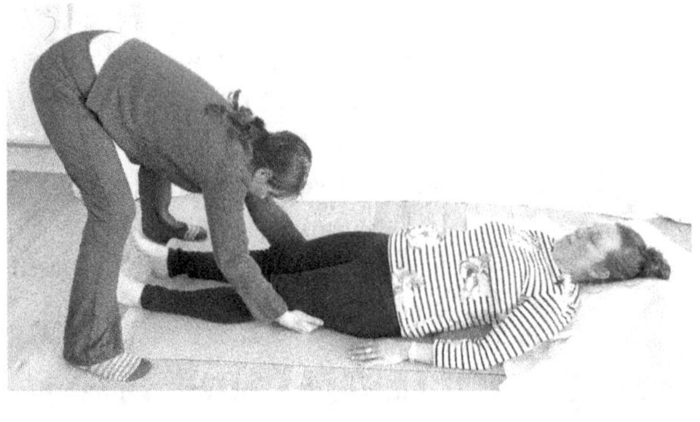

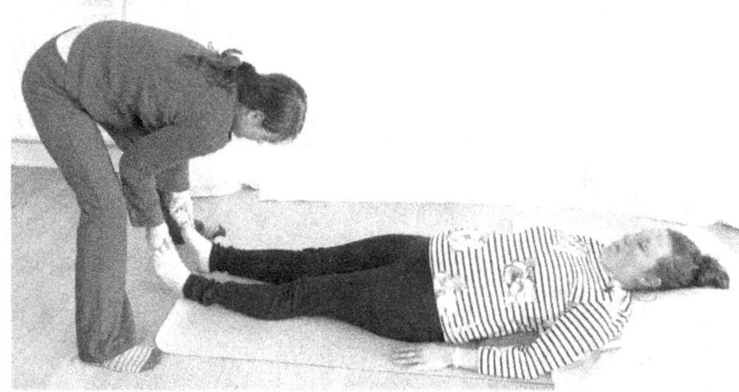

Leg and foot massage

If mum-to-be is comfortable on her back with the legs down, and the head should really be elevated or supported with bean bag/pillows especially in later pregnancy she will enjoy the partner squeezing gently down the outside energy/ meridian line of the leg and the middle lines that runs along the middle back, back of the leg.

Completing the legs with a good rub and squeeze to the feet.

Some gentle pressure on either sides of the hips, releasing with the out breath do a few rounds.

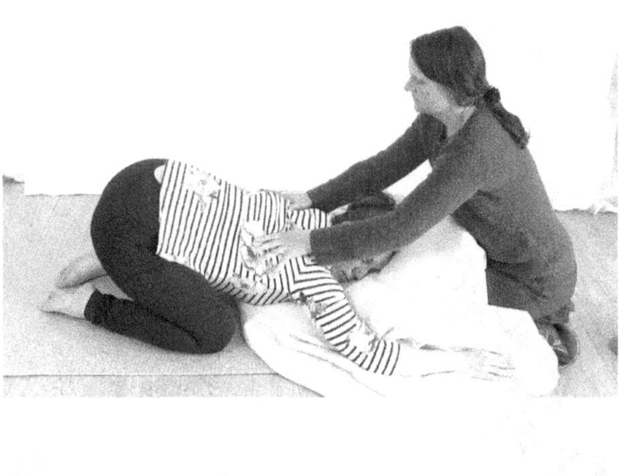

Its nice to complete the massage by allowing mum-to-be to turn ever and rest on a cushion or pillows on partners lap, who can release the shoulders once more, and this position will be good for mum and baby to rest in for some time before closing the session.

150

What is Pregnancy Chair Yoga?

Chair Yoga is another form of modified Hatha Yoga where you or your students cannot get down on the floor for any reason. Chair Yoga is another very helpful tool during pregnancy to improve flexibility, mobility and the health of your neck, shoulders, arms and legs. Also you may be able to work on your hips, groin and back with using a chair, wall or partner to support you in some standing postures like forward bends, modified triangle postures, etc.

Chair Yoga For Pregnancy

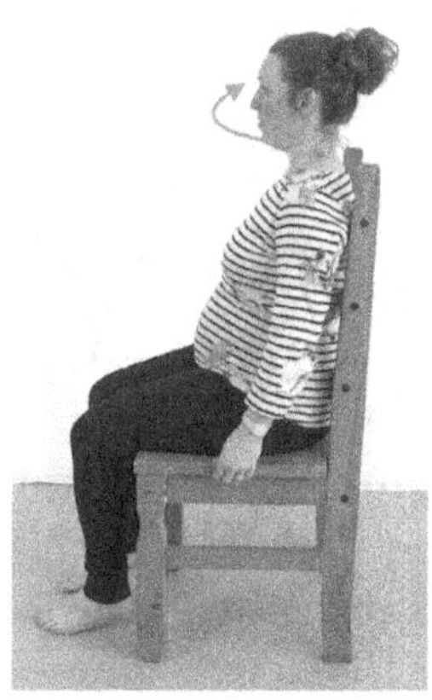 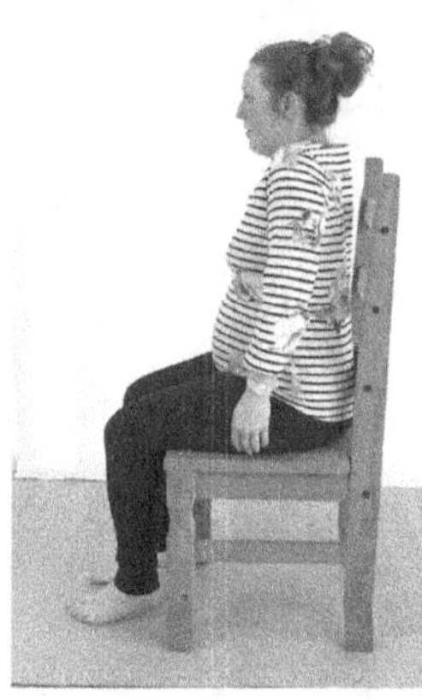

1.   Sit straight on a chair comfortably. Now flex your feet up and down with breath.

2. Turn your head right side with in-breath and to the left with out-breath.

3.   Turn side-to-side from your upper back, chest and shoulders to right with in-breath and to left with out-breath.

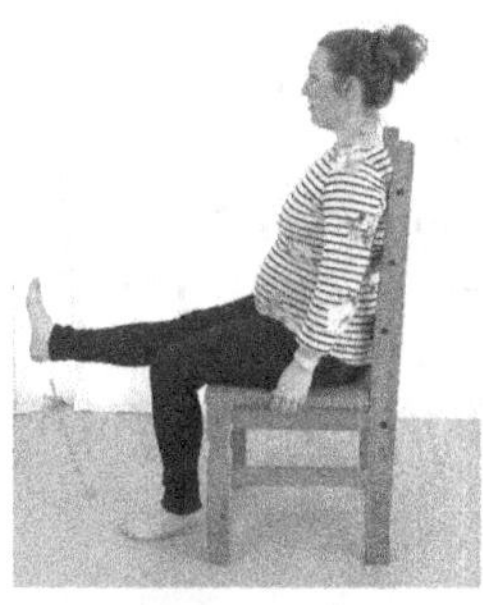

4. With in-breath extend your one leg straight and lift it up and release it back with out-breath. Repeat 3 to 5 times with each leg.

5. Lift and extend your both legs up together with in-breath if you feel strong and release it with out-breath.

6. Open knees wide with feet on floor. Now place your hands or arms on your thighs.

With an out-breath slowly bend forward with a flat back and hands on your thighs for support. Lift back to sit straight with the in-breath. Repeat this 3 to 5 times.

  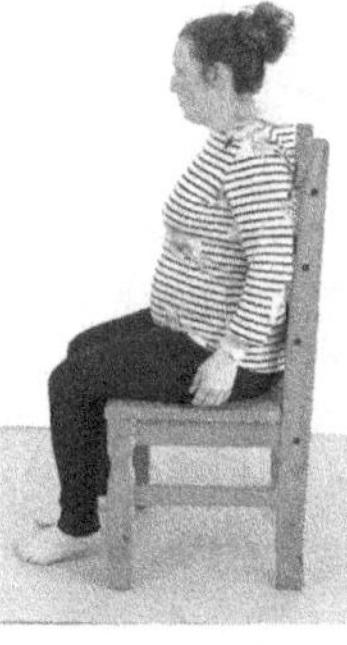

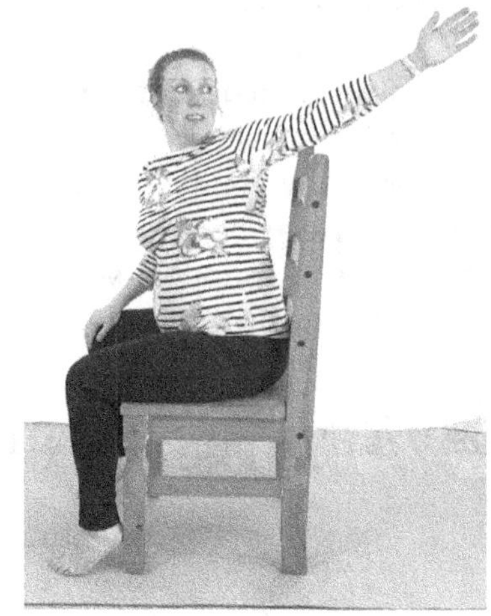

7. Keeping your one hand on your knee, raise your other arm from the side over to ceiling with a gentle twist through your back and opening your heart, chest and arms with in-breath. Release it with out-breath. Repeat 3 times with each side.

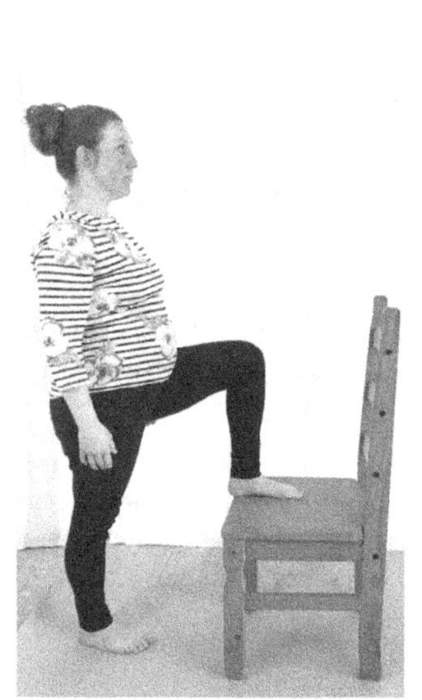

8. Stand straight with one foot on the chair if it possible with holding on to the chair support. With in-breath slowly raise your arms over your head and bring them back on to the chair support with the out-breath. Repeat 3 times.

9. With one foot on the chair keep holding on to the chair support. With the in-breath slowly move your knee forward with a gentle stretch in the thigh, groin and lower back and release with the out-breath. Repeat 3 times with each leg on the chair.

10. MERU-ASANA with support- as in the picture, gently place your hands or lower arms on the chair, bending over with buttocks pointing high. Keep your legs wide open and bend your knees gently if you need to.

11. VEERA-BHADRASANA-
Place both your hands and keep your arms straight and back flat. Here your head is in line with your back and buttocks.

12. UTAKATASANA- With the support of the chair slowly bend your knees and come to a squat. Keep your legs wide open. You come down to squat with the out-breath and come up straight with the in-breath or hold into the position for few breaths.

13. PARSVAKONASANA- Place your right leg on the chair with knee bend. Now place your left arm or elbow on your right thigh and raise your right over to ceiling.

This is a very good twist to ease your spine, open your chest and improve your shoulder flexibility.

Repeat three times to each side.

14. MATSYASANA VARIATION- Sit straight on a chair. Now bring yours behind and hold on to your wrists or interlock your fingers. With in breath stretch your arms downward, lift your shoulders up and open your chest forward as much as you can. Release with out breath. Repeat this 3 times.

This will help improving your mid and upper chest breathing, opening your heart and shoulders.

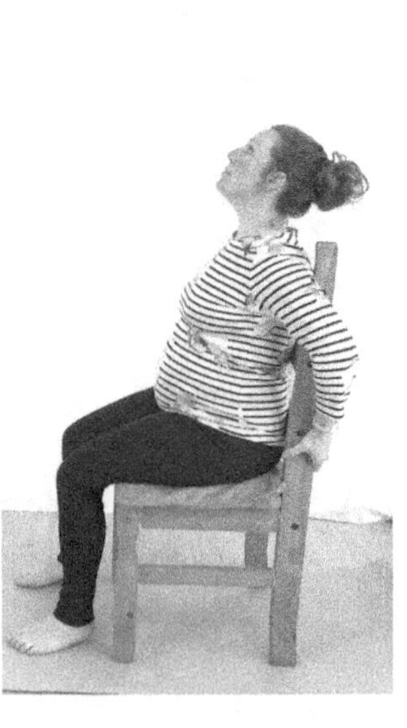 

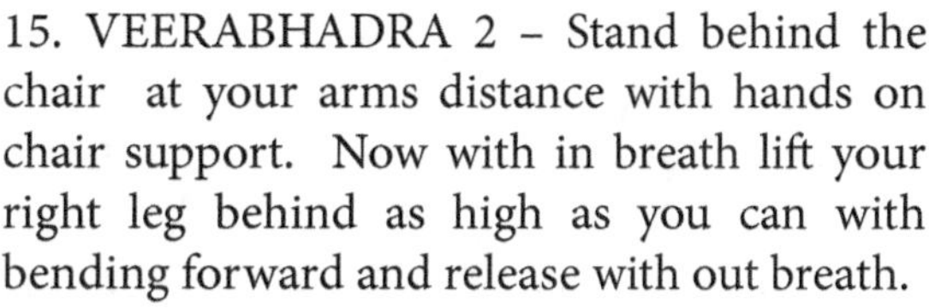

15. VEERABHADRA 2 – Stand behind the chair at your arms distance with hands on chair support. Now with in breath lift your right leg behind as high as you can with bending forward and release with out breath.

Repeat 3 times with each leg.

This is a good kriya for your legs, back and core strength.

16. TIRAYAKA TARASANA- With straight with legs slightly wide open. Raise your right arm over your head with left hand holding on the chair for support. Now stretch over to left side with creating a nice stretch along the right side. Repeat it 3 times to each side.

This is a good stretch for muscles along your side and waist. Also good for arms, shoulders and back.

17. Stand with both legs wide open to your own comfort. Now hold on the chair with left hand. Extend your right arm away from your shoulder with arm slightly higher to shoulder level. Stretch your arm and shoulder behind as far as you can.

This will help improving spinal, shoulder and arm strength, flexibility and mobility. It is also good for legs and groin area.

18. VRIKSHASANA- From standing behind the chair, keep holding on the chair with left hand. Standing on your left leg, fold the right leg to place your foot against the thigh as high as you can and raise your right arm over your head. Hold your posture for few breaths and repeat the same with switched arms and legs.

Beautiful balancing posture to improve body, mind balance.

19. RATHACHARIYA PROVRITTIS SAPURNA- Stand side ways near the chair with holding on chair support with the left hand. Now try to raise your right leg from side as high as you can with in breath and release with out breath.

Repeat 3 times to each side.

If you are more flexible, you can try to catch hold on your foot or leg and stretch and open out from side.

This will enable strong and flexible legs, ease and open groins and harmstrings.

20. PADAPRASARA- TIRIYAKA TARASANA- Sit on the chair with facing the support and legs wide open if possible. Keep your legs straight and stretched out to sides. Now hold on the chair with left hand. Stretch your right arm over and away from head to create a nice stretch from your right foot to right hand all along your side. Repeat the same with switched sides.

This is another good stretch for your side muscles, waist, arms and shoulders.

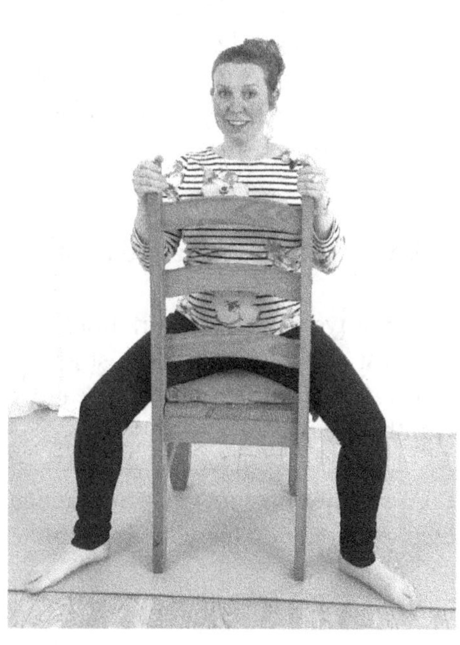

21. PADAPRASARA- Sit straight with facing to chair support. Now open your legs wide and if possible lift your fit up from floor. Hold your posture for few deep breaths with awareness in groin and pelvic area.

This will help open your groin and hamstrings. Also good for muscles in legs, lower back and buttocks.

22. ASHWACHALANA-SAPURANA- Stand with in foot on the chair. Now slowly bend forward to place both your hands on chair too with creating a gentle lunge from your back. You can try to keep your back straight and chest opened.

23. ASHWACHALANA PURNA- If above feels comfortable, you can raise both your hands over your head and hold the posture.

24. VAKRA ASANA – seated twist

Sit sideways on the chair, hold the back rest of the chair and twist aroud looking over your shoulder, repeat 3 x with the breath, then swap sides.

It is a simple and safe twist to practice during pregnancy for your back bone health.

CHAIR PROP USE

These are some simple examples, how to use a chair to make some yoga postures accessible to pregnant women if they cant do otherwise.

- As deep twists are not recommended during pregnancy, using a chair can help to twist and stretch upper back, shoulders and chest. Sitting on a chair, hold to bring both hands to one side and hold to chair. Turn behind from this side to look over the shoulder. Repeat the same to other side.

- Come behind your chair and taking a support with the chair slowly bend and open from knees to come down to squatting position. This will help preparing for labour and birthing.

- Place your hands on the chair and walk back to bring your back, and arms straight from buttocks.

Hatha Yoga with Nada or Sound

Hatha yoga provides us with tools on a physical, mental, psychological, emotional and spiritual level. Nada or sound is another beautiful aspect in Classical Hatha and Ashtanga Yoga. Nada has very simple Bija or root sounds to complex mantras. Sound helps us to be in-tune with, or align our body and mind, and open our senses; to have access to higher states of mind. It also stimulates our nervous system and brain and hence helps us to think in a much clearer and brighter way; helping relax our mind and release any stress, emotions and anxieties.

You may choose some simple kriyas or movements with the breath and release with one of the sounds, you may choose with out-breath. Kriyas or movements will help our muscles, joints and physical body to be more flexible, stronger and healthier. Nada or sounds with kriyas will help with releasing mental and emotional blockages, effecting our general health and well-being.

During pregnancy it can be more nurturing to practice them with your partner. It is not only just the Kriya or movement and sound with you partner but also creating the space to listen, wait and follow together in practices. This will help improve your relationship, as many couples due to changes in their life, can suffer with physical, mental and emotional disturbances.

If you are doing them with your partner, ideally one of you breathing into the Kriya and other one breathing out with the sound. This means one is creating the sound, nada while other one is listening and waiting. This improves understanding and communication.

For example, if you practice Vyagraha Pranayama with the nada aaa…., with your partner. You both come to Chatus-padasana (four-footed posture), facing each other. Now one of you, breaths into deepening your spine and opening your chest with lifting your head up, and the other one should lift the mid back up, draw the chin into chest as high as you can. Now while the first one breathing out with the sound aaaa…., reaching into lifting the upward arch as the other one breaths in into the lower arch. Repeat like this for five times. Each time you are making the sound, other partner should listen the sound, breath in and wait for their turn.

1. HASTA-PRASAR KRIYA- Sit straight in one of the comfortable postures, with hands joined in namaskar to your navel, Manipur Chakra. With the in-breath, open and stretch your arms behind and bring your hands back together to the navel area with sound aaa…, while you breathing out. Repeat this 3 times. This kirya is good for lower body organs, and helps releases fears, and anxieties.

2. AGRA MUDRA KRIYA- Sit straight in one of the comfortable postures, with hands joined to your heart, Anahata Chakra. With in-breath extend your arms in front and bring your hands back together to heart area with sound uuu…, while you are breathing out. Repeat this 3 times. This kriya is good for breathing and heart and helps releasing negative emotions, frustration and anger.

3. ANJALI MUDRA KRIYA- Sit straight in one of the comfortable posture with hands joined to your heart, Anahata Chakra. With in-breath extend your arms over your head in Anjali Mudra and bring your hands back together to heart area with sound mmm…, while you breathing out. Repeat this 3 times. This Kriya is good for neck, head and thyroid and helps clearing negative thoughts and mental weakness.

4. SHARBHA KRIYA- Come to Chatus-Pada asana. With in-breath raise your right leg behind and bring your knee back on floor with sound aaa.., while you are breathing out. Repeat this 3 times with each leg and rest in Shashankasana.

This Kriya is good for your lower body limbs, will improve blood circulation and energy flow in legs, hips and pelvic area. Sound will help releasing any stress from pelvic area.

5. CHIRI KRIYA- From chatus-padasana with in breath raise your right leg behind and bring your head and knee as close as you can with sound *uuu…*, while you are breathing out. Repeat 3 times with each leg.

This kriya along with lower limbs, also good for digestive system, breathing and spine. Sound uuu, will help with releasing stress from the belly and chest areas.

6. HASTA UTTANA KRIYA- From Chatus-padasana raise your right arm over the right side and bring it back on floor with sound *mmm…*, while you are breathing out. Repeat 3 times with each arm.

7. VYAGRAHA PRANAYAMA- From Chatus-padasana dip your spine down, raise your head with in-breath and reverse it all with sound *aaa…uuu…mmm, AUM* while you are breathing out. Repeat it 3 times.

8. EKA PADA PRASARASAR UTTANA KRIYA- Sit easy in Sukhasana or Cross-legged. Now hold to right leg with right hand. Extend your right leg out and away from your body with in breath and release it back with sound *aaa…*, while you are breathing out. Repeat 3 times with each leg.

9. STAMBHAMA ASANAM- Extend your right leg with-in breath and draw leg towards your chest as close as possible. Now release your leg with sound *uuu...*, while you are breathing out.

10. Neck Movement- With the in-breath let your head come down on to your right shoulder.
Bring your head back to centre with the sound *mmm...*, while you are breathing out. Repeat 3 times to each side.

11. PARIGRAHA KRIYA-
Bend over left side to place your left elbow and lower arm down on floor with the in-breath, raising your right arm over and down to left side. Bring it back to right side with the sounds *aaa... uuu...mmm, AUM*. Repeat 3 times to each side.

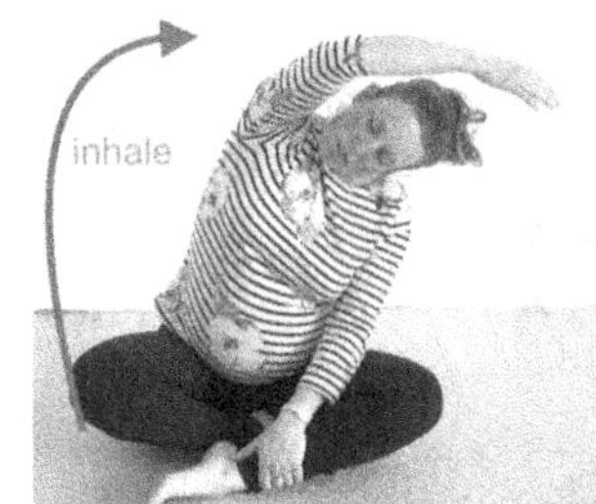

12. VEERA KRIYA- Come to warrior posture with in-breath with arms extended along the shoulders. Now raise your leg straight with sound aaa..., while you are breathing out and come back down to Veera-Asana with in-breath. Repeat it 3 times to each side.

13. VEERA- AGRA KRIYA- Come to Veerasana with one knee bent and join your hands together in Namaskar Mudra to heart. Now extend your arms in front of your heart in Agra Mudra with in-breath and release back to namaskar with sound *uuu…*, while breathing out. Repeat it 3 times to each side.

14. VEERA-ANJALI MUDRA- Like above raise your arms over your head in Anjali mudra with in-breath and bring your hands back to Namaskar with sound *mmm…*, while breathing out. Repeat it 3 times to each side.

Overview of musculoskeletal conditions and management in Pregnancy

by Jyoti Vora

Spinal and Pelvic Anatomy:

There are 33 vertebrae in spine including 7 cervical vertebrae, 12 Thoracic vertebrae, 5 lumbar vertebrae, 5 sacral vertebrae (fused) and 4 coccyx vertebrae (fused) and these are separated by intervertebral discs. Pelvis consists of three bones called Ilium, Ischium and Pubis; and three joints of which one is at the front (pubic symphysis joint) and two are at the back (L+R sacro iliac joint – SI joint). The bones form a protective cavity or basin for the bladder, uterus and bowel. The sacroiliac joints allow for the transfer of forces between the spine and the lower extremity. Joints of the spine and pelvis are supported by ligaments and muscles, which provide stability and help to maintain a good posture.

Hormonal changes during pregnancy soften these ligaments and joints become less stable; the resultant increase in movement can lead to aches and pains in the back and pelvis. As a result of the increasing weight of the baby and a change in the center of gravity, one's posture may also change, which may place further strain on the back.

Pelvic Structures:

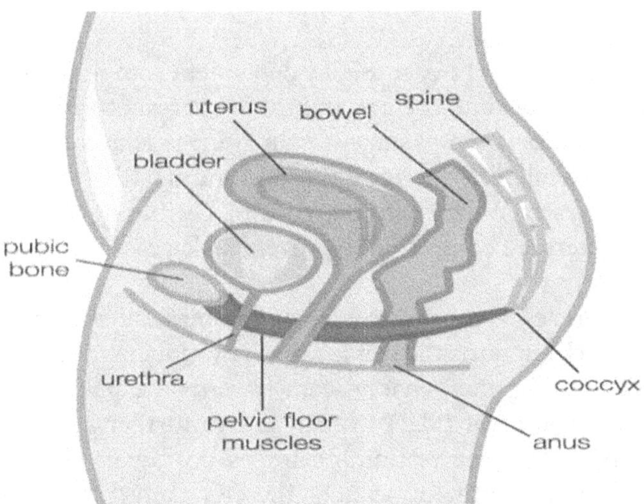

Pelvic cavity provides the basin for bladder, uterus and rectum. It is important to determine their position and placement in order to understand how pregnancy can impact their function.

- Intestine → colon →Rectum →Anus
- Uterus → Cervix → vagina
- Urinary bladder → urethra

Pelvic floor muscles:
This is the group of muscles spanning the base of the bony pelvis, held in place by ligaments that support the pelvic organs. They are important for:
• the control of bladder and bowel
• sexual function and pleasure
• the stability of the pelvic and lumbar joints
• the support of pelvic organs helping to prevent prolapse
• the support of the growing baby

The increasing weight of the baby during pregnancy, followed by the delivery, may weaken the pelvic floor muscles. If this support is reduced one may leak urine when exerting, especially after the baby is born. To try to prevent this exercising the pelvic floor muscles every day is essential.

Technique:
Imagine that you are trying to stop yourself from passing wind. You should feel a squeeze and a lift inside the vagina. Do not hold your breath. Do not clench your buttocks. You can check if you are using the right muscles by feeling inside the vagina with a finger to feel the vaginal walls tighten, or have a look with a mirror as you practice and you will see the area between the vagina and anus (perineum) move inwards. Pelvic floor muscle exercises (sometimes called Kegels) should include long squeezes as well as short, quick squeezes.

Urinary function:
The urinary tract comprises of two mutually dependent components: the upper tract, which contains the kidneys and ureters, and the lower tract consisting of the bladder and urethra. The urethra is the passage in which urine is excreted out of the body. The pelvic floor musculature encircles the urethra creating the external urethral sphincter, which operates under conscious control. During storage, both the internal and external sphincters are contracted to prevent leakage.

The Pelvic Floor muscles of continent women automatically contracts and shortens during a cough, which supports the pelvic organs by reducing the length of the Pelvic Floor (PF) and displacing the pelvic viscera towards the pubic bone. The urethra in Stress Urinary Incontinent (SUI) women moves further and faster in response to a cough, implying that the restraining forces do not increase as rapidly with displacement as those in continent women. Therefore, attachments of the urethra to the pubic symphysis are weaker in SUI women and/ or the PFM provide less support to stiffen the urethra from behind.

Bowel function:
As the stool moves through the colon the fluids are removed and absorbed through the body. The consistency of the stool is dependent on many things such as
– How long the stool sits in the colon
– How much water has been absorbed from the waste
Stool consistency can vary from hard lumps to mushy very loose watery stool. Fibre helps to add bulk to the stool and make it firmer but can also make them softer. Fluid also can affect the consistency of the stool. The amount of decaffeinated fluids determines how soft the stools are and how easily they are expelled.
Ability to retain and expel stool depends on the pelvic floor muscles; it depends on the tightness/looseness of the pelvic floor.

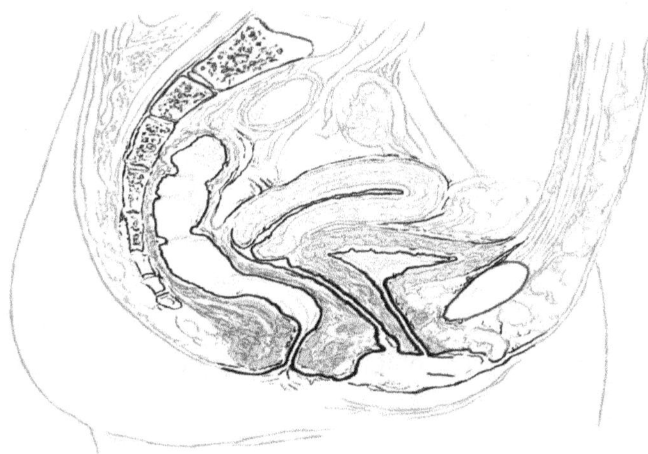

Observe the angle of rectum to anus

- Under resting conditions, the angle should be around 90 degrees but during straining and moving the bowels this angle increases to 135 degrees

- If these angles are not correct it can be more difficult to have a bowel movement

- If there is lack of control of the PFM or if they spasm constipation can occur

- They can block the anal canal making it difficult to have a bowel motion

- Also, if the pelvic floor is weak or fatigued it can result in bowel incontinence too

- Post-Bowel Movement Pain : This occurs because the anal sphincter over closes in a kind of spasm after a bowel movement in someone who has chronically tightened pelvic basin.

Abdominal wall:

Anteriorly abdomen wall extends from xiphoid process (which lies at the level of the 9th thoracic vertebra) to the pubic symphysis (which lies at the level of the coccyx). Posteriorly and laterally, some part is taken up by the thoracic cage above and gluteal part below.

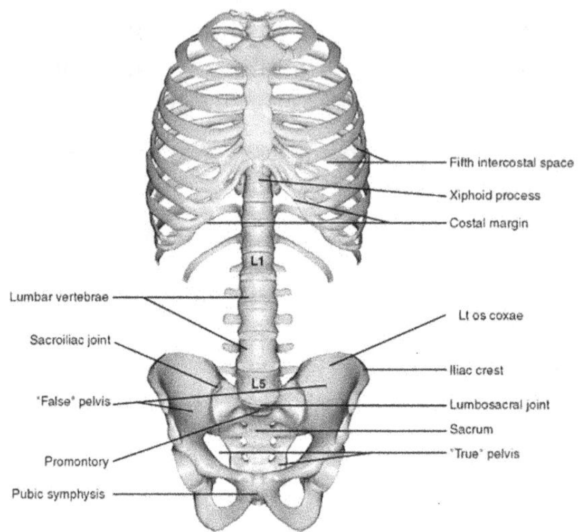

Muscles of the Anterior wall of abdomen

The anterior abdominal wall is made up mainly of muscles named transversus abdominis, internal oblique and external oblique muscles, rectus abdominis and pyramidalis.

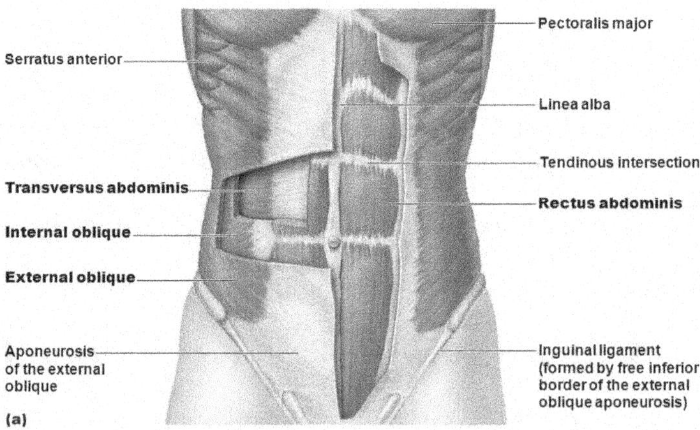

Transversus abdominis: The muscle originates from thoracolumbar fascia, inguinal area, inner lip of iliac crest, lower six costal cartilages. The fibres are directed horizontally and forwards. Insertion is into broad aponeurosis, xiphoid process, linea alba and pubis.

External oblique: The muscle arises in form of fleshy slips from the lower eight ribs and it runs downwards, forwards and medially. The insertion is broadly into xiphoid process, linea alba, pubis and iliac crest.

Internal oblique: the muscles originate from the intermediate area of iliac crest, thoracolumbar fascia and inguinal ligament; the fibres run upwards, forwards and medially. The muscle insertion is broadly into lower 6 ribs, xiphoid process, linea alba and pubis.

The fibres of internal and external oblique cross with each other at right angles. Rectus abdominis: The muscle arises from pubis area and the fibres run upwards and inserts into xiphoid process, 5-7th costal cartilages.

Pyramidalis: is a small triangular muscle located anterior to the lower part of rectus abdominis muscle within the rectus sheath.

Muscles of the Posterior wall of abdomen
Posterior wall of abdomen has Quadratus lumborum, Psoas major and minor, Iliacus and posterior dome of diaphragm muscles.

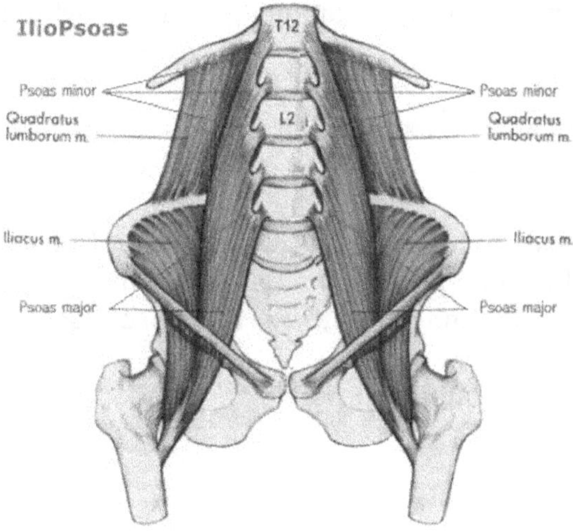

Quadratus Lumborum: quadrate shape on the lateral side of the posterior abdominal wall, originate from the ilium directed superior medially to insert into transverse process of L1-L4 and lower border of 12th rib. One of the functions of QL is lateral flexion and extension of the vertebral column and during the inhalation assist with the diaphragm and fixes the 12th rib.

Psoas Major: located lateral to the lumbar vertebrae, originates from the transverse process of T12-L5 directed inferolateral and insert into the lesser trochanter. It flexes the thigh at the hip.

Psoas Minor: originates from the T12-L1 transverse process and inserts into pubic pectineal line.

Iliacus: originates from the iliac fossa, and with psoas major they form iliopsoas muscle that is the main flexor of the hip.

Diaphragm: The diaphragm is a musculotendinous structure with a peripheral attachment to a number of bony structures. It is attached anteriorly to the xiphoid process and costal margin, laterally to the 11th and 12th ribs, and posteriorly to the lumbar vertebrae. The posterior attachment to the vertebrae is by tendinous bands called the medial and lateral arcuate ligaments.

Function of abdominal muscles:
-   Support the abdominal viscera

-   Expulsive acts like micturition, defaecation, vomiting, coughing etc.

-   Forceful expiratory acts- the external oblique can markedly depress and compress the lower part of the thorax producing forceful expiration as in coughing, sneezing, blowing, shouting

-   Movement of the trunk: a) flexion by rectus abdominis b) lateral flexion by one sided contraction of the obliques c) rotation of the trunk by combined action of same side external oblique and opposite side internal oblique.

-   Abdominal muscle helps maintain posture

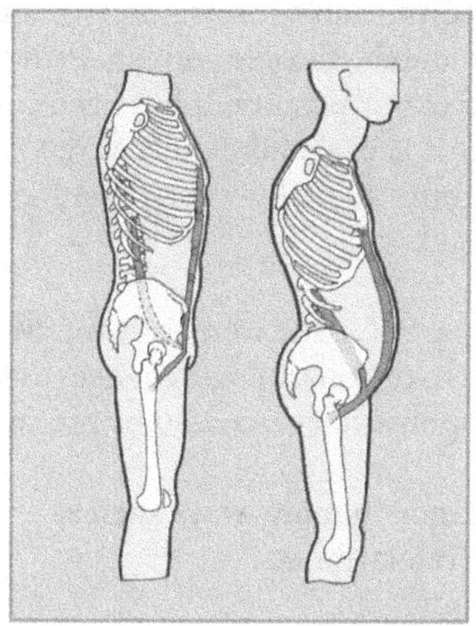

Our body is designed to move; the core muscles work together to control the movement of the spine, pelvis, and rib cage. During gait there is relatively a counter-rotation between the upper and lower part, and the arm and leg are moving in opposite direction to each other.

The contents of the trunk, below the ribcage and above the pelvis are suspended within a "box" of muscles. The diaphragm, at the top and the levator ani at the bottom of the box, and the psoas major and the rectus abdominis at the back and front of the box. The abdominal contents include the intestines, the liver, the bladder and the kidneys. The tone of the muscles that box the organs in can have a major impact on the way the organs function. Weakness or tightness of any of the muscles can affect posture, limit movement and function and cause pain.

To strengthen the abdominal muscles, just doing abdominal crunches is not enough. Effective training for abdominal muscles requires using movements that integrate the hips, trunk and shoulders to efficiently distribute the forces created by gravity, ground reaction and momentum during upright movements. The multiple layers of the abdominals are lengthened in all three planes as the rib cage and pelvis rotate opposite one another during upright movement in gait. This lengthening motion turns the muscles on reflexively, which is their natural way of functioning.

Poor posture and crookedness is one popular scapegoat for back pain. We hold our body in different shapes depending on what we are doing. This body shape is called posture. We talk about 'good' and 'bad' postures; however, it is not that simple. It seems obvious that posture is relevant. Many professionals assume that back pain is some kind of postural problem that you can exercise your way clear of. It is true that some postures are more symmetrical and can reduce stress on body structures.

However, any posture is uncomfortable if sustained for a long time. And to be able to change our posture we need to be flexible enough. Pain often makes moving more difficult and hence it can affect our posture. It has been suggested that bad postures can be the cause of pain, but it is in fact the other way. Our emotions can also have an impact on our postures. Think about how your posture is when you are happy and your posture when you feel sad.

Exercise has become a vital part of many women's lives. Mild to moderate exercise is good during pregnancy. Due to the physiologic changes associated with pregnancy as well as the hemodynamic response to exercise, some precautions should be observed.

Exercise benefits the pregnancy in many ways such as
- Cardiovascular and respiratory fitness,
- Control of maternity weight gain
- Maintain a stable body position, muscle tone and relieve tension
- Reduced subjective discomforts of pregnancy (swelling, leg cramps, fatigue, SOB)
- Positive influence on labour and delivery (decreased risk of operative or assisted deliveries, shorter active labour, increased foetal tolerance of labour)
- Possible reduced risk of preeclampsia (hypertension+proteinuria), GDM (Gestational Diabetes Mellitus)

Although exercise is beneficial, pregnant women need to follow some precautions.
- Drink plenty of water to avoid dehydration
- Have adequate diet
- Work within their own limits to avoid getting too hot or breathless
- Listening to their body- stop if uncomfortable, tired or feeling unwell
- If they were a runner-it is safe to continue at lower intensity upto 2nd trimester
- Gym-be cautious
- Competitive/contact and new sports may be risky, and should be avoided
- Do not overstretch
- Do not work to maximum ability
- Take support with chair, wall or support pole to help maintain balance
- Breathe out with effort, eg. when lifting weights
- Keep movement slow and controlled
- Vary the workout, concentrating on different forms of exercise such as yoga, pilates, swimming, walking and low impact aerobics
- Stretch and relax after exercise in sitting, standing or possibly left side lying - to avoid problems of lying flat on the back

Rest and Relaxation are very essential for healthy pregnancy. Taking rest more often is required during pregnancy. It is common to feel very tired in the early and late stages of pregnancy; and sleep can also be disturbed. Use of pillows is recommended to support areas of aches/pain/strain. Relaxation techniques can be very helpful to reduce tension and stress, and is useful during labour too.

Contraindications to exercise during pregnancy:
- Significant cardiovascular disease
- Poorly controlled type 1 diabetes
- Pregnancy-induced hypertension (preeclampsia)
- Restrictive lung disease
- Preterm rupture of membranes
- Preterm labor during the prior or current pregnancy
- Incompetent cervix
- Persistent second- or third-trimester bleeding
- Placenta previa after 26 weeks (low lying placenta)
- Intrauterine growth retardation
- Sudden swelling of ankles/ hands or face

Relative Contraindications:
- Severe anaemia
- Unevaluated maternal cardiac arrythmia
- Chronic bronchitis
- Extreme morbid obesity
- Extreme underweight (BMI < 12)
- Heavy smoker
- Previous miscarriage
- History of extremely sedentary lifestyle
- Poorly controlled hypertension
- Orthopaedic limitation
- Poorly controlled seizure disorder
- Poorly controlled hyperthyroidism

Warning signs to terminate exercise:
- Vaginal bleeding
- Dyspnoea prior to exertion (sudden SOB)
- Dizziness
- Headache
- Chest pain
- Muscle weakness
- Calf pain or swelling
- Preterm labour
- Decreased foetal movement
- Amniotic fluid leakage

Every pregnant woman is an individual with different level of pre-pregnancy fitness and varying degrees of fitness requirements both during pregnancy and after. She may be a complete non-exerciser or an elite athlete. In order to provide most appropriate advice, the service provider needs to be aware of the physiological and physical changes which the pregnant body undergoes.

Mechanical changes during pregnancy:
1. COG shifts upwards & forwards.
2. Posture:
- shoulder girdle becomes rounded
- scapular protraction
- Upper limb internal rotation
- increase in cervical lordosis
- knee hyperextension
- increase in lumber lordosis

3. Balance – Pregnant woman walks with wider BOS

Various biomechanical and hormonal changes occur during pregnancy that can alter musculoskeletal alignments by affecting the key areas of the body such as spinal curvature, balance and gait pattern and increase the risk of back pain.

The changes in the ligament laxity puts undue strain on joints leading to aches and pains in various joints such as hip/knee/fingers/wrists. The growing uterus, foetus, and breasts contribute to pregnancy weight gain that puts extra stress on their feet, especially the arches. Hence, it is common for pregnant women to have heel pain or plantar fasciitis because of the extra weight and stress on the arches.

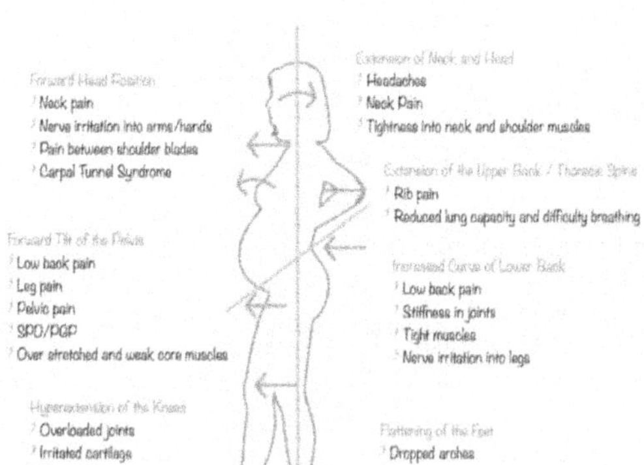

Postural Pain after Pregnancy:
It is easy to get give full attention to the newborn, but self-care is equally important. Self-care is not just about relaxing; self-care means taking care of one's own needs. It is important to allow time for good recovery and not to rush into getting back to life as before too soon.

Many new moms experience neck and shoulder aches as a result of many hours spent bending forward to feed the baby. The resulting hunched-over position can lead to the dreaded "forward head" position that may cause other problems such as headaches and back pain. Also, repetitive bending to change nappies, lifting baby, carrying baby can also lead to low back ache. Advice on appropriate posture for breastfeeding, appropriate lifting techniques, improving general fitness by exercising can help.

Post natal Exercise can be started gradually soon after the delivery when woman feels ready for it. All prenatal exercise can be performed safely in postpartum period considering that there was normal delivery. It is advised that, before starting exercise proper assessment of position and consistency of the fundus of the uterus and perineum should be done by GP and midwife. Extra care needs to be taken after c-section, and exercise should be done under proper guidance. Initial exercise post partum could involve breathing exercise, pelvic floor exercise, gentle abdominal exercises, ankle/foot and leg exercises. Exercise helps with postnatal depression, as exercise is stress-relieving. Ligament still exhibit laxity for upto 5 months after birth; therefore, care should be taken not to resume high impact activity too soon.

Pelvic Girdle Pain (PGP):
Around 1 in 5 pregnant women experiences mild discomfort in the back or front of the pelvis during pregnancy. Pelvic girdle pain (PGP) describes pain in the joints that make up the pelvic girdle, the symphysis pubis joint at the front and sacro iliac joints at the back. The discomfort is often felt over the pubic bone at front, below the tummy or across one side of the lower back, or both sides. Other signs and symptoms could be difficulty walking, pain when standing on one leg e.g climbing stairs, dressing/undressing; getting in and out of bath; pain and difficulty moving leg apart, e.g getting in and out of car; limited painful hip movements; pain during intercourse; clinking, grinding in the pelvic area. With PGP, the degree of discomfort one feels may vary from being intermittent and irritating to being very wearing and upsetting. The risk factors for developing pregnancy-related pelvic girdle pain are:
- a previous history of low back pain or pelvic girdle pain.
- a previous trauma to the pelvis or back.
- physical demanding work (e.g., twisting and bending the back several times per hour per day)
- multiparity - may play a causal role in the development of pregnancy-related pelvic girdle pain

PGP is complex and hence the management of it needs holistic approach. Physical assessment of spine, thorax, pelvis, hip and pelvic floor is required. Also, a routine needs to be assessed and advice needs to be given on sleep, diet, nutrition, stress management. Encouragement to varied form of exercise including walking, aqua natal exercise, yoga, pilates, pelvic floor exercise can be given. Ergonomic advice is necessary to reduce stress and strain on back and pelvic girdle. Education is key to management of any pain.

Diastasis Rectus Abdominus:
DRA stands for diastasis rectus abdominus muscle. This is where the two halves of one of the tummy muscles called the rectus abdominus, or the 'six pack' muscle, move apart and there is progressive widening of linea alba. During pregnancy, the pressure inside the abdominal cavity is greatly increased due to the size of the growing baby. As the baby grows, the muscles of tummy area start to stretch. It can happen at any part along the middle of the tummy muscle, from just under the rib cage, to just above the pubic bone.
Some degree of DRA towards later stages of pregnancy is normal. (a gap of 2.5 cm/2-3 finger is normal). This process is affected by the hormones, progesterone and relaxin. The amount of separation varies from one woman to another.
Symptoms of DRA:
- A bulging or doming in the centre of tummy during sit up from laying position
- Some discomfort along the centre of tummy, especially when being active
- A feeling of a gap when you feel along the middle of the tummy
- Poor posture
- Lower back pain
- Symptoms of incontinence
- Symptoms of prolapse

Generally, these are said to have returned to normal by 8-12 weeks, however if there is still a separation and its problematic the client may well be under a physiotherapist for specialist care and this should be discussed. For this condition we should avoid abdominal pressure work initially (e.g crunches, planks, high impact work). Also, avoid any activities that increase abdominal pressure, or cause doming of the abdominals, such as straining with constipation and repeated heavy lifting. Start with abdominal breathing exercise, Kegel's exercise, pelvic tilts and progress as able. Also, graded abdominal strengthening exercise is recommended.

Pelvic organ Prolapse:
Pregnancy and childbirth especially vaginal delivery is most common risk factor for pelvic organ prolapse. An episiotomy, vaginal tear or a delivery requiring forceps can also weaken the supporting structures contributing to problems at the time or in

later life. Pelvic organ prolapse, often referred to as 'prolapse', is described as a vaginal change where a pelvic organ which may be the bladder, bowel, rectum or uterus moves downwards in the vagina causing the symptom of 'something coming down' or a feeling of vaginal heaviness. The bulge may be felt inside or outside the vagina. A prolapse can be mild, causing little or no bother, or it may be severe causing many problems and badly affecting your quality of life.

Types of pelvic organ prolapse:
1. Front vaginal wall prolapse (cystocele) - The wall supporting the bladder bulges down into the vagina. This is the most common type of prolapse. Symptoms include problem emptying the bladder, increased urgency and frequency of urine, nocturia (needing to wee more at night), incontinence (leakage of urine) which may be due to straining activity, coughing or could also be associated with urgency. There could be difficulty in starting to pass urine or a slow flow when emptying the bladder.
2. Back vaginal wall prolapse (rectocele) - The wall supporting the rectum/back passage bulges down into the vagina. The symptoms include difficulty emptying the bowel or incomplete emptying leading to straining, bowel or wind leakage, bowel urgency, needing to press around anus or vagina to help empty bowel.
3. Uterine prolapse - The uterus moves downwards into the vagina due to the lack of support. The cervix will then sit lower in the vagina which might be mentioned during smear test.

Although pregnancy is most common factor for pelvic organ prolapse, other common factors include obesity, heavy lifting, family history, age, menopause, constipation, chronic cough, previous pelvic surgery.

Not all pelvic prolapses need treatment. Sometimes it is better to wait and watch and develop healthy bladder bowel habits which can resolve the problem in time. Pelvic floor exercise plays an important role in management of prolapse. If problem persists then vaginal pessary, women's health physiotherapy treatment or in more severe cases gynaecological surgery may be needed.

Pregnancy related incontinence:
It is important that bladder and bowel function is regulated. Regular emptying of bladder is necessary, particularly after having an epidural. Help from GP/Midwife should be taken if this is an issue. Do not 'stop and start' the flow of urine. Do not get into the habit of going to the toilet 'just in case'. Some women experience constipation; sitting in the right position on the toilet can help relax the muscles, and makes it easier to open bowels. For women with a Caesarean section operation, supporting a wound with a folded towel may also help. DO NOT STRAIN and DO NOT RUSH. Breathing out slowly while moving their bowels or passing urine may

also help. Advice should be given on drinking plenty of fluids per day to include water/squash, and eat plenty of roughage.

It is quite common to experience incontinence during pregnancy and after having a baby.

- Last trimester: 48% primiparous, 85% multiparous
- Post partum: 92% of those still incontinent at 12 weeks will be incontinent at 5 years
- 5-7 years after pregnancy 44.6% have some degree of incontinence

The symptoms can be very distressing and cause difficulty in all sorts of situations such as at work, going out shopping, exercising and caring for the baby. These symptoms can be improved with appropriate help and advice.

As the pelvic floor muscles stretch, they can weaken and not work so well. It is the job of the pelvic floor muscles to:
- Support the bladder, uterus and bowel
- Close the urethra and anus to prevent leak of urine or stool
- Allow urine and stool to pass when you want to
- Help with pleasure during sexual intercourse

For a vaginal birth the pelvic floor muscles have to stretch a lot for delivery of the baby. After the birth the nerves that make the pelvic floor muscles work may not be doing this so well and mean that the muscles feel weak.

Advice: Start by exercising your pelvic floor muscles as soon as you can during pregnancy. This can really help to improve and even prevent incontinence.

If you have the urgent need to rush and pass either urine or stool, try to squeeze your pelvic floor muscles at this time for 10 seconds. This can help to control the urge and prevent leakage.

Make sure that you empty your bladder and bowels well. Try to take your time and relax on the toilet. Sometimes gently rocking backwards and forwards or putting a bit of pressure on your lower tummy with your hand can help to fully empty the bladder.

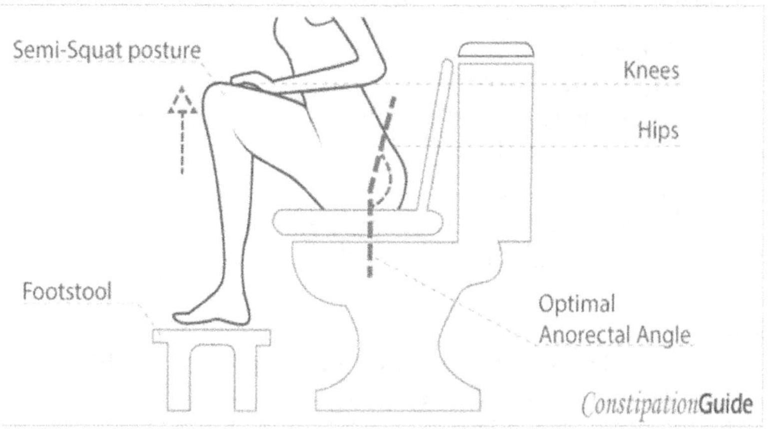

Ribflare:

This is the name given to discomfort over the lower ribs. It is due to the growing baby pushing on ribs away from their normal position. Advice is given on frequent change of position and avoid sitting on low chairs and in other positions which bring the ribs close to the pelvis. Temporary relief can be achieved by lifting the arm on the affected side and bending sideways away from the ache.

Carpal tunnel syndrome:

The carpal tunnel is an inelastic structure located at the level of the wrist. Many tendons which move the thumb and fingers pass through this carpal tunnel on their way to the hand. Median nerve also sits in this tunnel with the tendons, so there is very little room. The nerve is responsible for giving feeling in the thumb and fingers, and also makes the tendons work properly. Hormone changes during pregnancy causes extra fluid in the body, which causes pressure changes in many parts of your body, including the wrist and carpal tunnel. Swelling will increase the pressure on the median nerve inside the tunnel. This pressure on the nerve causes the symptoms known as carpal tunnel syndrome. Symptoms are most likely to occur from the fifth or sixth month of pregnancy and commonly disappear after the birth of your baby. Symptoms include pain, pins and needles, numbness or burning in the thumb, index middle or ring fingers, tingling or numbness in entire hand, weakness in the hand and forearm – dropping objects, trouble performing fine finger movements like writing, pain that shoots from hands up the arm as far as the shoulder, Swollen, hot and sweaty hands, symptoms are worse at night or first thing in the morning.

Management of CTS include:

- Elevate hands to reduce swelling
- Ice application
- Splints and support
- Avoid repetitive movements
- Carefully carry load
- Pacing activities
- Rest and relaxation to reduce pain
- Medication if pain uncontrolled

Varicose veins:

Varicose veins are usually caused by weak vein walls and valves. This causes the veins to swell and enlarge, and usually occurs in the legs. The veins may appear blue or dark purple, and are often lumpy or bulging.

Other symptoms include:

- aching, heavy and uncomfortable legs
- swelling in the feet and/or ankles
- burning or throbbing in your legs
- muscle cramp in your legs, particularly at night
- dry, itchy and thin skin over the affected vein

During pregnancy, the amount of blood increases to help support the developing baby. This puts extra strain on your veins. Increased hormone levels during pregnancy also cause the muscular walls of the blood vessels to relax, which also increases the risk. Vulval varicose veins may also develop as the womb begins to grow and puts increased pressure on veins in the pelvic area. Although being pregnant can increase your risk of developing varicose veins, most women find that their veins significantly improve after the baby is born. Varicose veins are rarely a serious condition and they don't usually require treatment. Calf strengthening exercises such as Heel raises can help.

Mastitis:

Mastitis is when breast becomes swollen, hot and painful. It's most common in breastfeeding women, but women who are not breastfeeding can also get it. Advice women to soak a cloth in warm water and place it on the breasts to help relieve the pain, a warm shower or bath may also help. With such conditions, avoid too much face prone work as the breasts can become very enlarged and sometimes sore from breast-feeding.

Summary:
Becoming a parent for the first time can feel like an overwhelming responsibility and it is very easy to feel inadequate. Advice women to find time to rest and eat a healthy nutritious diet as this will help them become physically and emotionally healthy. Things may not have gone as planned or expected either related to pregnancy, birth, feeding or bringing the baby home. It is important to inform them to remember some of these changes are beyond their control. Some women can feel a loss of things that haven't gone as planned, remaining positive about the here and now is important.

General advice on taking control, self awareness, planning and structuring the day, regular exercise, optimum nutrition and hydration and rest can help maintain emotional well being.

Reference:

'The Pelvic Girdle An integration of clinical expertise and research' book by Diane Lee
Physiopedia - universal access to rehabilitation knowledge (physio-pedia.com)
Foot Pain and Leg Problems in Pregnancy (verywellhealth.com)

Jyoti Vora

*Specialist Physiotherapist in persistent pain with special
interest in women's health physiotherapy.*

*Jyoti has over 20 years of work experience and also
provides educational sessions for yoga training courses.*

POSTNATAL YOGA

Baby arrival and big changes!

Advice around the labour is the duty of the midwife and whoever the pregnant woman wants to be involved. It is not something we should be giving instruction about or influencing decision making around the birth process, but some helpful encouraging positive tips should be fine.

Pranayama techniques for pain relief – deep breathing, follow the breath, focus on the breath.

Complementary therapies to aid pain relief (homeopathy, aromatherapy, massage) Keep moving, keep crawling, keep upright and keep breathing!

It's always good to share and listen to your birth experiences with other women after it's all happened! If it is the first baby most women who have had traumatic births thankfully tend not to share this, as they don't want to put any negative or frightening ideas into a new mums head! At the same time women find it therapeutic to talk it over several times. Depending on the area you live in there may be support groups around if the birth was difficult or had complications. Our expectation of the birth and our feelings around the whole event can definitely affect the process. If you are giving a new mum advice about the birth please be positive even if you have some horror stories, it's not the person to share it with! As we do not want her to be filled with anxiety during labour.

We can guide a woman mentally through labour and talk about how to breath well and focus in the body and most of all go with the flow of the body, our DNA and cellular memory has given birth for a millennia and we do know how to do it, but over time with modern day stress and pressure we have lost touch with our very self. There is evidence to show that natural home births for example are generally more successfully in delivering normally than when a woman goes into hospital. The stress the hospital experience brings on can be overwhelming and no-one wants to fight or disagree with a medical team when we are in such a venerable position and when it's a baby's life potentially at stake, which is fair enough.

Birthing
If it is a first baby let's face it, every woman simply has to go down this path and experience it herself! Although she may be with others at the time, it's her body, mind and emotions going through it all. It does not have to be a frightening event, which it is often portrayed as. The process naturally takes you inwards if you can stay with your conscious breathing, I would say it can be even quite meditative.

There are many methods that can be used to help women through the labour experience and many natural therapies. For my own first birth focusing on the yogic breath along with some Bach flowers rescue remedy and homeopathic arnica was really all I needed to get me through it. When it got to the point when I said, "I think I need some pain relief now!" The reply was "the baby is almost out" which kept me going for a few more minutes and out he came with a final push!

Ammaji our Guru tells her story of how she didn't even experience it as pain - just by breathing through it and crawling around on the floor using chatus pada kriya.

Other types of therapies are used successfully such as aromatherapy, birthing hypnotherapy, or the birthing pool is said to make labour a more gentle experience. Affirmations which work as a kind of mantra work well for some people too such as repeating 'each contraction brings me closer to meeting my baby' or make something up that's for that individual, again there are books with numerous suggestions.

Every mum is different and different tools will resonate and help them! In yoga our main tool is the breath for this intense period at the completion of pregnancy! With the breath your mind will become naturally focused and meditative if you can trust your inner abilities to birth. One thing I learnt the hard way following my 3 birth experiences and reflecting upon them is that you actually do not need to push baby with your own will, your body will naturally get to a point and push baby out and cause what can be described as 'tidal waves' through and down your body whereby you cannot help but push as it is naturally time! Just don't try to hold back, go with it, and keep focused on the breath.

Another experience I can share with you which may prevent other's miseries 'yet to come' (as we say in yoga!) is that labour can be greatly affected by our environment. It may sound obvious but if for example you have other children running around needing your attention whilst you are progressing in labour it can literally stop your contractions altogether – as your attention gets so divided! This is not uncommon. My advice is if labour starts, arranging for someone to get your other children or if you are a carer for someone else, make arrangements for someone to step in quickly! The more focused you are I believe the quicker and more easily you get through the labour.

The other obvious distraction from what can and should be an inward meditative labour and birthing experience is a medical team running around you, sticking monitors on you, testing you and generally panicking you whilst in labour about the birth! In my experience, situations can get quite stressful if there is any issue detected whilst in labour on the maternity ward. Obviously midwives and consultants are professionals and they have trigger points and steps they have to follow if certain things come up. All of my babies had fetal distress and this created quite an uneasy atmosphere in the room and does not help mum to stay calm, inward and focused!

With our third we had quite a fight to stay out of theatre for a C-section and in that case it was prayer that saved us I'm sure! The consultant even apologized to us afterwards for his less experienced staff tryingto take me unnecessarily to have a Cesarian! Unfortunately it would appear to be an easy option these days! It's quick, it's procedure, it's text book, and dare I say everyone will finish their shift on time.

My point here is that you can afford to ask questions and ask about your choices and options on the maternity ward, or wherever you are (at home). It has to be said of course that many mums out there even opt for C-section, but I'm confident also that many other mums would prefer to do whatever it takes to have a normal vaginal delivery. You have every right to ask about your options and for more explanation about what's going on. When we are in this vulnerable state however, we usually don't; so make sure your birthing partner is prepared.

For the final stages of labour mum just needs to know that when her body is 'pushing' during contractions, to work with that and push on the out breath. When the head is crowning (the midwife should guide) mum needs to help slow down the pushing for a few moments to prevent perennial tearing. Panting helps, or less deep breaths. Once baby is in mums arms the relief is overwhelming - for those of you who know- isn't it? Then the next part of the journey of parenthood begins with caring for baby outside of the womb and in the world, which is by far the most important part and lasts much much longer.

In India, the custom is for the new mother to have a full month's rest after the hard work of delivering a child, supported by an extended family the new mum will not leave her private space and focus solely on breast feeding her baby to give it the best of starts in life! The rest of the family will serve and support mum by bringing her food, doing her laundry, looking after the house etc. whilst she regains her full strength and bonds with baby.

The tradition in India (Hindus) is also for any visitors who want to meet the baby not to rush in and grab the baby as is often the case here in the West, but to respect the space and energy, they must wait in the house for sometime settling down their own energy from being outside in the hectic world and they can then go and see mother and baby when they are ready. The mother and baby are very much protected like a precious and rare treasure in the traditional Indian culture. Women are seen as the Goddess of every home and rule over their domain, which includes their husband! Although from the Western perspective looking in, things are usually not as they appear and many assume women in India are in a subordinate role, quite the opposite! A child in India is thought of as a GOD in the Hindu custom, and both parents are very willing to do anything to please the baby, as are the extended family. Of course, the culture is changing rapidly.

The baby is rarely laid down in any kind of separate cot bed or left alone, and if a baby is heard crying the whole family will attend to the baby until they see him/her contented once more! The newborn child is treasured especially in the first few months and will always have someone with them at all times even when they are sleeping.

The Hindu culture considers many other aspects of the child's wellbeing and considers it important for a baby's emotional and spiritual health to be held, loved and feel wanted in every possible moment. Indian women don't have such things as prams or buggies, they are simply carried in a type of sling on the body or held in the arms of father, mother or another close family member.

So new parents have some great changes to make in their life and it's good to be a little prepared! If we as Yoga teachers can help them to prepare it's all part of the good work we can do as we can often give some great and much needed advice.

Why Postnatal Yoga?

Post-natal Yoga has a variety of benefits for the new (or 2nd. 3rd time etc. mum) Firstly it's somewhere they can come and join a class without having to worry about having baby with them, it is usually a nice friendly environment where we expect and encourage breastfeeding in the middle of the class if needed or if mum needs to pop out to change nappies or rock a crying baby it's all part of the parcel and the teacher knows this, therefore mum can relax without stressing about disturbing people which I find is an important factor to help mums relax. If mum relaxes; then baby usually feels relaxed too! Mother and child are so interconnected on an emotional level in this early phase.

Being in a class with other mums is also hugely supportive to the new mum, who usually finds new friends she can talk to about the epic journey of motherhood! It is also a nice environment to get some advice about different aspects they may be struggling with such as breast-feeding or lack of sleep! The typical topics you hear women speak about and it helps to talk things though with some understanding 'been there and done it' other mums.

How Yoga can help regain health and well being after birth?
The body of a new mum is a 'new body' after going through 9 months of pregnancy. Mum now find herself recovering from the birth experience and the body slowly pulling itself back together after sustaining the life of a baby inside.
The physical practices of Yoga can really help with this. The pelvic floor work for example is not usually worked on in great detail by midwives due to their increased ties and pressure constraint of their roles; therefore I find most of the time I teach the pelvic floor the women have no idea about it in any real depth.
The sequence and movements we use for postnatal work are also all focused around re-establishing proper good breathing and working on our abdominal and pelvic area in a gentle way gradually strengthening and bringing mum into her original or better (in my case!) shape.
Some comments the mums make:

"This for me is special time with my new baby especially as I have older ones at home."

"The class gives me an awareness that my body is still healing."

"It's a place I can be with me baby and do something that's good for me."

"I love to bring my mind back into my body and breath."

"We are all in the same boat here and it's a safe place, I feel looked after."

Hindu rituals after birth

I have felt very lucky to be part of a Hindu family, I love and appreciate the Hindu lifestyle particularly in this post-natal time!

One of the first important parts is that the father cuts the cord after the delivery. Mother and baby are fully looked after (after baby is born) usually for a minimum of approximately 2-months; and is well protected and nurtured. The mother is escorted wherever she goes. Babies are never left out of sight or alone. Breastfeeding is seen as an auspicious dharma and the family will support and would not expect you to do anything whilst you are undertaking this duty. In public places (in India in our generation) it is seen as a very respectful and an acceptable practice, and people would support in any way they can. In my experience of breast feeding around Indian people, my duty of breastfeeding was always treated with a huge respect and support, everyone would try to make sure I was comfortable.

1st ceremony - 3rd day of Nuharta – This is the Astrological or Yantric auspicious day when the baby will have the first bathing ceremony.
Within the ceremony there is a yagya (fire) and mantra Vedic chanting (for health and well-being), the Gyatri mantras and the Mahamartyunjaya mantra. Close friends and family attend. This is the first opportunity for anyone else to see or touch the baby, other than the parents or close relatives that may also be living in the same space. Until this moment the baby is still covered in vernix (natural skin protection) from the birth. This is advised for health and immunity protection according to Ayurvedic teachings.

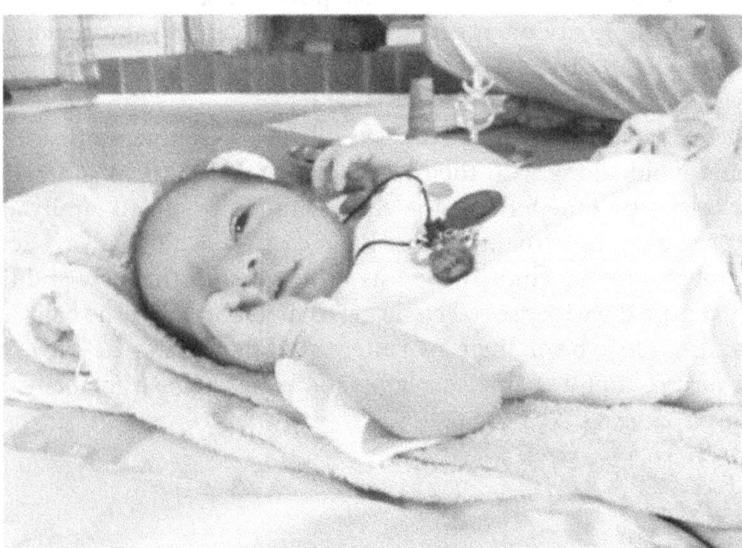

Pic - bathing ceremony with Krishna:
Baby is given some auspicious jewellery for ankles and waist and a pendant. Usually from the parents side.

2nd ceremony - naming ceremony - On an auspicious Muhurta (an auspicious moment or day in time, according to Indian astrology), the name will be given by the parent, grandparents or Guru based on Yantric calculations. The Guru may give a Beeja (a sound endowed with great spiritual powers), or the sound of the first letter for example. Folk songs are often sung and there is dancing as a social celebration. Again, only close family are invited.

3rd Ceremony – Dashothana- After 4-weeks, at the earliest, the health and well-being of mother and child, along with their Muhurta is taken into consideration. This is the time for celebrating the birth of the child with the extended family and friends. The family provide a feast, mantras are chanted again at the Yagya (sacred ritual), followed by music and dancing. The guests bring gifts for the baby and the mother. This is the first time the wider social circle get to meet the baby. The baby and mother after this are also free to be on their own after this if they wish. The baby could be left alone in the next room for example as far as someone can hear the baby or can keep a regular check.

Other thoughts about the Hindu culture and family.

In the Hindu culture the babies sleep in the same bed as the mother and/or father or even a grandparent. Generally there is no limit set for when co-sleeping ends, it is simply when the child wants to move into its own separate bed itself. Jnandev tells for example, left his parents bed by his own choice around 3 years to go and share with his brothers and sisters in another room as he preferred to be with them! So, his parents made him a bed there. It's important to note here that the typical Hindus, especially women would never consume alcohol; it was simply never a part of the culture and maybe this is why it was never considered a problem to co-sleep as in the West it is a bigger issue. The reason in Vedic texts as it explains, is for the physical mental emotional and spiritual nourishment of the baby to co-sleep that they are not lacking in feeling loved, a sense of touch and protection in these very early stages. I've often mused that this can be part of the reason that Indian people seem so open hearted and full of love and depth and confidence in comparison to the western people, which is obviously a sweeping statement however it has been my experience. Although the older generation is already very different to the younger generations who are sadly losing this. What is interesting is that now in the West people are becoming more open to these concepts, with all the studies that show the benefits of these types of practices, e.g. Skin to skin time, contact with baby, communicating with baby etc.

Communication with the baby is something I personally found very strange at first, as someone who was not brought up around any babies, throughout my childhood we were quite insular. So, I was blessed to have Jnandev, who I feel after our first baby taught me many things on how to 'be' with a baby. I remember loving all my kids to bits, but I didn't seem to have any confidence in what to do on an emotional level. Practically was no problem I was always pretty efficient, but I distinctly remember feeling almost shy to actually speak to my new baby and thought it seemed a bit silly as I had somehow assumed a baby can't understand anything anyway! How ignorant and laughable now I look back, and there was Jnandev twittering away at our little Siddha from the very moment he popped out with such ease (the talking part!). My point is that in the Hindu culture, it's very family orientated which creates a healthy, proactive and supportive environment for baby on so many levels. Jnandev was always so happy and hopeful to have a family in his mindset and no matter what, no matter if we had a fall out or anything at all his strong Hindu and family conditioning meant and means for him that there is no exit point on this family journey.

In traditional Hindu culture, divorce is considered the absolute last resort, which might seem like it should be the case in all cultures. However, as a Western woman, I've never felt more stable, secure, and safe in a relationship than I did in a marriage with a traditional Hindu Indian man. From the Indian perspective, there is a deep commitment to family and marriage. I faced many situations where, in a Western context, we might have divorced within the first year of marriage, but for him, even a big argument or disagreement would never signal the end of our union. That said, in the West, we tend to value open discussions, counselling, and mutual reflection to resolve conflicts and work toward harmony—an approach that could be beneficial for the Eastern perspective as well.

As we mature and grow on a spiritual path every challenge is a chance to evolve and take another look at ourselves. I've always felt that life will give us challenges whether we like it or not, we have to grow, that is why we are here to live and learn and evolve consciously or unconsciously, we are all on a conveyor belt back to the source or the Divine. We can just sit there and go along the conveyor belt (8,400,000 lifetimes according to the Garuda Purana), or we can open our eyes awaken and start to walk or even run toward this destination, or oneness! We have a choice to choose our challenges or if we try to avoid them another force will choose our challenges for us as we cannot live without them, this time however we will not have any choice on what life brings us.

Therefore, I would urge women who have chosen to take on the experience of becoming a mother, a deeply spiritual one that although it's not all 'peaches and cream' with the right attitude and surrender to fulfilling that Divine role of mother, allowing the life creation to flow in its dynamic harmony with the creative laws of nature. It is like the journey of the seed which starts with germination and ends with a mature plant producing more seeds. As Dr Ananda Bhavanani said it is the most spiritual state when we are surrendered to motherhood fully, we are ego-less, because we have forgotten ourselves, we are just existing for the baby in these early precious moments. That's not to say we are not important, but having this sense of oneness with the baby we lose ourself in that unconditional love and it is a truly special and profound experience.

Postnatal Yoga Classes

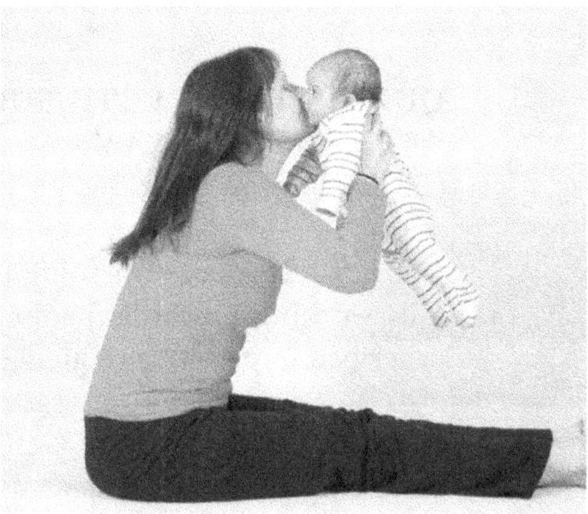

If you would like to run a post-natal yoga class, you may really want to consider a class which allows mums to bring their baby along! Especially if mum is breast feeding, it is unlikely she'll be going anywhere without baby and your class may be just what she needs with the freedom and support of other new mums there too. Having ran post-natal classes with babies in the class, it's not as distracting as you might imagine, in fact mostly the babies just sleep, or wake up for a feed so Mum just feeds and observes whilst the class continues! If a baby starts screaming, no-one really minds as we have all been there and as long as you re-assure mum not to worry about it, it stops sooner or later! Don't forget baby picks up on mums' tension straight away.

If mum did some yogic cleansing or asana work for some years before practice her body will probably go back to its normal shape pretty quickly! Especially if breast feeding any excess weight will soon be lost.

Depending on the birth, if mum had a caesarean we would recommend that no physical practice is undertaken for a minimum of 12 weeks – again this needs to be individual it may need to be longer! My middle child was a c-section and I was very aware of my body still healing its wounds for at least 3 months! The actual scar tissue will still be felt for up to a year later in my experience. After a normal delivery if mum's body is well used to the practices she can start again GENTLY please after just 2 weeks at home (as I did) but for mums that may not be in regular practice 6 weeks after a normal birth or the G.P post-natal checkup. Its safest to only allow attendance to a post-natal yoga class only after the G.P has confirmed it's ok.

Practices we use to get the body back into shape and rejuvenated! These are working with the body in a gentle and conscious way.

Postnatal Sequence
(you can create your own order in a flow)

QUIET SITTING WITH SUKKHA OR SAVITRI RYTHYM PRANAYAMA
(Pranayamas as described previously)

JATTIS - as usual! Warming up our body from the toes working upwards, jiggling, shaking, rolling as described in previous sequences

HAMSA MUDRA (Swan Gesture)
Following plenty of jattis as usual and refer back to the SHOULDER KRIYAS to really ease up the neck upper back and shoulders that will be under extra pressure now post-natal! e.g., carrying baby and breast feeding!

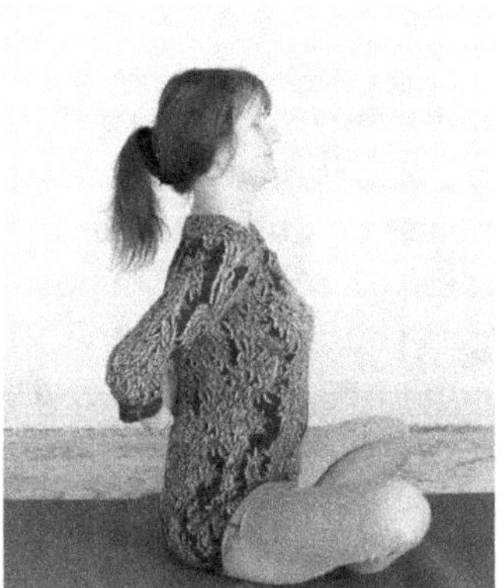

Bring both hands behind the back and if you can bring them into namaskar mudra. If this is not possible you can fold the arms over each other and hold onto the elbows with the hands.

Lengthen up the spine and take a few deep breaths, opening up the shoulders. This is very good for opening out chest up and breathing well. Our shoulders carry a lot of tension, and this posture will help keep us relaxed around the shoulders and upper chest.

GOMUKHA ASANA (cow faced pose)

Lift up one elbow and push it down with the opposite hand to assist your stretch and push your hand down your back as far as it can go. Then bring the other hand around behind the back to catch hold of the hand if possible, or you can even use some material (a sock) to connect the two hands or simply stretch as far as you can go.

Take a few deep breaths focusing on opening the chest and shoulder area.

GENTLE SITTING TWIST

Any type of twist is generally good, from any simple sitting positron, crossed legged or straight legs are also fine. Remember to lengthen the spine so we do not collapse or concave the spine and twist around using the knee or thigh for extra leverage to deepen the stretch a little.

Take a few deep breaths, use an out breath to untwist the spine. Always repeat the opposite side to keep the body in balance.

EKA PADA PAVANA MUKHTA

Start sitting up with the legs straight our in front. Bend the knee and draw the folded right leg close to your body with a squeeze on the in breath. Then whoosh the breath our as you release the leg throwing back the hands and arms.

Repeat this three times on each side.

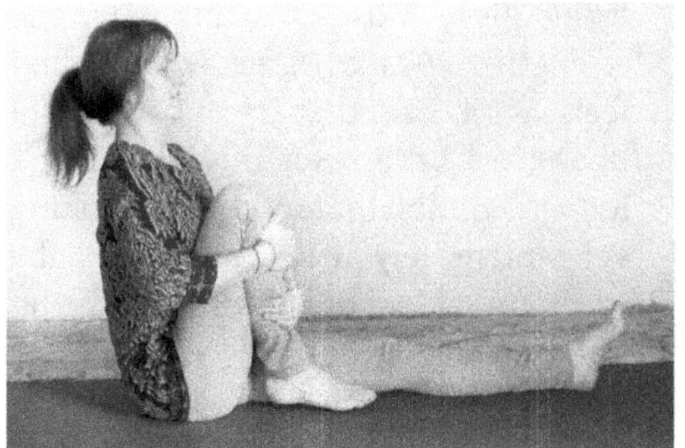

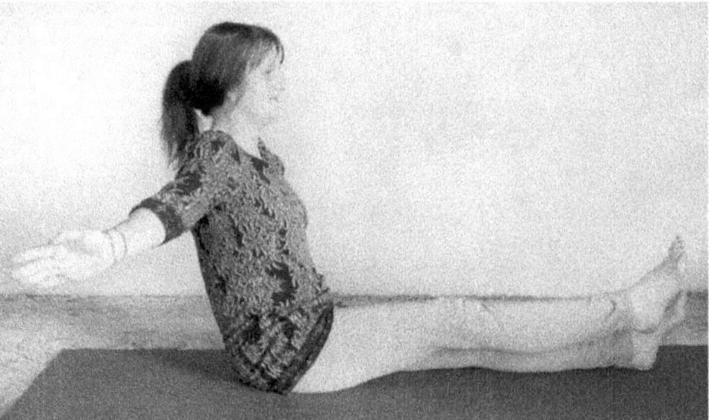

BADDHA KONA KRIYA

Bring the feet together and hold onto the toes, lengthen up the spine and bounce the knees out to the sides.

Here is also a good time to practice our Aswini Mudra or Moolhabandha to exercise the pelvic floor.

note: avoid with SPD

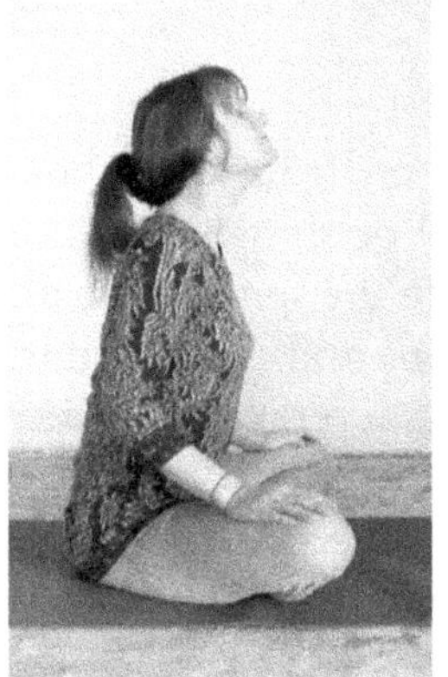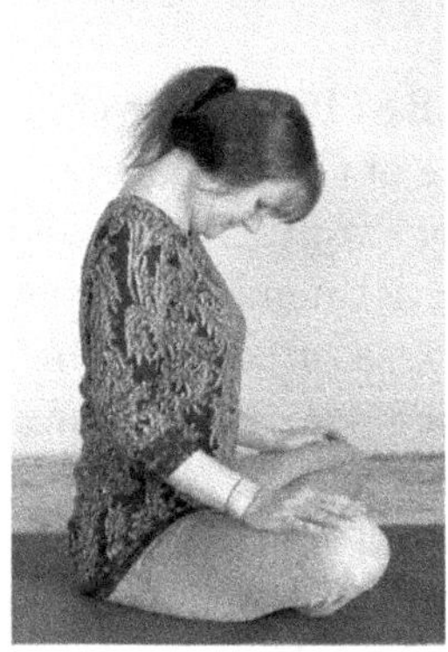

MAYURI MUDRA - The peacock gesture

Stretching the chin and neck forward on an in breath and then bringing the chin back down toward the chest on the out breath.

This is great to working out tension around the shoulders too, which tends to increase with all the lifting and carrying babies about!

CHATUS PADUS

Crawling around the mat in a conscious way, feeling inside the body, breathing deep and moving slowly! This movement is so beneficial for us on so many levels!

We are going back to baby crawling using these muscles to build up the strength to walk, or evolve! It often feels a bit like this in the postnatal phase, we have been through such a lot in childbirth, and then looking very intensively after a newborn baby can kind of feel a bit similar to being knocked off our feet!! We have to slowly build ourselves up again and this crawling around is very representative of evolving and growing. Once we have had the great honour of becoming a mother we are a new person all over again and we have to learn to walk again as a new person!

CHIRI KRIYA - The cricket action

From chatus padus (four footed) we extend the leg back on the inhale and on the exhale bring the knee and forehead towards each other.

Repeat 3 - 6 times each side. This movement is one to put in every sequence really as it is so beneficial, we are working on our lungs, stretching and compressing the rib cage working with the breath. We are actually working with all parts of the body in one way or another but it's a very good movement for the spine also. When we get down on all fours particularly after childbirth it can help all our body organs to get properly back into position.

VYAGRAHA PRANAYAMA - Tiger breathing

From chatus padus we breath in and dip the spine, lift with the chin and we can push on the hands a little.
On the exhale we can arch the back, bringing the chin in towards the chest again pushing on the hands for some extra pressure.
Repeat this for 3 - 6 rounds.

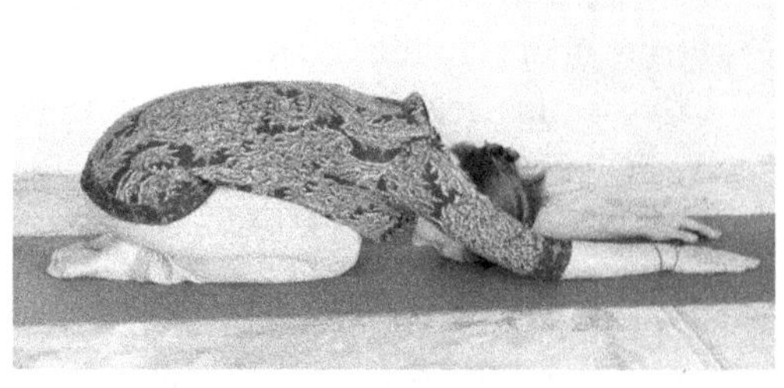

SHASHANGA ASANA - rabbit pose

After practicing Tiger breathing relax down into Shashanga for a few deep breaths, sitting back on the heels and stretching the arms away in front of the body.

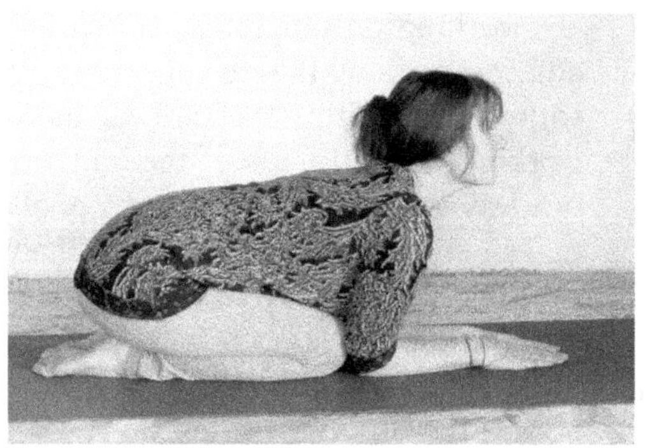

SASHA ASANA - rabbit variation

Bringing the elbows to the knees, palms flat down on the mat, looking upwards this posture will direct the air into the lower lobes of the lungs thus increasing our vitality. Take 3 - 6 deep even breaths. Then relax the head and neck down.

PURNA SASHA ASANA - Hare pose

Bringing the backs of the wrists to the knees straighten the arms and look up in Purna Shasha asana. This will primarily direct the air flow into the mid chest thoracic region increasing the blood flow around the heart.

Take 3 - 6 deep even breaths here then relax the head and neck down.

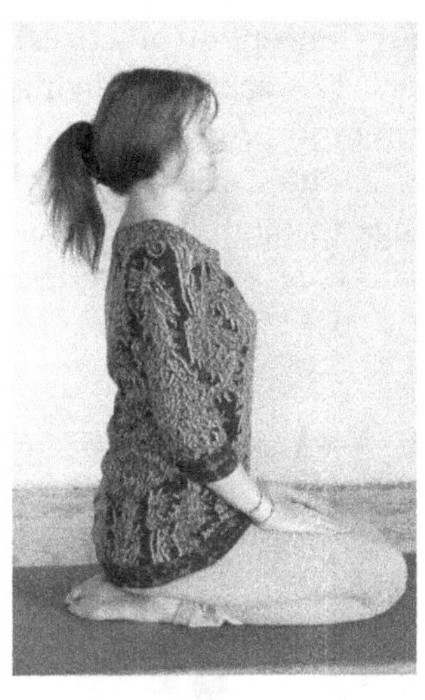

DANDA KRIYA SEQUENCE
- VAJRA ASANA
- USHTRA ASANA (gentle variation)
- VAJRA ASANA
- PARI PURNA SASHA ASANA
- DHARMIKA ASANA
- VAJRA ASANA

Starting in Vajra asana take a few breaths here to start. Then lift up onto the knees into a back bend Usthtra asana gentle variation on the in-breath. As we breath in try to feel the air flowing down into the lower lobes of the lungs. On the out-breath release back down into vajra asana.

Then inhale in Vajra asana and on the exhale come forward brining the head down onto the mat, arms are back alongside the hips into Dharmika asana

On the in-breath lift up the buttocks and roll up on top of the head into Purna shasha asana. As you breath out roll back down into Dharmika asana. As you breath in lift back up into Vajra asana.
Repeat this sequence 3 rounds.

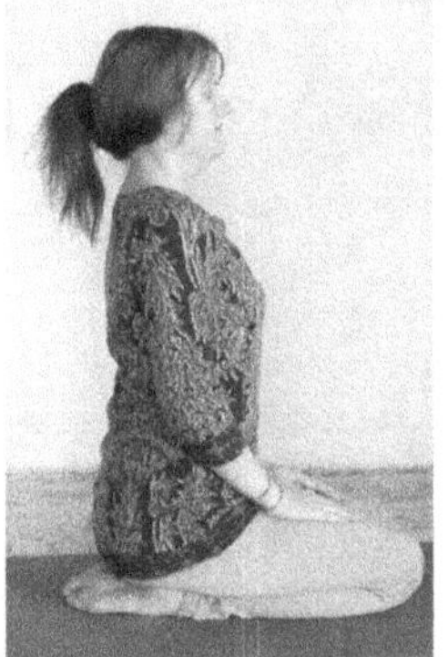

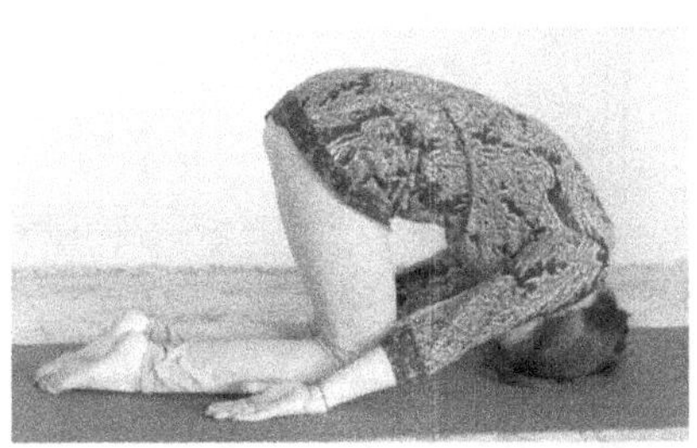
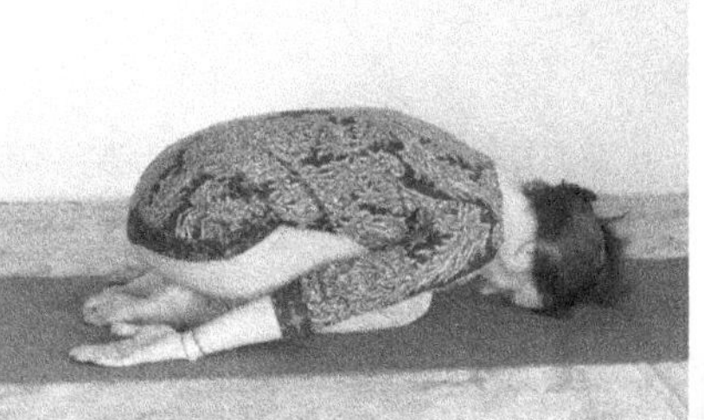

Here we can bring in the Sun salutation described earlier (in pre-conception practices) if the woman has practiced the rest of this sequence in the first 12 weeks after giving birth (or more after a Cesarian). Again every woman is different some may be ready for more physical work earlier depending upon her own abilities, recovery, pre conditioning to Yoga etc. which you should be able to gauge through listening to her situation and watching her body language, and how she is responding to the practices. Otherwise, this page can be skipped.

Vajra asana - tuck under with toes - slowly place hands on the mat and push up into meru asana - slowly walk the hands back and uncurl upwards to standing.

(Do the reverse to come back down to sitting)

ARUNA SURYA NAMASKAR

- VAJRA ASANA
- NIKUNJA ASANA
- SHASHANGA ASANA
- DANDA ASANA
- PASCHIMOTTANA ASANA

From Vajra asana come forward with the upper chest on the mat turning the head to one side. Take a few breaths here and lift briefly up again to turn the head to the other side. Then sit back into Shashanga asana and relax for a few breaths. Lift back up into vajra asana, then stretch the legs out in front and stretch up with the arms into Danda asana lengthening the spine taking a few deep breaths. Then fold forwards into Pastimottana asana on an out breath and lift back up on the inhale. After a few rounds you can hold Pastimottana asana.

Take a few deep breaths here.

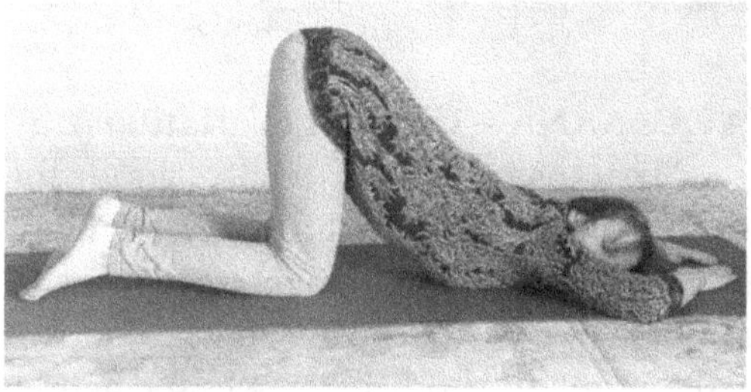

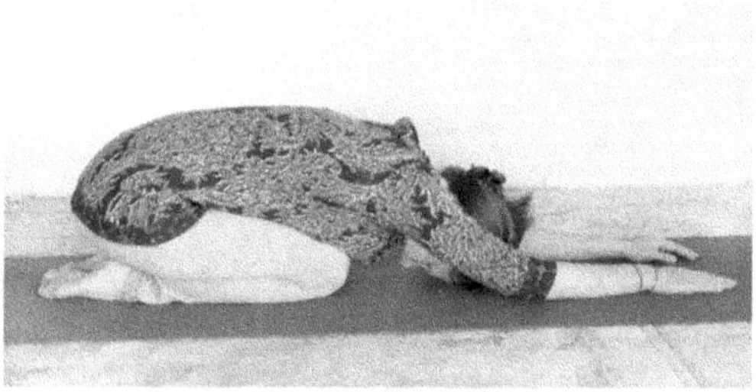

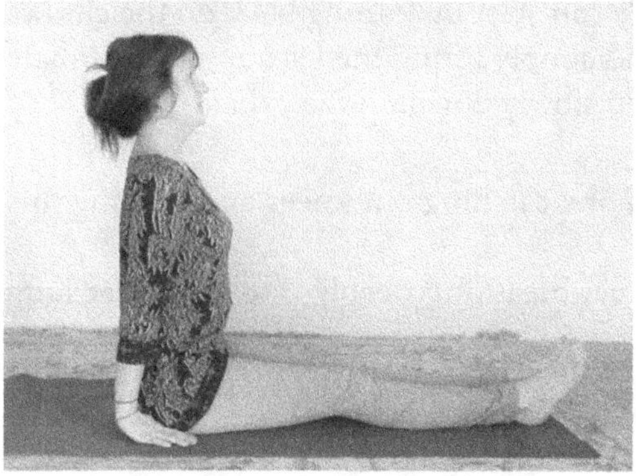

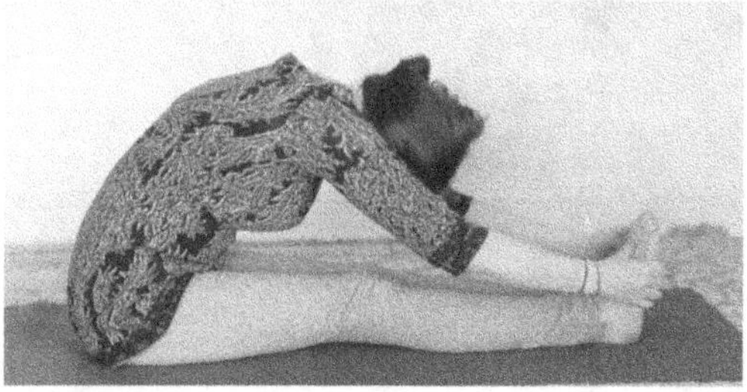

Stretch up again into DANDA ASANA
Then lean back, planting the hands behind the back and lift up the hips on an inhale into PRATIPAHALASANA and release back down on the exhale. Repeat a few rounds and hold for a few breaths once mum is feeling strong again.

Release back into sitting up and loosen up jiggling around and shaking for a minute or two.

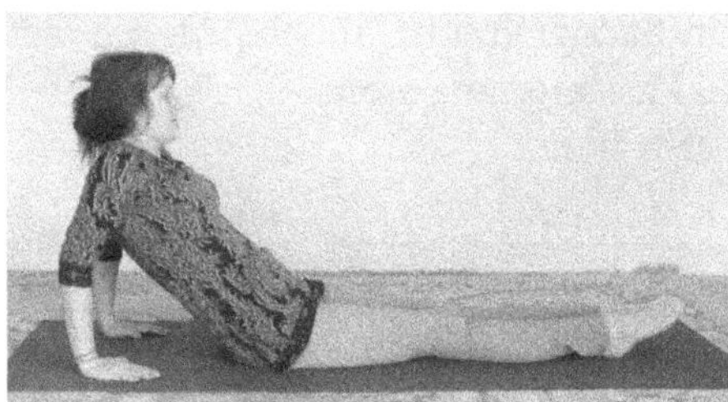

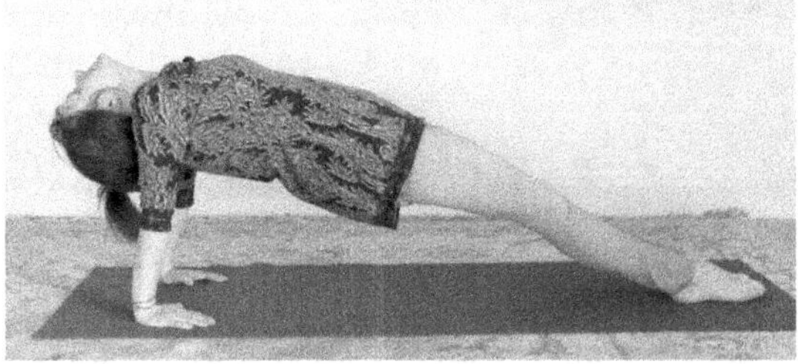

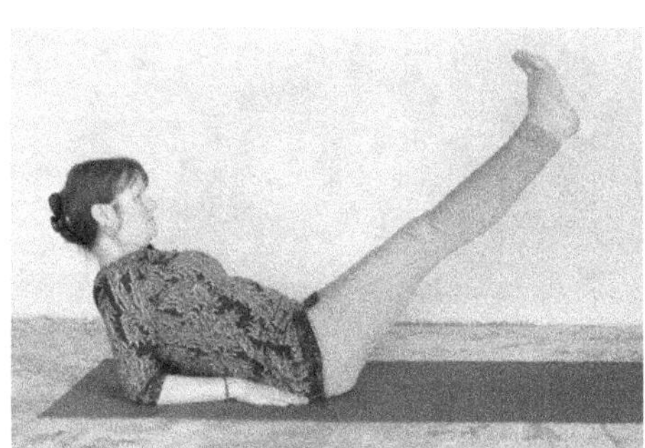

NAVA ASANA - The Boat (Variations)
The Nava asana is especially good for working on our abdominal area. We can use several variations but remembering not to go too strong in the post-natal period, we need to build the body up slowly and gently. We can start by leaning back on the elbows and simply lifting the legs up on the inhale and slowly down on the exhale.

Next we can sit up and balance on the tailbone catching out knees and holding this variation for a few breaths.
Then we can catch hold of our ankles or feet breathing deeply into the lower lung region.

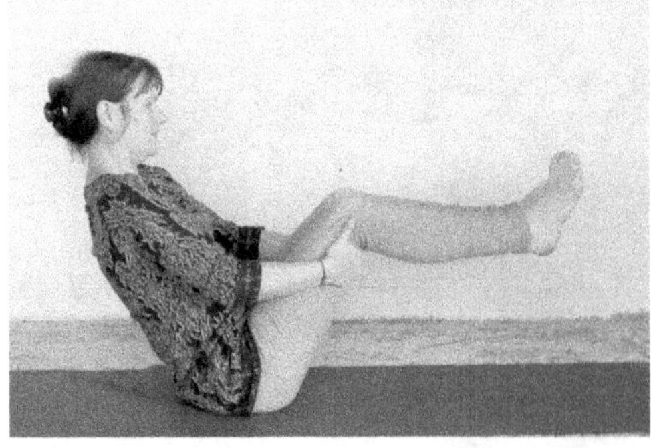

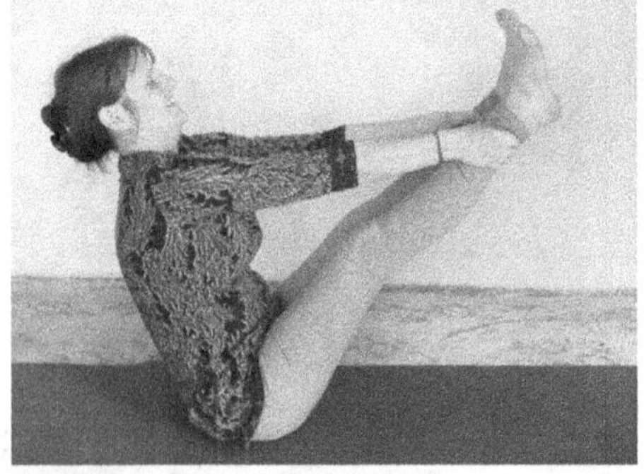

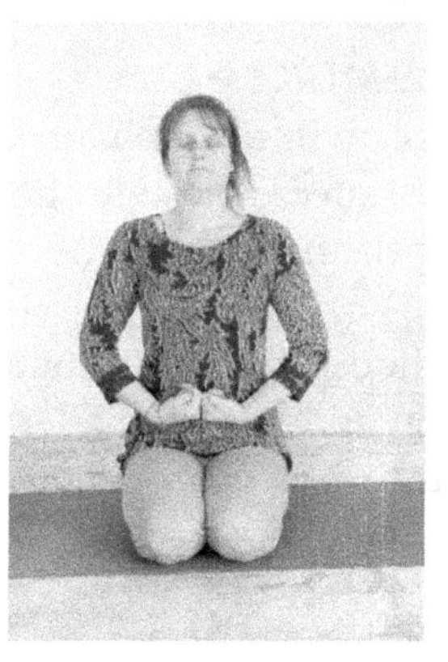

Pranayama time!
Its good to bring one of the pranayama practices in around here before we lie down on the mat. It also prepares us for a deeper relaxation.
Use one of the practices from the Pranayama section here.
Bramha mudra and Pranava Aum are both great!

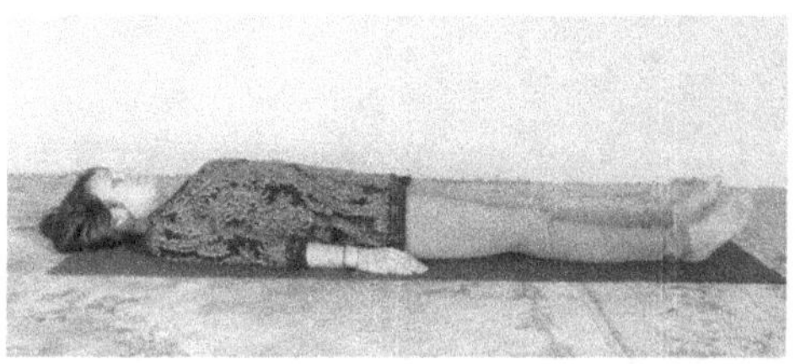

SHAVA ASANA - take a few breaths let the body relax in this position.

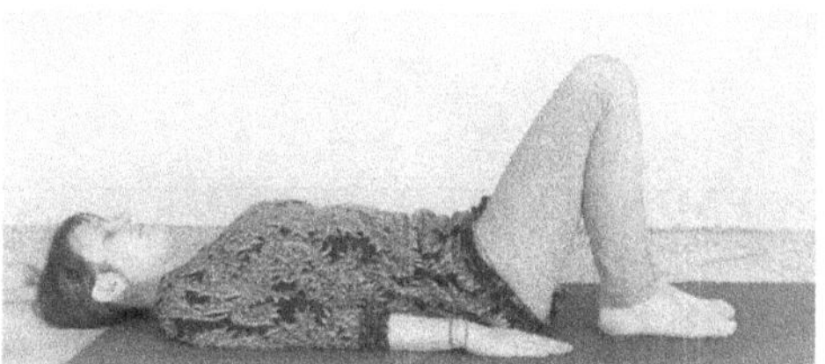

SETU KRIYA - The Bridge
Bringing the heels to the buttocks bending the knees, as you breath in lift up high with the hips, as we exhale uncurl the spine back down onto the mat, try to feel each vertebrae and rock slightly forward onto the pelvis when you reach the floor again.

KATI CHAKRA KRIYA
Starting with the knees in the centre, as you breath out drop the knees to one side, lifting on the inhale and switching sides on the exhale. Repeat for several rounds.

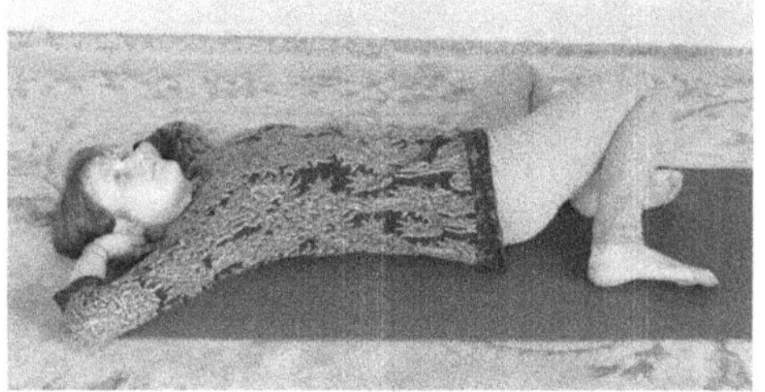

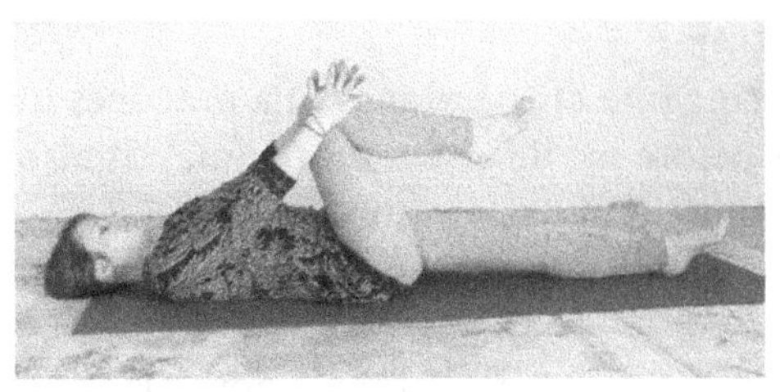

EKA PADA PAVANA MUKTA

From Shava asana, breath in catching hold of the bent knee and squeeze close to the body whilst bringing the head up to meet the knee.

On an out breath whoosh the breath out in a bhastrika fashion and release the leg back down rapidly throwing the arms out to the sides.

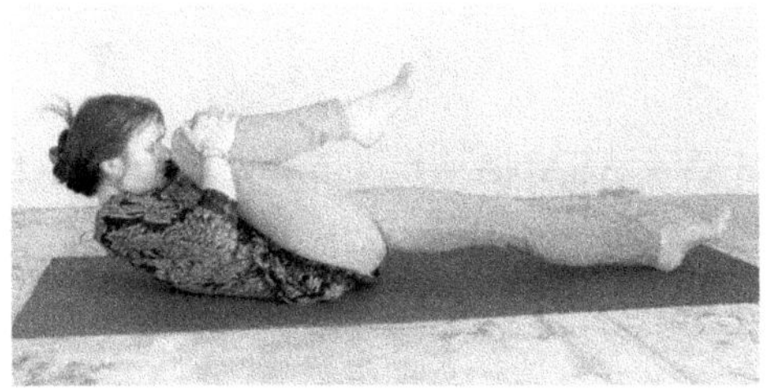
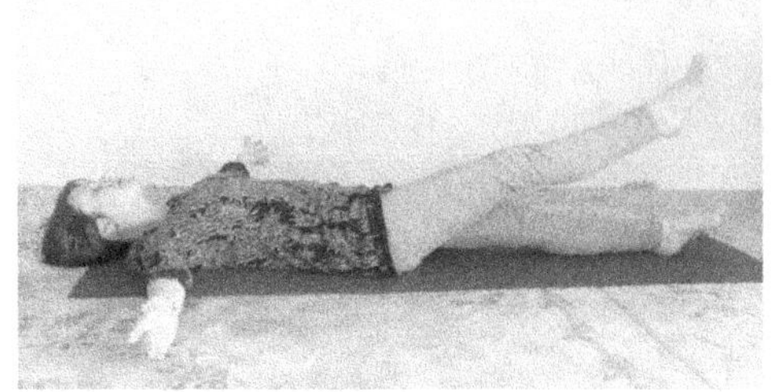

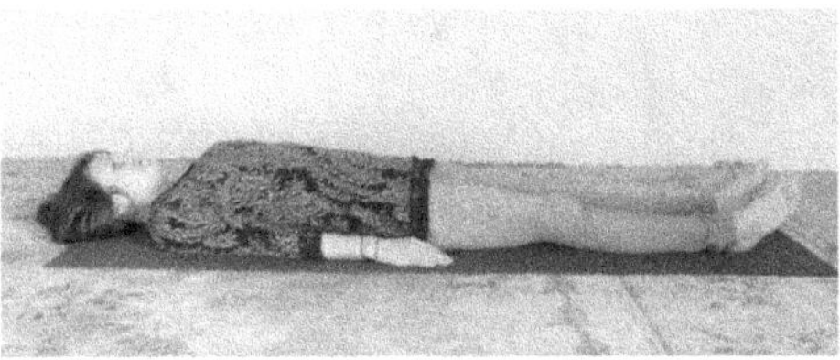

EKA PADA UTTANA ASANA - single leg lifting

From Shava asana use the Sukkha rythym 6x6 breathing to lift and lower the legs with the breath in a slow and controlled way. in this way we can build up the muscle tone again to the entire abdominal region.

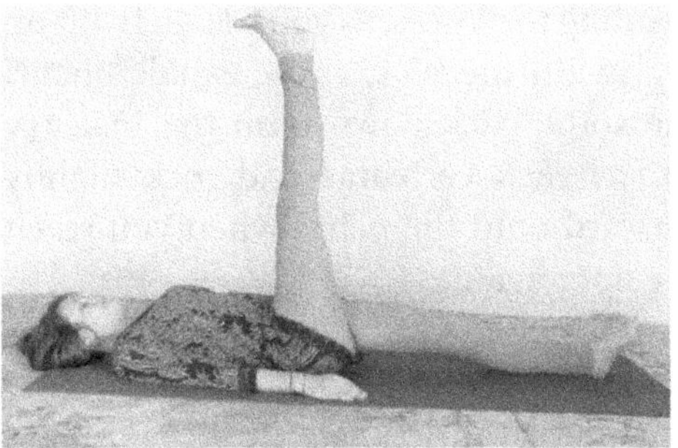

As you breath in lift the right leg up slowly pointing the toe and flex the foot back when you reach the top. Point the toe again and on the exhale slowly release the leg back down.

Note: If this feels uncomfortable or if there is any back pain, issues it is better to start by bending the knee first then straightening on the lift and lower.

You can also add in some side leg lifting.

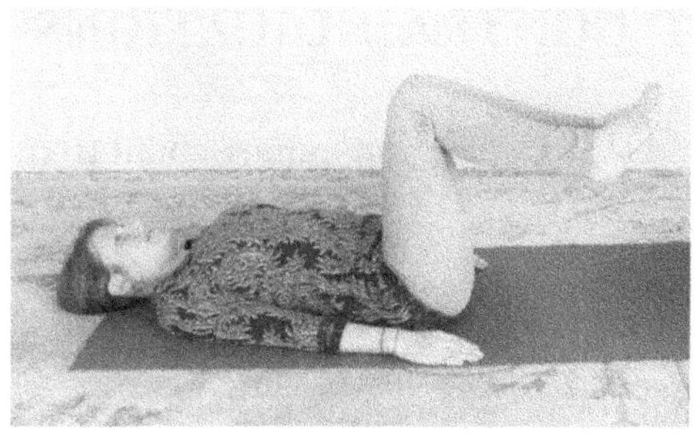

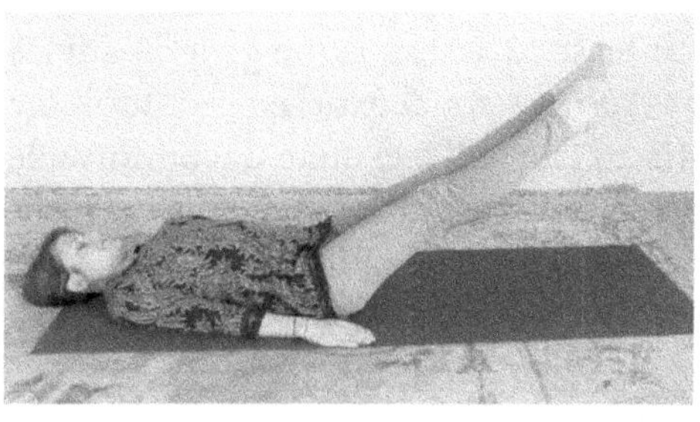

DWI PADA UTTANA ASANA - Double leg lifting

As with the single leg lifting we are moving slowly and consciously with the breath. On the inhale we can start by bending the knees and then straightening the legs together and lifting them up. On the exhale bend the knees and slowly release back down.

Once we are used to this we can start lifting and lowering with straight legs. It can be quite tough work so only do 3 rounds to start with and take a few relaxing breaths in-between each round.

This can be built up week by week. This is excellent for rebuilding those abdominal muscles.

SHAVA ASANA

Using jnana yoga kriya - relaxation technique

After several weeks of practicing these more gentle kriyas you can start moving along into some more vigorous work such as sun salutations but only if mum feels like it – don't forget for breast feeding mums who aren't getting a lot of sleep on a regular basis they probably just need to stay on the floor and are just needing some time for themselves and quality rest! Personally, until I finished breast feeding I just felt dizzy every time I tried to do something very active or strenuous asana work mainly due to lack of sleep! When mum is ready she can join your regular class.

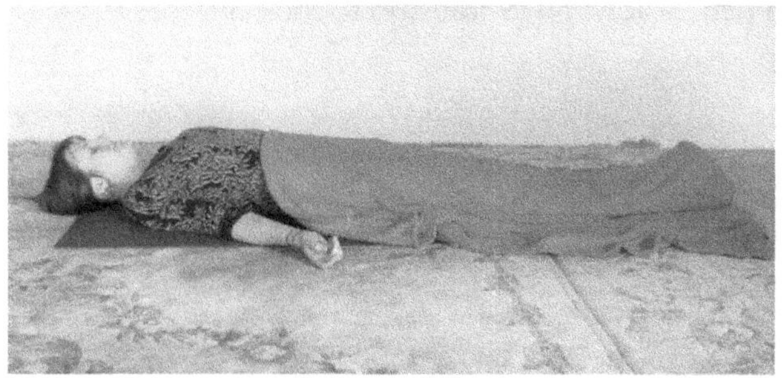

POSTNATAL CHALLENGES AND CONTRAINDICATIONS

There are some important conditions we should look out for and inquire about from the mother with a new baby.

To reiterate they should not attend class until their GP check which is usually around 6-8 weeks. It is best as a yoga teacher to make sure your students have signed a health form confirming they are fit to attend post-natal yoga following their GP check.

If they did have a c-section they should wait at least 12 weeks is the general advice and as my middle son was a c-section I can say from personal experience it took me a good year to feel 'normal' again and the scar tissue can still feel quite uncomfortable for years after. I was able to have a normal delivery with my third after this however although this did feel like a bit of a battle as there was very much a sense of once you've had a c-section following babies will be delivered in the same way!

Post-natal depression
Is real! The dramatic changes the woman's body goes through is immense and even those lucky enough to have a good supportive structure around of friends and family can still experience unbearable dips in moods and their coping mechanisms seem to fail. I have personally not experienced this I can attribute this to the preparatory work and so many hours of yoga practice in all its aspects! I definitely personally had quite a difficult time after all my babies with sleep! My first seemed to wake hourly or less though the night and after 6-months I had to return to work for various reasons which was also very difficult feeding through the night in the end I got quite sick and had to be signed off work for some time. Although the physical struggles were tough, and the lack of sleep affects your day to day functioning I still had a very deep love for all my children and this love somehow kept me mentally stable and able to keep going on regardless. I feel blessed that I was married to a traditional Indian man who respects the roles of mother as a scared role where the act of sex was just not on the cards for either of us, I was a new mother and all my energy was engaged in being a mother. The absolute last thing I could want or think about would be sex (every woman is different, no judgement here). It was good to be in relationship that supported this way of living. I know many other new mothers who feel this too, that said the hormonal changes can affect everyone in different ways.
Here are some signs of post-natal depression (NHS website) to look out for:

- Frequent crying
- Difficulty bonding with baby
- Withdrawing contact with others
- Negative frame of mind
- Self-neglect e.g. hygiene

- Loosing sense of time
- Lost sense of humour
- Constant worry that something is wrong

Encourage a woman to seek help and speak to their GP, health visitor or a family member. If you think a baby or child may be in danger you must contact your local social services, this may be necessary if the woman has postpartum psychosis which is a combination of bipolar like symptoms, delusions and/or hallucinations.

Symphysis pubis dysfunction (SPD)

This is pain and discomfort around the low back and pelvic girdle which can also radiate to the inner thighs. The joint itself separates and we need to be careful not to intensify this by practicing a lot of open leg and hip work and use postures that encourage the SP joint to be drawn back together eg. Gomukha asana (leg part only) or twists crossing the legs over to the opposite sides. This can be quite challenging in a general class as it would limit the class practices so it may be better to have a 1:1 session with these students and then after they have advice perhaps they can join in the general post natal class and manage to avoid certain postures themselves.

Note: you can try other sitting positions if the mother has symphysis pubis disfunction (SPD) such as crossing legs inwards so knees parallel. Such as the leg position for Gomukha asana.

When a child is born, the entire Universe has to shift and make room. Another entity capable of free will, and therefore capable of becoming God, has been born.

Ina May Gaskin - 'Spiritual Midwifery'

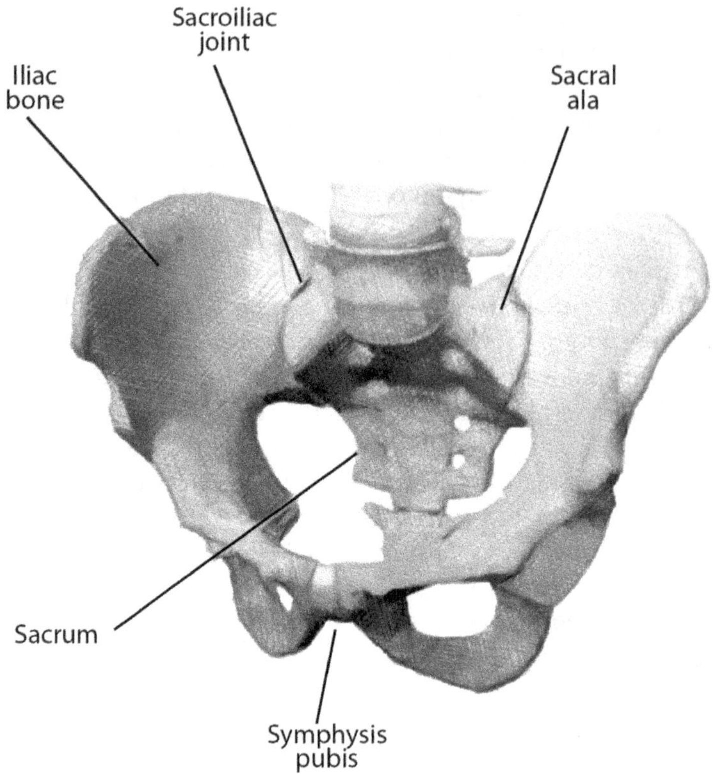

Diastasis recti

This is when the separation of the rictus abdominal muscles occurs due to the growing uterus pushing the muscles apart. Generally these are said to have returned to normal by 8-12 weeks, however if there is still a separation and its problematic the student may well be under a physiotherapist for specialist care and this should be discussed. For this condition we should avoid abdominal pressure work (crunches, planks etc).

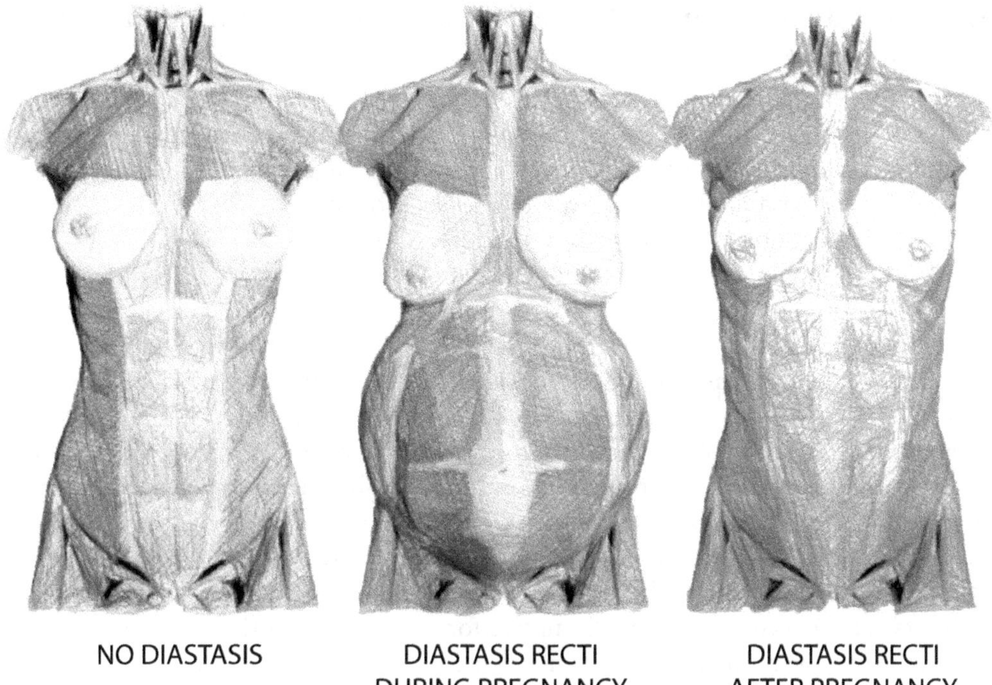

please note oblique work needs to be avoided if the new mother has Daisis recti.

During pregnancy, the pressure inside your abdominal cavity is greatly increased due to the size of your growing baby, the uterus growing, and all of your organs being squashed together. That pressure can only build and build until, eventually, it cuts loose. Think of it as bending a pencil-you can bend the pencil so far until is snaps into two pieces. Your abdominal muscles are no different! Too much pressure in your abdomen can cause both halves of your tummy to split apart (avoid crunches, planks, sit ups in pregnancy which can apparently cause this)

There are some of the main issues that we can come across though there are others. Another point I will mention it to avoid too much face prone work as the breasts can become very enlarged and sometimes sore from breast-feeding so take care.

How long does the student attend post natal yoga or mother and baby yoga for?

Well this is an interesting question! How long is one 'post-natal'? Well, the postpartum period for example (after normal delivery) is in three stages:

- Initial phase: 6-12 hours after childbirth
- Subacute postpartum period: 2-6 weeks
- Delayed postpartum period: up to 6-months

In this sense we would say that the postnatal time frame will be over after about 6-months. However when you're trying run a class and I have experienced it myself, you will meet women who gain such a lot from the class it's very difficult to ask them to stop coming! After teaching for several years my personal method is to allow women to come up to around 9 months or crawling age, as once the baby starts moving around the room it does create a different kind of energy and the idea of a post-natal class is holding that space for the very sacred earlier weeks/months of mother and baby time. As the babies start to develop and head towards becoming toddlers, I have found it can be disruptive for new babies mothers to have an older baby crawling over and grabbing its nose etc.!

You could create another class for mothers and babies which could be very similar to any normal yoga class just with lots of 'racket' and noisy toddlers crawling and stumbling about the room! I usually provide a basket of children's toys for them to play with, go for the less noisy ones and ones that will not be too hard - soft toys!

THE YOGA OF MOTHERHOOD:
MY OWN EXPERIENCE

Yogacharini MEENAKSHI DEVI BHAVANANI
Director: International Centre for Yoga Education and Research (ICYER) at
Ananda Ashram, Pondicherry. South India.www.rishiculture.org

Introduction: Though I often jokingly refer to myself as a "reluctant mother", I must confess that bearing, delivering and raising our son Ananda Balayogi has been the single most significant spiritual experience of my life, my first real initiation into the blissful state of Yoga – a oneness and communion with the Universe on a nearly mystical level.

At, the age of twenty-eight, I had "practised the techniques of Yoga" for nearly four years before my son's birth. Yet, it was in the most real sense only a "practice", and not a realisation. It was a preparation for the experience of that sense of oneness, rather than a realisation of that blessed state. I can, with all honesty, say that from the moment of Ananda's entrance to this Karma Bhumi (earth plane), I have experienced an "inner wholeness", a "completeness", a fulfillment and a peace which I would never have dreamed possible.

This personal account of the pregnancy and delivery of my son thirty-two years ago may inspire some of our modern ladies to take up the practice of Yoga in order to prepare themselves for the greatest spiritual experience of them all – mother hood.

Born in the USA, I traveled to India in 1967 to take up the study of Yoga. Luckily, I found my Guru and I took to the practice of Yoga as easily as a bird on wing takes to the sky. The concepts of Yoga which I encountered through my Guru (later to become my husband) were those thoughts and feelings for which I had hungered for my whole life. In those days, I saw Yoga as Tapas, difficult austerities – long periods of silence, meditative practices, solitude, extreme Hatha Yoga Asanas, Pranayama and fasting. This I felt would culminate in that blissful state of Samadhi, which I assumed I could achieve within a year or two of intense Sadhana!

After three years of marriage, I found myself pregnant. My pregnancy was very easy, thanks to my Yoga Abhyasa. I had been practising Yoga Asanas, Pranayama and the usual Yoga Tapas, fasting, Mauna, etc. for four years prior to the pregnancy, so my body was strong, flexible and healthy. Indeed, it was not till the end of the sixth month that anyone other than my husband even realised my state. At the end of the fifth month, however, one of our good friends, a Swamiji, had casually remarked, "Meenakshi, you are getting a little fat. That is not becoming to a Yogini". I simply kept quiet, and suppressed my smile.

Yogic Life Style Prepared Me Well for Delivery: I kept a good figure and never did become too big, even at the time of delivery. I was able to carry out all my normal, heavy workload, including riding on my bicycle to Pondicherry town, nearly five kilometers away, once and sometimes twice a day up to the end of the eighth month. I participated in all the Ashram's daily 6 a.m. Hatha Yoga Asana classes right up to the very day of delivery, and was able to do all of the Asanas, Kriyas and Mudras up to the end of the fifth month.

After that time, my body began to change its shape, so that some of the face-prone positions, such as Dhanur Asana, Shalabha Asana, where extreme pressure is placed upon the abdomen, were not possible. After that, I performed whatever Asanas, Kriyas and Mudras that my body shape would allow. I was able to do Hala Asana up to the beginning of the eighth month, and the Sarvanga Asana, Nava Asana and its variations, Nikunja Asana, and Vyagraha Asana, with relative ease. I found those positions done from a four-footed position (hands and knees-Chatus Pada) were especially beneficial. I worked hard on strengthening and loosening up my pelvic area and lower back and strengthening my stomach muscles. I performed Aswini Mudra (tightening and releasing the anus) and also Mula Bandha regularly. I did many standing postures. I worked hard on sitting postures and sat often in the Utkat Asana, the Squat, at any time of day or night, whenever possible.

Baddha Kona Asana and variations were very useful in loosening the pelvis. I concentrated on performing as many Pranayamas as possible, especially using the various types of Bhastrikas to cleanse the body of toxins; Savitri Pranayama, the Rhythmic Breath, to calm and harmonize systems; Loma Viloma, Aloma Viloma, Nadi Shuddhi, to clean and purify the nervous systems; I felt Sukha Purvaka gave my mind great depth and clarity. The various Vibhaga Pranayamas, Sectional Breaths, and Mahat Yoga Pranayama, the Complete Breath, stimulated Pranic flow into body organs. I also used often the Kukuriya Pranayama, the Dog Pant, sticking the tongue out and panting like a dog, breathing in and out through the mouth, to deliberately strengthen the solar plexus.

Goals for a Healthy Pregnancy. I wished to keep my system relaxed, flexible, and free of toxins, my pelvic area and lower back flexible, my lower back and stomach strong. I wanted my legs to be strong enough to support the added weight and prevent varicose veins. I wanted plenty of Pranic energy flowing through my body and breathed as deeply as I could whenever possible. I participated in as much Mantra chanting as possible and tried at least to begin and end my day with a short period of concentration. I actually only had two hours in the morning for my Hatha Yoga Sadhana, though by participating in the Ashram Sadhana, I also had some time at the high noon Sandhyam for concentration-meditation and again at the sunset Sandhyam for Mantra Chanting. The rest of the day I carried on my busy work load: Ashram administration, Swamiji's private secretarial work, supervising the printing of books and our monthly YOGA LIFE magazine; teaching classes, receiving visitors, etc.

I did not go to a doctor until the eighth month. I only went then because I wanted to have some idea of the delivery date. At that time, the doctor told me I was in good health and should have no trouble. I found that my body did start to feel heavy towards the end of the eighth month and I found it difficult to take the deep breath to which I was normally accustomed. Swamiji told me this was because the child was now pushing up against the diaphragm. Two weeks before the actual delivery, the child dropped in the womb and the pressure against the diaphragm and lungs lessened considerably, allowing me to resume once more my various Pranayama routines. About that time I was starting to feel "crowded" in my body. I gave vent to my feelings in a poem to my unborn child, asking the child how it had the audacity to choose me to be its mother without consulting me! In the poem I complained to the child, that there was "scarcely enough room for me in this body, let alone for thee! " I was feeling cramped for space, in spite of all my Yoga! During that last month my husband would often take me to the sea-beach where I found taking bath in the salt water made my body feel light and buoyant and gave a great relief from its heaviness.

Diet During this Important Time: I was careful of my diet, eating much fresh foods and drinking much fruit juice and vegetable juice and eating many salads. I was eating only whole grains and chewed the food carefully. If I was what I ate, then surely, my child would be what I ate as well! I was a vegetarian, and though my parents expressed concern that there would not be enough protein in my diet to build a child properly, our little Ananda later proved that all their fears were false.

I used to see, occasionally, European women in Pondicherry who were expecting, sitting in the coffee shops smoking, and gorging themselves on pasteries and ice cream. Many of our students coming from the West had horror tales to tell of the life style of many expectant mothers in Western countries, who thought nothing of drinking alcohol, smoking cigarettes, taking drugs and eating the grossest of foods during their confinement.

Swamiji cautioned me that I must be very careful of what I put into my system, for he explained that everything which entered my blood would pass via the umbilical cord into the child's body! "Those women who smoke in pregnancy are pouring nicotine into the clean, pure tissues of their child! Then they wonder why their child cries so much after delivery!

The poor thing is suffering from "nicotine withdrawal", he said. Apparently, pregnancy in the West is a traumatic time for most women. What a terrible shame! I was most grateful, when I heard those tales, and remembered my own experience, that I was privileged to experience this wonderful time in "Mother India", where a pregnant woman is treated as a "priceless jewel". The Hindu style of life, spending much of the time squatting on the floor, or sitting on the floor; the light, cotton saree, which makes such a graceful and beautiful maternity dress, the vast amounts of time spent outdoors in lovely, cheerful sunlight and fresh air, and the great innate respect that the Hindu people have for all "mothers" is a reassuring, comforting and supportive atmosphere in which to bear one's child. I felt sorry for all those women in "less civilized countries" who found pregnancy so traumatic that they needed tranquillizers to get them through the experience I was finding so rewarding and spiritually enlightening!

Importance of Positive Emotions and Thoughts: I was fortunate to have my Guru as my husband, for it was he who really initiated me into the spiritual subtleties of "motherhood" and made me aware of the more subtle aspects of mother-child relationships. 'You must be very careful of your emotions and thoughts during this time', he said, "If you are happy and contented, your child will also feel those positive feelings as surely as if he is being bathed in sunlight. If you keep your mind on a high level of thought, your child will also imbibe those spiritual aspirations from his birth itself." He told me stories of the wives of Rishis in ancient days, and how they would sit for hours during their confinement, listening to their husbands chant the VEDAS and the sacred scriptures, deliberately exposing the unborn child to the holiest of vibrations. I especially loved the beautiful story of Ashtavakra, who, when he was but a child in his mother's womb, not only listened consciously to his father chanting the sacred scriptures, but actually called out one time, "Father, you are making a mistake! It is not chanted like that at all!" much to the amazement of all. Such charming stories with a moral such as that are common in India, and delightful paintings, drawings and sculptures of the various gods and goddesses in their infant stages abound, drawing the mind and the heart to rest on their beauty.

Folk Wisdom Is Sometimes Real Wisdom: Thus, my time drew near. I had no senior woman friend or advisor close to me in whom I could confide, and for those things that only women know I could turn only to my old Ayah, a village lady of considerable personality. I had some misgivings about emerging from my experience with a misshapen body, and was gratified to meet later in my pregnancy a young woman who not only looked trim and slim, but had returned to her practice of Bharat Natyam only four months after delivery. Meeting women like this, who had come through this experience intact, joyous and loving, had a profound effect upon my state of mind. I received advice from all quarters, however, and was always happy to listen to the experience and thoughts of others. One old
Russian lady in particular pleased me with her folk wisdom and humour. "You should treat your son, " (she naturally assumed my first born would be a son,) "as a god for the first six years of his life; like a king for the next six years; like a slave for the next six years, and as a friend ever after. " This attitude towards the "ego development" of a child at various stages I have found quite accurate and have seen its wisdom in the passing years. This same woman also gave me a formula for producing a genius. "If you want your child to be brilliant", she said, "you must breast feed him for three years and during that time have no sexual contact at all. This power from your own body will pass through your milk to the child". As things turned out, I later fulfilled these conditions and our little Ananda today does have a rare brilliance of mind. I used to ponder these concepts carefully, for they also had their harmonic thought in Yoga philosophy.

Motherhood – Nature's Way of Subjugation of the Ego: The various students and friends passing through our Ashram used to share their experiences with me, and I slowly built up confidence that I too could go through what women since Eve have endured as their part in perpetuating the race. It was a sacrifice, giving up my own body to another being for nine months, and I understood full well why the Hindus had so much respect for motherhood. Is there any other human experience in the world in which one can so willingly and joyously put every single need and desire of another living being before one's own welfare? This constant subjugation of one's own ego to the needs of another is itself a spiritual discipline unparalleled. I slowly felt the presence of another life growing close to my own and empathized with the Biblical description of Mary, the mother of Jesus, who "kept these things in her heart and pondered them deeply". One does feel an immense closeness to the Universe at this time, a feeling of the utter mystery of creating, the perfection of the unfoldment, which has nothing to do with one's mind. I could never consciously "create a baby"; even the most brilliant scientist with all his test tubes could not create life. Yet, here I was, on automatic pilot, so to speak, bearing witness to the slow unfoldment of another human life within the protective cocoon of my own. I could not help but meet each new stage, each new development with awe and thanksgiving for this rare opportunity.

The Yogic Experience of "Labour": One day in the middle of April, the 16th of the month, 1972, I was wakened about 3 a.m. with strange rippling sensations in my lower back. They were pleasant; my mind was drawn naturally to dwell on them, to contemplate their movement in my body. They were similar to the swells of the ocean, the mighty rhythm of waves beating upon the shore. I lay awake till dawn, absorbed in the sensations, which were like none I had ever felt. I attended the Hatha Yoga class and participated in whatever postures were possible for me in that state. After breakfast, I sat at my typewriter to take dictation from my husband, for we were working on several books, our monthly magazine as well and had to do several pieces of mail before lunch. The "rolling sensations' in my lower back became more and more pronounced, but they were not painful and I wondered if this could possibly be the "labour pains" about which all women speak. There was nothing painful about them, but they were becoming more and more intense. I started to squirm somewhat uneasily in my chair, but continued with the typing. Finally, when I felt they were becoming too powerful to sit still, I told my husband. "I think the labour pains have started, though they don't hurt." They were coming very closely by then, about one minute apart. "I think we had better go to the nursing home", I said. My husband sent for a taxi and by 10 a.m. we were on our way to the nursing home, about five kilometers away.

This clinic was run by Catholic nuns in Pondicherry, and they took one look at me, and directed me to the delivery room. By 11 a.m. the sensations had become very intense, by that time breaking through the pain threshold and I became conscious of very powerful, now painful muscular thrusts of the body. I was "working very hard" even involuntarily and could appreciate the significance of the term "labour" pains. The body was hard at work to sever a connection, which it had maintained so intimately between two bodies for the last nine months and the partition would not be easy. The nuns did not give me any medication nor did I ask for it. I wanted to be conscious and aware. I walked around the delivery room. I did the Kukkriya Pranayama, much to the astonishment of the attendants, who had to be reassured that it was a Yoga practice and I had not indeed gone mad. I performed some shallow Nasarga Bhastrika and Nasarga Mukha Bhastrikas. I even got down on my hands and knees and crawled about the delivery room. These were rather strange antics for the staff and I suppose I should have prepared them better for the sight. I simply gasped, "Yoga practice" between breaths, through my clenched teeth, and they relaxed their anxious glances in my direction. I was in the delivery room for one hour, when at 12:45, the little one made his "big break" into Karma Bhumi, and let out a lusty cry to let us all know that he had arrived. My husband was standing directly outside the room on the balcony of the second floor of the clinic, and rushed into the room at the sound. The nursing sister put the small red bundle with an immense mop of black hair on its head into his hands, and he took it to the balcony and showed his child to the sun, chanting appropriate Mantra all the while.

Sahaja Samadhi – A Natural State of Bliss: I really felt as though I had slipped into a Samadhi by mistake. Completely drained, relaxed, limp, receptive, I felt a bliss, which I had never felt before in my whole life. As though a purpose had been accomplished, as though I had achieved what I had set out to do, difficult though the task had been, as though I had somehow repaid a debt, which I had contracted by my own birth. I felt tremendous love for everyone, for my husband, for the doctors, for the nurses, for the Universe, for the good green earth, and the beautiful warm sun…but most all, I felt an immense, overpowering love and devotion to the small little creature that the doctors immediately put into my arms. It was mine, and from that day, I would be responsible for the growth into light of another little human soul. My baby smiled at me, he really did, even though he could not see, and I smiled and smiled back at him, for surely, he was the most beautiful, perfect, intelligent and fantastic child ever born to the Universe! And even as I thought that thought, I realised how many others must have experienced the same feelings, looking for the first time at the first child born to them, and I felt wonderful communion with all mothers who had ever lived and all those who would ever pass through this marvellous experience. Certainly, we shared a secret; certainly, we had something more precious than the rarest of gems; certainly, we were blessed by life itself to be brought so close to that mystical core which creates, out of nothing but a few cells of matter and a few sparks of energy, such a marvellous creature as the new-born child.

Little Ananda, whose name means the "Universal, Blissful State of Cosmic Consciousness slept." I laid him carefully by my side, for in Indian clinics and nursing

homes, the child is given to the mother immediately after delivery and never separated from her again. I took my pen to paper and wrote these words. "I was given life… I gave life… a debt repaid with interest… I have returned what I was given a hundred-fold. Was there such perfect beauty in my own body… once, long, long ago…Did my mother also see…God move one step beyond herself…in me?"
And thus, on the crest of these overpowering, ecstatic emotions, did the Yoga of Motherhood rush into my life… a whole new phase of my Yoga Sadhana had begun…
with
Ananda!

*Enjoy the blessing
to be able to
connect with the
new Souls coming
into this world and
enriching
mother and babies
life through Yoga!*

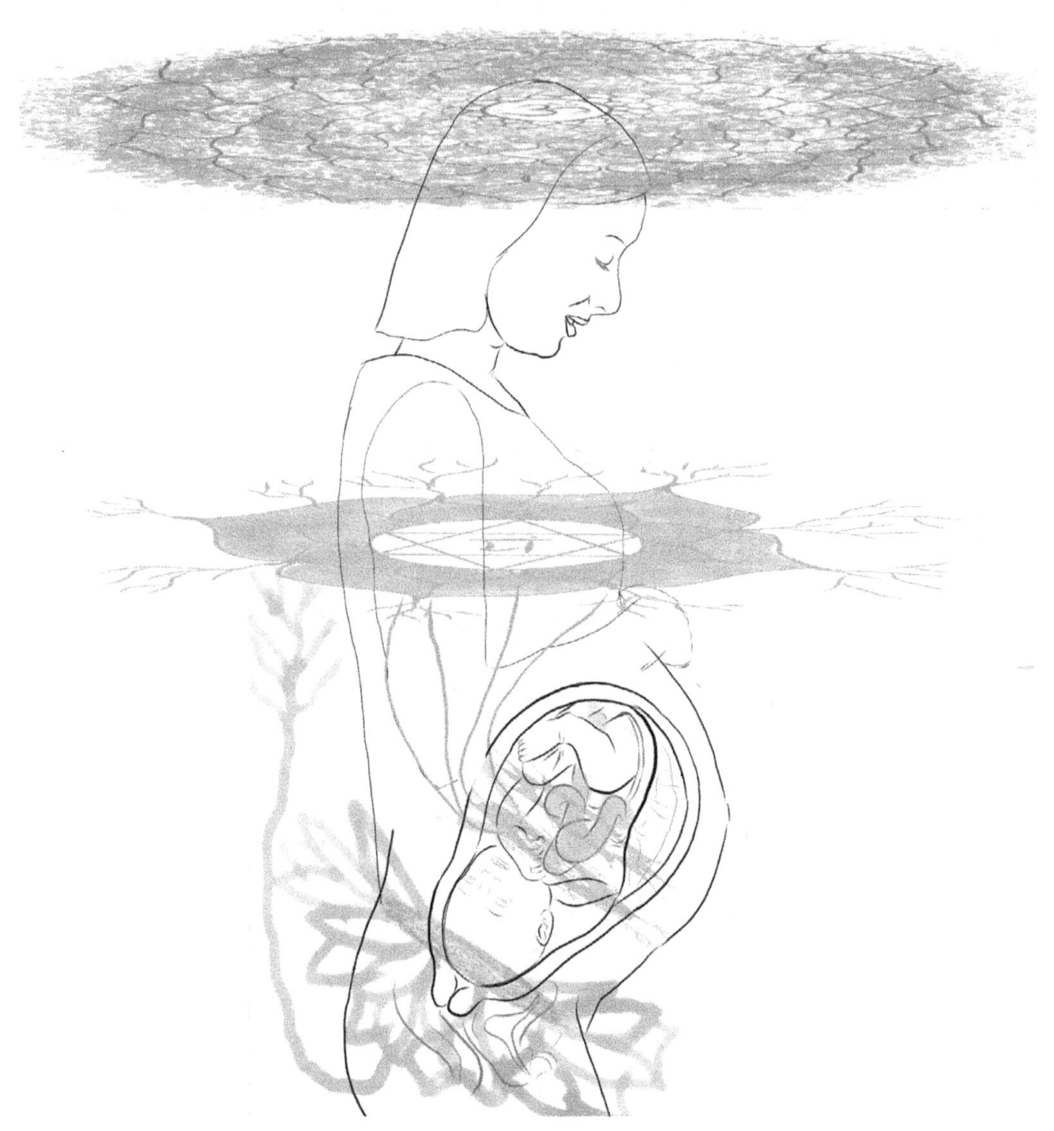

'*The universal umbilicus connects
to mother, connects to child*'